"*How to Raise a Feminist Son* has practical to-do lists about how to tackle some of the hardest conversations."

—NPR

"A beautiful and honest ode to imperfect parents everywhere who are trying to raise kind, compassionate, confident feminist sons."

—*MS.* MAGAZINE

"Explores race, gender, pop culture, and power dynamics, and consistently acknowledges the imperfections inherent in pursuing ideals. By weaving moving, personal stories about her own life and her son's life together with research and interviews, Jha encourages readers to embrace the difficulties and the joys simultaneously."

—*SEATTLE TIMES*

"Raising a boy? Then you absolutely have to read Sonora Jha's just-released book *How to Raise a Feminist Son* immediately!"

—PEGGY ORENSTEIN, AUTHOR OF *BOYS & SEX*

"A feminist manifesto steeped in personal story that seeks to unwind and reweave the way we make men."

—*THE RUMPUS*

"Part guide, part memoir, Sonora Jha's book is for anyone trying to raise a feminist boy in a world that's generally designed to produce the opposite."

—SEATTLE MET

"Jha issues an urgent, fervent plea to raise feminist sons in this trenchant guide. At times touching and always impassioned, this is an excellent resource for like-minded parents."

—PUBLISHERS WEEKLY

"Part memoir, part parenting guide . . . [the book] combines Jha's life story and her indispensable advice and is essential reading for today's parents."

—BOOKLIST

"*How to Raise a Feminist Son* focuses on how Jha developed positive parenting practices rooted in feminist values. Committed to building a 'gentle and vital masculinity from the ground up,' Jha shares tactics for parents interested in raising boys with emotional intelligence. She conspires with readers to cultivate a new generation of men—allies capable of questioning masculinity and violence against women. . . . [This] is fundamentally a book about cultivating love and connection. Not just as a vision for our sons, but for ourselves, so that each of us might experience, and express, the whole spectrum of human tenderness."

—SEATTLE'S CHILD

"Essential reading for any parent, loved one, or teacher seeking to raise feminist boys in these times."

—V (FORMERLY EVE ENSLER), AUTHOR OF *THE VAGINA MONOLOGUES* AND *THE APOLOGY*

"Combining the insight of memoir with sound advice, *How to Raise a Feminist Son* is a glorious map to a better future."

—MIRA JACOB, AUTHOR OF *GOOD TALK*

"Sonora Jha takes on the hardest questions and the most-fraught conversations with nuance and grace. Here, when addressing the deepest anxieties of parents raising boys committed to a fair and just society, her insights are invaluable."

—SORAYA CHEMALY, AUTHOR OF *RAGE BECOMES HER*

"A fierce, elegant, necessary book . . . *How to Raise a Feminist Son* scorches, illuminates, and above all challenges us to do better."

—CLAIRE DEDERER, AUTHOR OF *LOVE AND TROUBLE* AND *POSER*

HOW TO
RAISE A

A MEMOIR & MANIFESTO

FEMINIST
SON

SONORA JHA

SASQUATCH BOOKS

SEATTLE

Originally published in hardcover in the United States
by Sasquatch Books in 2021

Printed in the United States of America

SASQUATCH BOOKS with colophon is a registered trademark
of Penguin Random House LLC

26 25 24 23 22   9 8 7 6 5 4 3 2 1

Editor: Hannah Elnan
Production editor: Bridget Sweet
Designer: Anna Goldstein

This book grew out of material that appeared in the form of the essays "To Raise a Feminist Son, Talk to Him About Aziz Ansari" (Establishment, January 17, 2018) and "We Need Boys to Dismantle the Patriarchy" (DAME, October 16, 2018), parts of which became chapters eight and six, respectively.

Interview with Ijeoma Oluo originally occurred live at Town Hall Seattle on April 7, 2021 and is reprinted here by permission.

Library of Congress Cataloging-in-Publication Data is available.

ISBN: 978-1-63217-410-9

Sasquatch Books | 1904 Third Avenue, Suite 710 | Seattle, WA 98101

SasquatchBooks.com

FOR MY SON

CONTENTS

AUTHOR'S NOTE

In using "son" in the title and sons/boys in the theme of the book, I am choosing to focus on the urgent task of raising cisgender boys to be feminists, but I also address other intersectional identities within these chapters. This book is for anyone with an interest in feminism, but it's especially for those who have influence on the raising of boys. Most of us do.

I have changed the names of most people I know except for the experts I have quoted, public figures, and some friends. I have collapsed some time spans and have focused on those people and those parts of my story that I believed were central to the theme. I have relied on my memory to tell my truths of moments in my life and in the life of my son. Others may recall some of the shared moments differently.

HOW I RAISED A FEMINIST IN THE DARK

In Jordan Peele's *Us*, there is a scene quite early in the film when a boy says, "There's a family in our driveway." If you have seen the film, you know this is the pivotal moment that sets the mayhem in motion. We see a man, woman, and two children holding hands, standing silhouetted in the driveway of a vacation home, looking in on the people inside.

All hell is about to break loose in the film, but I am distracted. How did the boy know to call that group of people in the driveway a "family"? Is it because that's all he knows and sees reflected, being part of a wholesome American family himself? Is it because there's that sticker on his family car of a stick-figure man and woman and boy and girl holding hands—you know the one I'm talking about—depicting a family? If my son and I showed up in someone's driveway to stand, holding hands quietly, silent and backlit for some reason, would we be as eerie? Would the boy looking out at us call *us* a family?

I know the answer to that question and it is no. *I* don't even call our single-mother-and-only-child unit a family. I should, but I don't.

As I lean back into watching the film, shaking off my spoiler thoughts, suspending disbelief so I can hand myself over to the deliciously escapist terror reserved for wholesome families, I sneak a look at my adult son in the seat next to me and then back at the screen as a family attempts to kill a family, and I wonder if Jordan Peele doesn't care for traditional families either. I am oddly comforted by this thought.

This is why we go to the movies, my son and I. These beautiful things that glow in the dark, these reels of thought and story sent to us from imagination factories, connect Gibran and me in our reimagined life together. Here, we are far from my violent family in India, from the poor role models of masculinity there to which I would have had to hand my boy over had we not found our temple in these seats at the movies.

You could argue, of course, that Hollywood, Bollywood, and any other film industry in the world are hardly temples of feminist thought and representation. In fact, they are mostly quite the opposite. And yet, although I didn't know it for years, I was building a tenderhearted, sharp-witted feminist boy at the movies.

The task of raising a boy into a man with a feminist consciousness sometimes involves stealing him away from the quotidian misogyny and its twenty-four-hour infractions, and leading him into the fantasies conjured up by twenty-four frames per second. Feminism, like film, requires a suspension of disbelief. It requires that we trust that a little girl can use her wit and courage to rescue her parents when her father makes a wrong turn into a ghostly world in Hayao Miyazaki's *Spirited Away*. It suggests that my son trust that Nancy Chan, who sat next to him in his third-grade classroom, is smarter than him and will one day be President of the United States.

For every such film that lent a flicker to our feminist imagination, there were scores of films that doused it with their rampant misogyny.

Both kinds served the feminist cause. Films gave us an activity to do together, just mother and son. They gave us a way to talk about things, first in simple terms of fairness, and eventually love and sex and representation and erasure. Films are a social force, fantastical and yet dictating normativity. In toddler terms, that translated to: "Gibran, why does *The Jungle Book* have so many boys and only one important girl, Kaa the snake, and she is sly and mean? Mama wants to see more girls in the movies doing important things! Don't you?"

As Gibran grew, he witnessed the movies and he witnessed his mama's female spectatorship at the movies. On the bus ride or drive home afterward, I'd ask the teenage Gibran why we would see women sexualized for men's pleasure or for men's violence or for men to get revenge upon each other. The adult Gibran had to dwell on the matter of why we see so little of women's own pleasure at the movies. And why didn't we get served visuals of men's bodies for the heterosexual female gaze?

We squirmed at these conversations and we laughed through the squirm. We watched the films that centered girls and women with power and agency (*Mulan, Ponyo, Matilda, Mirch Masala, Zootopia, My Neighbor Totoro, Brave, Eighth Grade*), and we watched the ones that didn't.

I told Gibran about the Bechdel test—author and cartoonist Alison Bechdel's set of three questions to determine if women are represented fairly in a film: (1) Does it contain at least two women, who (2) Talk to each other about (3) Something other than a man? Later, Gibran informed me about the concept of "fridging," a term coined by comic book writer Gail Simone referencing a 1994 *Green Lantern* comic in which the DC hero comes home to find his girlfriend murdered and stuffed in a refrigerator, which then motivates him to seek revenge while the woman is, quite literally, frozen out of the story.

We went to the movies for fun, but we returned speaking of them as both mirrors and mind-snatchers. I overheard him once explaining to a friend how learning to recognize sexist tropes essentially reduced them to ridiculousness and humorousness, and spotting them became like something of a game. Gibran was equal parts fan, film critic, cultural critic, and feminist at the movies. Spotting the erasure of women at the movies (as characters, as actors, as auteurs, and as spectators) alerts you to their erasure in real life.

<hr />

The first film I watched with my son was when he was one year old: *Babe*, about a pig. The last movie I watched with him just before he left for college was *Stardust Memories*, starring Woody Allen, so also about a pig.

My baby was weird at the movies. When I took him to watch *Babe*, I was a film critic in Bangalore and had to go weekly to the cinema to review Hollywood and other foreign films for the *Times of India*. I was also their chief of the metropolitan bureau, a rising star in journalism. I had a husband, a home, friends. I found that I could have all these delicious things and also sneak some time in with my baby if I took him to the movies with me. Technically, I'd be at work, but I wouldn't be in the office, I'd be with my baby.

I sat him in my lap and cradled him with my left arm while I took notes with my right hand. In the dark of the movie theater, I sniffed the top of his head. I did this for years after the new baby smell had faded. The best place to do that was at the movies. Always, like that first time in *Babe*, he was too rapt to notice.

His father and our friends had warned me against taking my baby to the movies. "It's not healthy," they said. "He will get addicted to movies."

I could think of nothing better.

"He will cry. It's a nuisance for other viewers," they said. My baby sat wide-eyed. Quiet as a mouse the whole time. I still remember the back of his neck, erect in the way babies manage to keep their wobbly necks erect when they are taking in their world.

What did he see on the screen that had him so mesmerized? The pig being adopted by the sheep? The farmer's troubles? The politeness of the child pig when he talks to the lady sheep? The hope in the film? The despair? The triumph of the pig who was the outsider at the dog show? Nothing?

Baa-ram-ewe! Baa-ram-ewe! To your breed, your fleece, your clan be true.

On a recent Mother's Day, some twenty years after that screening of *Babe*, my now strong-necked boy wrote me a letter on Facebook Messenger (this is often his last resort on the day of, when mailing cards from college is not an option). The letter was brief, and within that brevity was this:

And, perhaps best of all, I learned how to appreciate and critique art through all the time we spent together watching TV and movies on the big screen or on our various couches, pointing out plot holes, ridiculing the stupidity of different characters, and laughing. These are probably the fondest memories of my childhood, and they'll always be with me, that I may rely on them in those times when I fear I am alone, or I feel life is too lonely, or boring, or painful to persevere through.

I never want him to feel that life is too lonely. But I do want him to know loneliness. It helps grow that muscle called empathy. It has him pick up the phone when I call him after sending the desperate text: "Just watched *Beatriz at Dinner*. I'm crying." It has him listen. It has him say, "I cried like that at *I, Daniel Blake*. That movie broke my heart."

May voices of young men all over America and India and Ireland and Saudi Arabia and Nigeria rise up together in a big, thunderous chant: *Something broke my heart.*

At *Babe*, and for the movies that came fast and faithfully into our life together thereafter, for as long as I could, I sat him on my lap and let my heart beat against his tiny back as I bobbed him gently on my knee. My heart grew strong. His back grew steady. When he was old enough to sit in the seat beside me, I'd lean over for the popcorn and sniff his head.

His father got a job in Singapore. I resigned from my rising-star-in-Indian-journalism role and followed him with our baby. The three of us went to movies together then, but something was wrong. For one, I had no job. For another, my husband was having the time of his life, doing well in his career, traveling a lot, going to parties to which I was oddly never invited. I grew listless. I was prescribed antidepressants. My little boy cried at the movies. Yes, his father and I shouldn't have smuggled him into *The Devil's Advocate*, where he was miserable because he was hot. In *Titanic*, he was anxious, frantic—"Is the ship going to sink, Mama? Will they all drown?"

"No," I said, and walked out with him and waited for his father in the lobby. For a few years, in my son's imagination, those people on the RMS *Titanic* arrived at their destinations just fine and went on to live long lives. When my boy learned later in books that the ship did indeed sink and those people did, in fact, drown, he never questioned me about why I had lied. Movies had, by then, become those joyrides where not just disbelief but all the dysfunctions of truth too were suspended.

The next few years of his childhood would see my son move with me to the United States, watch his parents get divorced, and witness his mother being taken into trauma surgery after a car crash from which he escaped unhurt. He and I would survive life's uncertainties time and time again and head to movie after movie. Having already reimagined and recast something as colossal as the fate of the *Titanic*, I now assembled the detritus of our small lives and reimagined how my boy and I would live and who we would be thereafter. I worked on a PhD, then got a job as a journalism professor in Seattle and moved there to build a life for him and me, whatever we were, because I still didn't imagine we were a family.

We developed a ritual—any time we'd travel, we would go watch a movie in that town. It was one way of exploring that town, he said, through its film-going spaces. Uh-huh, I said. It was just his way of getting to the movies, no matter what. And, although I did not voice this to him, I knew it was his way of finding something routine, normal, familiar, no matter where on the map he found himself as his parents' worlds fell apart. In our everyday life, we had worries. At the movies, we had wonder.

When we would visit my family in India, and the trauma of the past would land on me afresh in the form of physical violence from my brother or harsh words from my mother, we still had movies starring the dreamy Shah Rukh Khan. In India, our movies had intermissions in which you ate samosas. I hadn't taught my boy Hindi, so I had to whisper rapid translations into his ear as the movie played. "I love her," Shah Rukh Khan said in *Kabhi Khushi Kabhie Gham*. "She is not from our class or caste but I love her and you will not humiliate her," he declared with delicious melodrama to his father, and left home to build a life where his wife would be respected. My boy nodded in the shadows.

I believe he could tell that movies were his mother's heartbeat. It was also where I felt safe and my feet felt steady. Back in Seattle, his friends' parents would take their kids to their lake houses, or at least fishing at the lake. They'd take them to ski resorts in the winter and go canoeing in the summer. They'd take them camping. Being in nature is vital to a child's growth, they said. And yes, you can grow a feminist in the great outdoors. I also tried to go camping, to be in nature. I went sledding. But I'd had polio as a child and crushed my ankle in a car crash as an adult, so my damaged legs slowed everyone down.

At the movies, I was strong. On the way home, Gibran was chatty. When the sullen years of adolescence came, he still leaned in with wide eyes at the movies. So we met there, the best of him and the best of me. *To your breed, your fleece, your clan be true.*

My boy saw me happy at the movies. Perhaps happy isn't the right word. He saw me give myself over. As the world outside confused me and I took him along for the ride in my confusion, the world inside, in the dark, was one in which we placed our trust.

Tell me a story; I am here. Take me away from my story for a while.

For years, I'd look over at him when we were at the movies and Gibran would look back, nod or smile. Yes, Mama, we're here. We're both still here.

And then one day, Gibran took me to a movie so he could watch *my* face: *Rise of the Planet of the Apes.* He was sixteen and he had started to go to movies with his friends, so he had seen it already. Going to the movies wasn't exclusively our thing to do anymore. And I was trying to be gracious about it.

But he wanted to watch this movie a second time, with me, he said, because "there was this scene in it."

"I don't want to watch a movie about apes," I said. "You saw how I was with wizards and hobbits." I had fallen asleep in the *Harry Potter* movies and in the *Lord of the Rings* movies.

"Trust me," he said.

Within the hour, we were watching an ape grow smart. And then Caesar was in a cage, pacing, trapped, enraged at the way he and his fellow apes were shackled and starved. Caesar escaped. The zookeeper arrived and set at him with the taser. The actor was someone I recognized as a boy from the *Harry Potter* movies. This wasn't going well.

"Go on, back in your cage!" he commanded the ape. I shrank back in my seat. My neck turned stiff. Caesar grabbed the zookeeper's hand.

"Take your stinking paw off me, you damn dirty ape!" the zookeeper hissed.

Caesar pulled up to his largest size and bellowed: "*No!*"

Caesar says no. Caesar speaks. Caesar has language. Caesar has rage.

I gasped, too loudly for a movie theater, the adult equivalent of a noisy baby at the movies. My son's hand squeezed mine. I tore my eyes from the screen to look over at him. His eyes were shining. He was smiling from ear to ear. He had been looking not at the screen but at my face. This was why he had brought me here. This was why he was here. We resist. The ape resists. We learn to say no.

Later, I would read books and academic essays on that film. I would be gratified that Caesar's "No!" represented a mutiny against oppression. That scene would become something I pulled up regularly on YouTube and circulated to my friends and on social media as a cinematic battle cry for revolution. I doubt that it was as cathartic for most others. You had to have seen the movie. You had to have seen the movie with us.

But more profound for me than all of this was that my son saw me that day at *Rise of the Planet of the Apes*. No, he *watched* me. He anticipated my gasp and my catharsis. His face beamed. He loved Caesar's triumph twice over. He was telling me that we, together, saw the value of dissent. We sat there at the edge of our movie seats as Caesar and his tribe broke free and swung from the redwoods in California.

Movies gave us a way into conversations that weren't about us but *were* about us. Stories led my son to reading. He became a formidable reader. But reading is a solitary activity. Movies are in your face. Movies are shared in the moment. Shared as, maybe, say, a family.

The feminist reel has its bumps and scratches, though. After the #MeToo revelations, when Gibran asked me to watch Woody Allen's *Stardust Memories* with him, I did, but I said it was the last of that man's films for me. Gibran put up an argument. You know, the one about separating the art from the artist. We exchanged some heated words. As we fought, I realized *Why had I believed it would be easy?* My job of raising a tenderhearted, sharp-witted feminist son would never be done. Fighting back years of patriarchy—or white men's art, for that matter—was not a job accomplished in eighteen years.

I'd bide my time. I'd take heart in this: The movies gave us other people's stories like branches to swing from in glee, to hold the weight of our own stories. The movies were where my child met *Babe* and learned empathy, the foundation of feminism for a boy.

Masculinity can be a cage, a gilded one, in which Woody Allen has hooked up a projector and hands out popcorn. My boy would have to break free. I would throw him the key.

When my boy visits now, we quickly make plans to go to the movies. On the drive to the theater, I think of this—only time will tell if my boy has grown to be a tenderhearted, sharp-witted feminist man. And my time with him, in the dark of the movie theater, is running out. This child is the only family I have in the vastness of the United States. I must ignore the half-truths of stick-figure decals and lean into the glorious truths already lived by same-sex parents and adoptive parents and the many other iterations of family, and see my own little enterprise of familial bliss. I'd have to be a tenderhearted, sharp-witted feminist woman and say, of us, in the same definitive tone as that little boy in *Us*, "There's a family watching a movie."

Chapter One

HELP, I JUST FOUND OUT I'M HAVING A SON!

In India, when a mother has a baby, she is given postpartum massage to soothe her from childbirth and help her regain her strength and shape. Then, when the baby is around a month old, the mother is encouraged to massage her baby. It is said to help bond the baby and mother while also removing toxins from the baby's system. When done right after the baby's bath, it eases the baby into a deep sleep— and we all know how badly we want that.

For my baby, I would use a mixture of olive oil, coconut oil, Ayurvedic oil, and Johnson's Baby Oil. I would coo to him and he would gurgle. He would blink at me with his huge, long-lashed black eyes as if wondering if this feeling rushing over him was love. Yes, it is, I would whisper as I folded his chubby left leg over his right and gently pressed them into his tummy, the way the woman who had taught traditional Ayurvedic massage for generations had instructed me, to aid the baby's digestion and promote suppleness in his joints.

In those early months, I looked at my baby and knew he was the most beautiful thing in the world. I thought I would die from this love. This was in the days before Facebook and Instagram, so I couldn't share it with the world. And so I could just quietly believe it and bask in our moments of gurgle and coo.

I also had time to wonder how to turn this beautiful, dough-limbed, ink-pool-eyed miracle of mine into a mighty warrior of feminist revolution.

I wanted nothing but the best for this boy (thus the combination of massage oils). A part of me then paused to wonder if my plan to raise him as a feminist would be good for the world, yes, but perhaps set *him* back? Why not let him stay in a deep sleep instead of use his tender heart and limbs and brain for a cause that didn't celebrate *him*?

Fortunately, I started to read everything I could find about feminism and its benefits for boys. I sought out both poetry and research that would help me stay the course. I talked with friends. Over the years, as Gibran grew and grew, I kept all of that close.

Twenty years later, when my friend Julie found out that she was pregnant with a boy, she went through somewhat similar emotions. This was going to be fun, she concluded. (And of course, the boy would grow up to be a feminist.)

Perhaps your friends are cheering and buying cute onesies for your baby shower that say "This is what a feminist looks like." Or, after too many Trump years and in the reckoning of the #MeToo movement, perhaps they can barely manage a steely "Yes!" and a grim nod. Either way, we know that more and more of us are on board and aching to raise feminist boys.

This desire doesn't span merely the twenty years between Julie's boy and mine, of course. Feminists have been imploring men to be allies for centuries, actually. Let's harken back to Britain's "first feminist," Mary Wollstonecraft, when she wrote in her essay *A Vindication of the Rights of Woman*:

Would men but generously snap our chains, and be content with rational fellowship instead of slavish obedience, they would find us more observant daughters, more affectionate sisters, more faithful wives, more reasonable mothers—in a word, better citizens.

Centuries later, a little bit has shifted in that we are now trying to convince men—and some women—that we'd like to be characterized simply as human, rather than appeal to men as daughters, sisters, wives, and mothers, but yeah, Mary, I get you: feminism will help my son be in a rational fellowship. To this reasonable mother, that means that he will be given permission to be wrong sometimes, to fail, to fall, to cry, to be protected rather than always be protector, to be provided for rather than always be provider, to seek and receive wise counsel, to be chastised as much as he is cheered, to be led to wild fun, to be held and to be held responsible, to get schooled and to get laid.

I greedily, reasonably, wholeheartedly want all these things for my son.

Is this even possible? *Can* boys be feminists? Are they doing it for the greater common good, in selfless solidarity, or is there something in it for *him*?

A pertinent and eloquent response to this question came from a gentleman on Twitter, when I shared an essay about raising a feminist son. "Raise a feminist son? Why didn't you just cut his dick off at birth?" his tweet said, blinking at me in rage. I didn't respond at the time. I imagined his question was rhetorical.

I realized soon that the man was addressing an important and rising question in the universal zeitgeist. Boyhood, especially in America, has become some sort of battleground. An odd battle, this, in which boys are both the soldiers and the spoils. Tweet-Man has his finger on America's pulse, perhaps better than I. Tweet-Man demands a response.

So, dear Tweet-Man: I didn't cut off my baby's dick because that would be sexual violence. (Feminists are sort of opposed to sexual violence.) And, to be a feminist, my son would need his brain, his heart, his hands, his feet, his tears, his voice, his breath, and definitely his dick. Make no mistake—he would need his dick to "fuck like a feminist," a call put out to our men by political commentator Samantha Bee in the wake of the #MeToo movement.

I can see why Tweet-Man wouldn't want to trust me on all this. To understand why the time has finally come for boys to be raised as feminists, I'd point him to the opinions of someone with a dick. To be precise, I'd like him to hear what Pope John Paul II said in a letter he sent to women back in September 1995 as they gathered for a United Nations conference in Beijing. It was a letter he wrote on June 29, less than a month after my son was born:

> There is an urgent need to achieve *real equality* in every area [of women's personal rights]: equal pay for equal work, protection for working mothers, fairness in career advancements, equality of spouses with regard to family rights. . . . The time has come to condemn vigorously the types of *sexual violence* which frequently have women for their object.

This love letter from the Pope was more widely published than the words of any woman saying the same thing, whether in whispers or in clear-eyed articles or in screams. And it was certainly never said by any Catholic woman priest ever, because even the Pope couldn't go so far as to heed his own call for fairness in career advancements and, gasp, ordain a woman priest.

Enough about dicks. In the same year the Pope wrote his letter, as my baby was fattening himself on the milk of my human kindness, I first heard of Gloria Steinem's suggestion that men should embrace feminism because it could add four years to their lives by reducing the stress associated with traditional masculine roles. All right, then. Breast milk would turn my baby strong and feminism would give him a long life. *Jiyo, mere laal.*[1]

▀▀▀▀▀▀▀▀▀▀▀▀▀▀▀▀▀▀▀▀▀▀▀▀▀▀▀

So perhaps I can just be straight with Tweet-Man: the reason I didn't cut my boy's dick off is that I want him to live. To be more precise, I also want him to have a *good* life, filled with love, lasting love. The man may ask: Why would your son listen? Why would he want to be a feminist? Why would he risk being uncool and learn feminism from his mom?

True to Tweet-Man's worst nightmare, yes, it's because I never gave my son a choice. Respect and equity for women are not things I was willing to have him evaluate, cautiously weighing the pros and cons. Rape and violence are not something you mull over before you take a stand. All the evils that besiege women even before they step out of their front door—and in some parts of the world they don't step out—are easily traced to the fact that we are still hemming and hawing about whether women are actually fully viable human beings.

To raise a feminist son, you take away this choice. Feminism has been the water that my little baby swam in while in my womb, back when he looked like a fish. Feminism was the time—the hours—I spent chasing my own goals, dodging bullets as a pregnant reporter

---

1. A traditional Hindu blessing for a long life given to sons in India. No such common and exclusive blessing exists for a daughter; women are blessed with *saubhaagyavati bhava*, which means "be a fortunate wife."

covering riots in India and then writing papers as a tenure-track professor in America. Feminism is the space we traveled between continents so I could protect him from our patriarchal relatives and grow a whole other set of values for us to live by. Feminism is like the protein boost in the smoothies we drink now in cafés in Seattle. Feminism is how we roll. Ask my son to describe our feminism and he will look at you, smile, shrug, and walk away, his dick intact.

▪▪▪▪▪▪▪▪▪▪▪▪▪▪▪▪▪▪▪▪▪▪▪▪▪▪▪▪▪

Feminism has a history across the world, as a concept and also as a lived experience for many who do not know that particular word. It has been studied for its four waves in the western world and has been lived as whispered dissent in places where such things are not necessarily documented.

If you were/are a feminist during the four waves in America, your to-do list looked something like this:

1830s to early 1900s: Struggle for equal contract and property rights;

1960s to 1980s: Struggle for workplace, sexuality, family, and reproductive rights, and demand the Equal Rights Amendment (still not passed);

1990s to early 2000s: Struggle against inequities based on gender, race, and class; embrace the nuances of intersectionality (a term introduced in 1989 by feminist scholar and activist Kimberlé Crenshaw that helps us understand how the intersections of different social identities such as race, gender, and sexuality may affect the way one experiences societal structures);

2010s to present: Struggle to overcome gender norms, to involve boys and men; use social media for radical grassroots solidarity.

If you were/are a feminist during the four waves in India, your to-do list looks something like this:

Mid-nineteenth century to 1915: Be a reformist and begin to speak of women in public life, focused on education;

1915 to 1947 (Indian independence): Join activists like Sarojini Naidu, who joins Gandhi in the struggle for independence from the British while highlighting women's struggles in India as well as launching class and anti-caste struggles;

1947 to 2010: Work with or support women's organizations that demand fair treatment of women in the home and at work, especially on issues of dowry, rape, and property ownership;

2012 to present: Call for anti-rape laws and gender equity; join and support queer activism; highlight oppression of Dalit women; and launch transnational feminist collaborations over social media.

Pick a place on the planet. Feminists made it better for you.

For me, as it is for many of us, feminism was a feeling before it was a focus. When it became a focus, I started this project of raising a feminist son out of fear of him becoming like the men who had neglected me, beaten me, abandoned me, preyed on me. Today, I see my son has turned into a man who looks a lot like those men, but I don't see in my son an oppressor. In fact, my son is vulnerable.

He is a young man in the United States with brown skin. Audre Lorde said back in the 1970s that white women's feminism may not be appropriate for women of color, and I believe that it may not be adequate for my boy of color.

I grew up in awe of feminist writers like Ismat Chughtai, who wrote of lesbian passion in 1942, and Mahasweta Devi, who wrote of women under colonization and caste oppression. I came into adulthood in a time of the courage of Bhanwari Devi, the rural grassroots activist of a scheduled caste (considered a "lower" caste in India), who tried to stop an upper-caste family from marrying off their infant daughter. As punishment, she was gang-raped by upper-caste men. Bhanwari Devi and her husband had the gall to go to the police. She was ostracized by her people, abused by the police, and brutally rebuked by the justice system, but her case finally won a victory when the Supreme Court of India recognized that she was targeted for her work as an activist, which then led to changes to sexual harassment laws in India. When asked in an interview how she overcame the shame of rape, Bhanwari Devi said: "What wrong did I do? It's their shame, not mine."

Both heartbroken and heartened by such feminist stories in my homeland, I now live in America, working—alongside white feminists and feminists of color, trans feminists and cisgender feminists, straight and queer feminists—to tailor a beautiful, sleek, custom-made, expandable, steeped-in-history and yet timeless feminism for my child.

Which is where you come in. If you are reading this book, you probably have a boy in your life whom you want to raise as a feminist. I hold you in happy solidarity. And I tell you we are not alone. We can snuff out toxic masculinity, which is defined as a cultural concept of manliness that glorifies stoicism, strength, virility, dominance, and violence, and that is socially maladaptive or harmful to boys' own mental health. We can build a gentle and vital masculinity from the ground up. We can raise our children without gender stereotypes, perhaps even without gender binaries, so that they are free to experience and express the whole spectrum of human emotion. And we can be people of any gender building all sorts of family as we do it.

Most of my rearing of Gibran was done as a single mother. Perhaps that made my job of raising him as a feminist easier, perhaps it made it harder. I have witnessed the strengths and weaknesses of the feminist enterprise in all kinds of families.

In 1996, when my boy was one year old, researcher Phyllis A. Katz published an article titled "Raising Feminists" in which she pointed to one significant contributor that determined whether or not a child would grow up to be a feminist: parental behavior. For one, Katz pointed out, many children rely less on gender-role stereotypes if their mothers have been employed outside the home. I do not believe that my stay-at-home-mom friends will fail to raise feminists, but I have come to see that mothers who seek and find fulfillment of any kind outside a homemaker role are more likely to phone home and ask their sons to fold the laundry. I made it a point at least once a week to call my teenage boy and ask him "What's for dinner?"

Katz and her fellow researchers found that at three years old, a child was less into gender stereotypes if the parents displayed "a more positive parenting style—they granted their children more independence and they were less demanding, less authoritarian, and warmer than parents of more sex-typed children." The report from my friend Julie and her husband, Ragan, is that they are doing well in raising their son (and their daughter) to be feminists. For one, they are modeling for their children a different gender-role equation. Julie has a PhD and is a professor. Ragan is a musician who works odd construction jobs. Julie is putting Ragan through college to be an engineer so he can bring those skills to his music production career.

They also redistribute the chores at home, bring in gender-neutral books, and praise gentleness and respect in both kids, especially in their son.

In the battle to straitjacket boys' masculinity, feminists like Julie and Ragan are seeking an armistice. No, actually, they're going a step further and seeking an ally in their boy. Fourth-wave feminism, researchers tell us, is going to bring boys and men along. Moms on Twitter are saying *Yes, please*. All over the globe, parents, teachers, activists, and boys are building a league of male feminists and allies that will, very soon, laugh in the face of misogyny.

Take students Matt Chen and Matias Benitez, who answered actress Emma Watson's call for male feminist allies and started a HeForShe club at their all-boys Regis High School in Manhattan. When the boys heard that some girls had felt uncomfortable and had been touched inappropriately at some of the Regis High School dances in previous years, the HeForShe club collaborated with the nearby all-girls Catholic Marymount School to host a conversation about how to shut that kind of thing down at the school's dances going forward.

Take Urvashi Sahni, an educator who developed a special curriculum for teachers of working-class boys in the Prerna Boys School, a K–12 school in Lucknow, India. Her teachers go through rigorous training so they can teach boys how to demonstrate "responsive care" to one another. Boys caring for other boys is a first step toward teaching them self-awareness and social-emotional awareness, so they can examine masculinity, violence against women, gender, and marriage. The teachers ask the boys to look around in their community and notice how gender injustices crush their own dreams and feed their own fears and those of the girls and women in their lives.

Take the men across the world leading the "Man Box" study, which, in 2017, showed that young men ages eighteen to thirty feel pressure to "act tough," which then causes harm to those around them and to themselves. The study went deeper to find that these behaviors led to a cost of $20.9 billion that could be saved by the US, UK, and Mexican economies if there were no "Man Box." What were these behaviors and what did they lead to? Sexual violence, bullying and assault, suicide, traffic accidents, binge-drinking, and depression. A private boys' school in Croydon, England, drew a link between male learned behavior and the fact that suicide is the most common cause of death among men under forty-five in the UK. They brought in volunteers for a charity called the Great Men campaign, where trained men follow lesson plans to teach boys about gender issues.

Take Fatma Özdemir Uluç, who led a British Council–supported study of gender equality in Turkish schools. One of her social science teachers gave the students homework to observe their family for a week and report back on who was getting the most tired. A sixth-grade boy reported that his older sister and mother were the most tired because they were doing all the chores in the house. His older sister was preparing for her university exam and was still expected to bring him his tea. Once the boys woke up to this gendered injustice around them, the teachers brought in the families and talked about how they could treat boys and girls equally. One of the schools put on a play about Cinderella, casting a boy in the lead role to find out how this changed the story.

Take an initiative in which thirty-six Kenyan preschool teachers participated in a study to see if they held gender-stereotyped views and if they communicated these views to children during selection and use of play materials.

In short, the world is conspiring to raise feminist boys. You and I and the whole wide world.

The part of me that wants to raise a feminist son is the same part of me that wanted to make sure his Hercules blanket was tucked in well enough around him so he wouldn't be cold as a three-year-old. It's the same part of me that made sure I put an egg on his plate for breakfast every day before school because research said that kids who ate protein for breakfast stayed alert in class longer. It's the same part of me that tells him to call me if he and his friends have been drinking and need a ride; I'll be there, no questions asked. I wanted my baby warm, I wanted my boy well-fed, I want my young man alive.

I want to send a good man out into the world and I want for my grown son a good life, with mutually supportive relationships and a fulfilled and happy partner. I want him to be loving and I want him to be loved. Simone de Beauvoir, in *The Second Sex*, said: "When we abolish the slavery of half of humanity, together with the whole system of hypocrisy that it implies, then the 'division' of humanity will reveal its genuine significance and the human couple will find its true form." In a world where relationships are jaded, fraught, and short-lived, I want great love for my son. I want him to be fully shaped so that when love arrives, the human couple can find its true form.

It hasn't been easy to raise a feminist boy, and it isn't over yet. I'll say this much—I see signs of it every day. I know how much you want to do this too, and the chapters that follow are an invitation.

TO DO:

- Make a list of reasons why you believe feminism is good for your boy.

- Complete this sentence in your own words: "I aspire to raise a feminist boy because . . ."

Chapter Two

WHAT IF I'M NOT A GOOD FEMINIST?

I am twenty-three years old and I am standing completely naked in front of a tap trickling water in the middle of a busy railway platform in broad daylight at Allahabad Junction. Yes, in the middle of the platform—not inside a ladies' restroom, but in an L-shaped concrete enclosure that is tall enough to hide my body but not my face. People are milling about the railway platform in this second-oldest city of India, where both Hindu gods and Mughal emperors have left their patriarchal seeds, and if I can dare to lift my eyes from the water trickling down at my feet, I will look into the faces of men who have stopped to stare fixedly at my face as I try to collect enough water in a plastic mug to wash myself down. I am trying not to think of how easily any one of these men could step into the zig and then the zag of this enclosure I am in and see me naked. I have chosen to take the risk because my skin has been baking under the 106-degree Allahabad sun and I have not showered in two days. My clothes, covering me from neck to ankle and designed to give me the highest degree of modesty, are close to giving me a heatstroke instead. So, my twenty-three-year-old girl brain has chosen to let me take off all my clothes and run cold water down my body as I fight back hot tears. *What am I doing here?*

Years later, I would learn that these taps of water and these bathing areas were provided as facilities for the 120 million or so ascetic sadhus who arrived at Allahabad Junction, mendicants congregating at the Kumbh Mela, the largest pilgrimage known to humankind, religious men with their hair in dreads as long and knotted as tree trunks, their bodies thin and naked but for sacred ash, and their minds afloat under the influence of gods and ganja. Where they washed their feet to rid themselves of the mud settled between their toes from miles of devout procession, I am now washing the soot and dust and layers of dried, rancid sweat from hours of listless railway travel.

These showers on the railway platform were meant for men. Almost all public spaces in India are meant for men.

My family is far away in Bombay and they have no idea that I am standing naked and ashamed at this railway station. Not that they have been stellar at protecting me from men or malaise in the past. Still, I feel like they should know about this current situation. But this is 1991 and neither cell phones nor the internet are ubiquitous yet. My family has no idea that I was thrown off the train along with a handful of other reporters—all of them male, mind you. Four of us are traveling home to Bombay after a few days in a remote village inhabited by a cult of skull worshippers who are hated and feared in these parts.

The general feeling in my group is that *I* am the reason we are thrown off the train. My sex was listed as "male" in the railway ticket collector's list of oddly detailed demographic information. This discrepancy did not raise any eyebrows on the journey in, but one particularly diligent ticket collector, when he squinted up from his clipboard, saw me as flagrantly female. One of the skull worshippers, responsible for outreach and public relations, had prebooked the train tickets and had listed all the news reporters as men because he had never imagined that a woman reporter would be assigned to go into the dangerous interior villages of West Bengal bordering the lawless state of Bihar. He never would have imagined that the father of an Indian girl would agree to let her go on such an assignment. Besides, what kind of name is Sonora anyway? Definitely male.

The ticket collector was having none of this. The skull worshippers were up to no good, he decided. This beautiful twenty-three-year-old girl with them might be someone they had kidnapped, he said to everyone in the railway compartment. They nodded. The ticket collector's way of dealing with this situation was to throw the skull worshippers and their four male accomplices as well as the kidnapped girl off the train at Allahabad Junction.

Everybody in my group is now furious at me. This is what happens when you bring a woman along. And look at her now, shampooing her hair in the middle of the railway platform. If someone rapes her, it will be on us.

I know what they are thinking, and I feel for them. I am filled with a bitter hatred for my newspaper editor, a man named Behram Contractor, who, while I am showering in terror on a railway platform, is probably getting dressed for a cocktail party hosted by some celebrity in a penthouse suite at the five-star Taj Mahal Palace Hotel in Bombay. I cannot fathom his faith in me as a cub reporter whom he sends around the country as a roving correspondent to cover the most outrageous of stories in the most far flung of places where it's no country for young women.

"You can do this," he says each time. "You're the best roving correspondent I've ever hired. Better than any man."

I am angry for what he sees in me or wants to see in me that he says I don't see in myself yet. I trust instead my teacher from first standard (first grade), who had failed me in that class and handed my parents a report card that declared me "far below the standard." My father had pleaded my case with the school principal (although it wasn't *my* case as much as his, for failure and success meant a lot more to the rising officer in the Indian Army than to the six-year-old). I had been grudgingly promoted. Ask me about impostor syndrome.

In this moment of hot shame at the railway station, I hate my father, who ought to have been stricter, like my friends' fathers, instead of letting me go—in all my fragility and femaleness—to roam places with people who foraged in cremation sites to find human skulls. And how about my mother? Yes, she was scared for me, but her central belief about me is that I am a reincarnate of one of her heroes, Dr. Martin Luther King, Jr., who was assassinated five days before I was born into this world in April 1968. My mother, an educated woman with heroes in the western world and religious beliefs in the eastern, believes that his soul had wandered from America to India in search of a worthy vessel to carry his work forward. Naturally, this baby of hers was that vessel, and, at twenty-three years, the child's time had come.

These parents of mine should have known better. They come from these very parts in which I am now afraid for my life. The villages of Purulia district, the place we were returning from, are bordered by the Dhanbad district of Bihar, the land where my mother and father were raised, where the only thing more common than lawless gun killings is lawless rape. But my parents had come to live a modern middle-class life in Bombay, as an army officer and a five-star hotel executive. As I packed my bag for the trip, my father had told me he knew all about these skull worshippers, the disciples of the Ananda Marga, a socio-spiritual organization that promotes meditation, yoga, social service for the transformation of society, and the public performance of the Tandava dance of Shiva the Destroyer, which involves dancing with skulls and snakes. My father also told me they are hated and often murdered by people who hate them. Or is it they who are doing the murdering? He couldn't recall. He wanted me to go have an adventure, be a strong woman. An adventuress.

They are the ones being murdered, my reporting tells me. They and the people who visit them. I spent two nights lying awake reading newspaper reports of how people from the same fucking room in which I was lying awake, from the same fucking bed, had been abducted to later turn up dead, their bodies dismembered or raped or both. By whom? The cadres of the Communist Party of India (Marxist), which was the ruling party in this state in 1991. I spent two nights convinced that I heard a comrade breathing heavily outside my bedroom window. I practiced screaming "I love Marx!" at my imminent abductor. I practiced screaming it in Bangla, the regional language: *"Ami Marx ke bhalobashi!"*

I didn't get abducted. My body was not dismembered or raped. I am whole. But, when I am thrown off the train with the other reporters, I feel a rage with this whole self of mine. My mind is swimming with confusion over communism, capitalism, and whether the Ananda Marga truly wanted to present a middle path. I have met nuns who taught the village children and I have met monks who talked down to the nuns. I know the west (and even urban India) exoticizes my country for things like skull worshipping, but I have also just learned how this practice is rooted in spiritual meditation. I have questions and they come at me so fast and hard, I feel a fear for the first time that I will be pulled far into their orbit.

This is not my calling, I tell myself as I struggle to put my clothes back on over my wet skin in the railway platform shower. My audience of men grins at the obvious actions of me pulling on my underwear. They clearly have no train to catch.

Nope, not my calling. World leaders like Václav Havel and Lech Wałęsa have asked the CPI(M) to lay off the Ananda Marga, but these are not *my* stories. I am no Gandhi being thrown from a train.

I have no souls to channel and no souls to save. I want to find a good man and get married. I want to wear pretty clothes and shower in a private en suite bathroom in which my husband has scattered rose petals. I have always hated the slightest bit of adventure, let alone revolution. I have a deep dislike for travel. I am fucking terrified of strangers. The only news stories I want to cover from here on out will relate to fashion, I decide, or maybe something even safer, like the market price of summer mangoes. I never want to leave home. If they agree to let us board the next train out of Allahabad and if I ever do find my way back to Bombay, *I will never leave home again.*

It's not like I didn't know of feminism at twenty-three years of age. It's not as if, upon being told about feminism, I didn't experience a rush of relief that this feeling I had had for the first two decades of my life as a girl, this feeling that something was *terribly wrong*, that this knot that rose in my chest, a rage and a sorrow and a mad yearning coiled desperately together, growing, growing so I could barely breathe anymore, hadn't found its salve in this thing called feminism. So my father's regular beating of my mother and his children wasn't him being "a good disciplinarian" but a violent patriarch! So my brother being allowed to have a string of girlfriends but my never being allowed to be alone with my male college friends was a policing of my sexuality! So me having to tie a string on my brother's wrist on the festival of Raksha Bandhan was a twisted celebration of his bravery and a plea for him to protect me, even though he was my most frequent violent tormentor!

I first heard the word "feminism" when I was twenty years old from a professor in my all-women mass communication postgraduate program in Bombay. The head of my department, a woman named Jeroo Mulla, smiled at my comments in class and told me I was a feminist. I wasn't alone in the despair I had felt for years, she said, and I should read a book by someone named Simone de Beauvoir and interview an Indian feminist lawyer named Sheela Barse. I fell upon feminism with a hunger I had thus far not understood and had tried to wish away.

It's not like I hadn't taken myself on a feminist journey before either. As I started to devour books on feminism, I had, on a visit to my uncle and aunt in Bangalore, begged my uncle to let me stay alone overnight for two nights in a cottage at the Mysore Race Club. I wanted to be alone to read my copy of Germaine Greer's *The Female Eunuch*. I wanted to be alone to deeply feel the feelings I knew the book would stir up in me. I wanted to retreat into the kind of solitude that feminist practice recommended, years before I read of such a recommendation. I was twenty, and Greer's Western feminist call from the 1970s—to imagine ourselves as more than wives and mothers—echoed perfectly into the imagination of a Bombay girl in the late 1980s. I wouldn't quite heed her suggestion to taste my own menstrual blood, but everything else in that book made me feel less alone than I had in my whole life, sitting there all alone in the shade of a banyan tree in Mysore.

But while my feminism had been a salve and a retreat, it had been an intellectual exercise until that day when I was naked on a railway station platform. That day, I learned that feminism would strip you down sometimes and ask you just how badly you really wanted to take up space in a man's world. How far do you want to roam from "home"?

<hr />

I roamed. You could say I was just a person who roamed, but, no, I was a *woman* who roamed. A woman roaming far from home had better have a good reason. She follows her husband, and I, too, did, when I followed mine for his career, to Bangalore and then Singapore.

But to roam away from home and husband and protection and head on to nothing, *who does that*? A sixteenth-century mystic poet like Mirabai does that (but she, too, left her aristocratic home only to go about singing of love and devotion for a man-god, Krishna). And, a feminist sometimes does that.

The reason feminism made it feel like I was finally breathing is that it gave me a flicker, a sensation that I could perhaps move my body through the world on my own terms. My policed body, my body that had been publicly taunted (people in the streets of India would shout "*langdi*"—cripple girl—because I limped from polio), and my body that had been privately and publicly invaded (by predators on the streets and at home), this body now had the knowledge of a solidarity across continents, across decades. Feminism told my body that what happened to me hadn't been my fault. Feminism whispered to me about the possibility of resistance. Feminism laid out a series of risks and smelled thickly of ruin, and I couldn't even tell how good or bad a feminist's life could be. I had no role models for quite the mess I was about to make.

In *Living a Feminist Life*, Sara Ahmed says, "Feminism is DIY: a form of self-assembly. No wonder feminist work is often about timing: sometimes we are too fragile to do this work; we cannot risk being shattered because we are not ready to put ourselves back together again. To get ready often means being prepared to be undone."

I was never ready and I am never ready to be undone. Like the Copenhagen mid-century microfiber sofa in sage green from Overstock.com that I assembled on my own in a temporary apartment after my second divorce, my feminism has legs but they are screwed on wrong, askew, pointing neither neatly inward nor brazenly outward (if this sofa were walking down the street in India, it would be taunted). The legs are still askew because I have gone from being too tired from sobbing to being too busy from achieving to being too disinterested in seeking perfection. I just can't bring myself to reassemble and screw things on right. My DIY is always shaky, and even when I sit back and relax on my feminist laurels, something feels just a tiny bit wobbly.

I still want a loving husband. I don't need protection, but I'd love those rose petals.

I still hate traveling alone. I love trains and I love ticket collectors.

There's no arrival in feminism, only departures upon departures. In *Seeing Like a Feminist*, Nivedita Menon reassures me that feminism is not about a moment of final triumph over patriarchy but about the gradual transformation of society so decisively that old markers shift forever.

If you think I have gone too far, perhaps you are a bad feminist. If I think I am still lost, perhaps I am a bad feminist. When I am lost, I read writers like Roxane Gay, who tells us, in her book *Bad Feminist*, not to identify with any prescriptive "essential feminism," which makes rules for feminists and thereby defeats the purpose. When I am searching, I talk to other feminists. So I asked some of them how to be better bad feminists.

My friend Cleo in Louisiana says she has never used the word "feminist" for herself. I am stunned, because she is one of the best intersectional feminists I know, or maybe I just need her—a Black journalist turned academic at a historically Black university in New Orleans—to be an intersectional feminist hero *I personally know*. But she was taught to serve the men, she says. "Black men were treated so badly outside the home that we women would have to rebuild them when they walked in the door. I remember bringing my father his slippers. My mother would cook a delicious dinner and he would put his feet up and watch television." Cleo is in her sixties and is close to retirement. She and her husband shared in household duties and taught their boys to do so, she says. But a feminist? She's not so sure.

My colleague Victor Evans, a Black gay media scholar, says his mother doesn't call herself a feminist, and he's disappointed too, because she raised her children with such strength and grace, she had to have been a feminist.

I am also somewhat challenged by the feminism of a woman who *does* call herself a feminist, the woman who introduced me to the term and the identity and the books, my professor in Bombay and now my friend, Jeroo. When Gibran and I visited her in Mumbai in 2018, she took us out to lunch and, as we caught up, she wondered if the #MeToo movement may be going too far and ruining some good men's lives. Gibran and I exchanged a glance. I'd wanted to introduce my boy to my feminist guru. The next day, after I spoke to her class and rejoiced with the students about their radical stand on the #MeToo movement, Jeroo had tears in her eyes and said she was moved by how her students over generations were advancing their feminism. This constant learning and unlearning between feminists is where I rest my head and heal my heart.

For Roxane Gay, dancing to "Blurred Lines" (a song that is said to glorify rape culture) felt good, and the label "feminist" felt uneasy because it had, historically, "been far more invested in improving the lives of heterosexual white women to the detriment of all others." Given my own colonized education growing up in India, I am still struggling to emerge from under the influence of white feminism and commit myself over and over to feminism that centers Black and brown bodies.

For Max Delsohn, a young white transgender person and rising stand-up comic and writer in Seattle, their mother was definitely not a feminist. Feminism saved Max when they identified as a lesbian woman, and feminism was there for them in their trans identity like no mother could ever be. "Where would I be without feminism?" Max says.

A similar tension comes up for Gibran's friend Cal, who has recently been struggling with what he calls his mother's "TERFy (trans-exclusionary radical feminist), second-wave feminism." Cal was in a relationship with a trans, nonbinary person and his mother kept insisting on referring to them as "she," even after Cal asked her repeatedly to respect his partner's pronouns. Cal had grown up with his mother as breadwinner and his father as homemaker pursuing his career as an artist. But now Cal saw the limits to his mother's feminism and then was faced with the limits of his own as he navigated romantic and sexual relationships. "I expected certain things from my first girlfriend that I didn't demand from myself," he says. "Feminism has been like being under water and coming up for air and then having to go under again and again." But, ultimately, it's been fulfilling and made his life easier, he says. It enables him to explore his own white masculinity outside of societal norms.

The poet Anastacia-Reneé tells me over dinner that she is a bad feminist because she judges women on conventional beauty standards, but maybe that's because she feels judged, she says; for instance, when the other women writers show up at a reading dressed to the nines, dresses, makeup, heels, and all. We talk about how the pressure to look good is real. I tell her that when I am invited to speak at an event, I decide what I am going to wear before I decide what I am going to speak about or before I put a word down on the page. Sometimes I go out and buy something new because my over-stuffed closet still tells me I have nothing to wear. So, who is the bad feminist here: Anastacia-Reneé, the women who judge her, or me?

Can we go through any gathering of women without comparing ourselves to one another?

When I am in a group of South Asian women in Seattle, the conversation invariably shifts to where our kids are going to college. Oxford, Cambridge, Princeton, Stanford, Harvard, Swarthmore.

I grow uneasy. The women shift to talking about the suicide of the daughter of one of the members of the community. They very gently blame the mother. "She ran a tight ship," one of them says. The others nod. I want to say something about how they are being judgmental, but I want to have them, at least as some kind of community.

To be in the company of women can be the most beautiful, empowering, raucously fun thing. Sooner or later, though, the cracks start to appear and the patriarchal norms seep in, like hidden instructions on the Evite to the potluck. We're underdressed for the occasion. We're unmarried for too long. Our children are killing themselves.

When I was a girl, the teachers in my Jesuit-Catholic high school in Bombay believed in corporal punishment. They would use a wooden foot rule to whip us on the palms of our hands if we'd been bad. The back of our hands if we'd been worse. The instrument that was used to measure was turned into an instrument of torture. With feminism, we are doing the same at once.

Let's just admit that we do not yet have the lens, the language, or the socialization to comprehend what an unquestioning love for women would look like. It took me years of struggle to even learn to catch my own sexism and internalized misogyny. I sometimes said terrible things about other women within hearing distance of Gibran. I often said terrible things about my body instead of just enjoying that ice cream with my toddler. I always felt ashamed when my boy cried on the playground in front of other boys.

Feminism, like yoga, is a practice, and perfection is an illusion. You were a good feminist on Tuesday, but on Sunday you think your feminist friend may have gone "too far."

These days, though, I am drawn to a sport called Extreme Feminism. (Just kidding. We're not calling it a sport yet.) But yes, I am drawn to the feminism of women like Mona Eltahawy, a self-described "impolite feminist." In 2011, this Egyptian American writer was in Tahrir Square, covering the Egyptian Revolution during the Arab Spring. She was detained by the police and then physically and sexually assaulted by them. Since then, she has chosen to be uncivil, curse, call people on their shit. On Twitter, she tells institutions, governments, and white feminists who try to shut her down to "fuck off, kitten."

I am also still grieving the death of a Pakistani feminist model named Qandeel Baloch, who fashioned herself into a social media star within the patriarchy of Pakistan. "Love me or hate me, both are in my favour. If you love me, I will always be in your heart, and if you hate me, I will be in your mind," she told her detractors who couldn't bear to watch her flaunt her sexuality. In 2016, she was murdered by her brother.

"It's time to bring change because the world is changing," she had said.

Our brothers are beating or murdering us, and yet, somewhere inside me is still the twenty-three-year-old who just wants to go home and pretend everything is OK. But almost thirty years after that naked moment at Allahabad railway station, that moment of wanting to swear off roaming, of wanting to run right back into the brawny but brutal arms of patriarchy, I have this to say—the greatest feminist resistance I have had to launch has been within myself. It gets easier and then it gets suddenly harder, over and over until it turns almost into muscle memory. Feminist struggle becomes pleasurable.

Good feminism feels good even if mostly just in the head, ineloquent and incomplete. Bad feminism is like the soot that's curled into the cuticles of our toes, but if we see it, we know it will one day come out in the wash, and watching it run down the drain will feel so, so good. When feminism turns to love, we can lavish it upon those for whom we want a good life. Like the ash-cloaked, mottled ascetic of the Kumbh Mela for whom those showers on the railway platform were built, I, too, was meant to roam. Raising a good, feminist man and then sending him out into the world has been my truest pilgrimage.

TO DO:

- I urge you to track your feminist journey: When did you first hear the word? When did you first feel it warm your bones? When did you say, "I don't really call myself a feminist; I'm a humanist"? When did you throw yourself in like your life depended on it?

- Make a list of your feminist moments. Do you reflect on them differently in hindsight? Can you acknowledge the "bad feminist" moments and build something good from them?

Chapter Three

WHAT WOULD THE GODDESSES DO?

———————————————
··································

Some years ago, my mother gave me a selection of childhood photographs to keep for myself. One of these is a black-and-white picture of my brother walking on a Bombay beach with my mother. The year is 1971; he is around four years old. His chubby palm is locked in my mother's hand, smiling the slightest smile at the waves at his feet. Sweet baby boy.

He now physically threatens our mother. My country, my father, my own mandated silence and my mother's raised him to do this. My father was a wife beater and child abuser. My brother trained under the best and practiced on the easiest—me.

When I got pregnant at twenty-six and found out I was having a son, I wept while my husband rejoiced. I wanted a daughter whom I could raise to be strong, secure, and sassy. I wanted two of those. What would I do with a son? I was afraid. What would he do with *me*? What if he grew up to be like the men I'd known? What if he assaulted women? What if he assaulted *me*?

I remember clearly the evening at the ultrasound clinic in Bangalore, when my ob-gyn barely looked at me as she slathered cold gel on my belly. The gel both soothed and singed the fresh stretch marks there, red and angry from my incessant scratching, even though I had been warned that the more satisfying the scratch, the more lasting the scars. My body had been besieged by change—glowing skin, shiny hair, yes, but also treacherous bowels and swollen ankles that would only fit into the ugliest flip-flops—it was as if pregnancy was turning my body into a Disney movie in which I was both the beauty and the beast. Pregnancy is the real tale as old as time.

The ob-gyn looked at the ultrasound image and her face broke into a wide grin as she turned to my then-husband and told him we were having a boy. I asked her to check again. My husband, Rajat, leaned over the image along with her and they exchanged a look and laughed and said yes, definitely a boy.

Let me take a moment here to say that this was some twenty-five years ago, and in my world then, a penis in the ultrasound led to the assumption that you were having a boy, and the general practice was to conflate sex assigned at birth with gender identity. We know better now, so we know gender is more fluid. You may think you are having a boy, raising a boy, and that your boy will grow up to become a man. But your child may feel differently. You may actually have a trans girl. Or a nonbinary kid. And that's an adjustment and celebration for your family to have. This book proceeds with the assumption that you are the parent of a boy or are a family member or friend of a boy, or in some other manner have some influence on the raising of a boy. Feminism works for all genders and you'll do great as long as you stay open and accepting of your child.

Back in that ultrasound room in 1994, though, this is what happened—I burst into sobs. I broke from the tradition of wild celebration in India at the news of being blessed with a boy, and I cried.

Hormones, said the ob-gyn.

Absolutely, said the husband, who is now an ex-husband.

I already knew Rajat wanted a boy. "I wouldn't want to raise a girl in this world of ours," he said as we left the clinic. The skin on my belly was still clammy from the gel. He twiddled his thumb at me in a mocking gesture indicating the unmistakable embryo-penis he had seen on the screen. My sobs turned inward.

The lab assistant, a middle-aged woman, approached us as we walked to our car. She asked my husband for a baksheesh, a little tip for the good tidings in the birth of a boy. I turned my tear-soaked eyes into her startled face and hissed "No."

The next morning, I woke up and shrugged off the dream of birthing a million daughters. We would adopt one, I told myself, not daring to share this idea with Rajat. Then I put my hand on my belly where my child and his penis were growing strong, and I swore I would raise one heck of a feminist son.

In the months that followed, I realized that all the most memorable stories around me about raising children had been about raising boys. It was as if my country, my womb, and my imagination had been in a tight umbilical conspiracy all along. I found myself taking those stories, recognizing their problems, rejecting their misogynistic messaging, and repurposing them to suit myself.

I wasn't raised religious, although Hinduism floats thick in the air in India. I didn't hear the stories through scripture, although references to deities spring up everywhere: in brand names of cars (Maruti) or the idea of the birth of a girl as the arrival of Lakshmi, the goddess of wealth, as if to begrudgingly offer comfort—she has some use!

I got the stories from comic books that took tales of Hindu gods and goddesses, and all their mortal dreams and failures, and placed them in the hands of Indian children. My '70s girlhood afternoons handed themselves over to these comics. I lay on cool cotton printed bedsheets and waited for my brother to finish reading each comic and toss them over to my waiting hands. The vivid illustrations of muscular gods wielding shiny gold weapons and slim-waisted, busty goddesses clad in filmy fabrics captivated my heart. The speech bubbles were written in a quasi-pious but perfectly approachable home-grown Indian English.[2]

Hindu mythology was awash in stories of mothers raising sons but had few tales of mothers raising daughters. When I held the baby Gibran in the crook of my elbow, guiding him to my milk-swollen breast, the goddess-mothers came leaping and dancing over my imagination and placed a guiding hand on my shoulder. I hardly trusted my own poor mother to teach me how to raise a boy, because by age twenty-seven, I had seen enough of how she and my father had raised my brother. So I looked back at those mothers from the four-rupee comic books. The three best-known stories of mothers raising boys told me that those boys had turned out OK (for the most part, for their time, for the misogyny of their moment and all).

One of the greatest love stories in Hindu mythology is the one between Yashoda and her adopted son, Krishna. The baby's birth mother, Devaki, was in prison, thrown there by her brother, King

---

2. Amar Chitra Katha comics comforted any anxiety I had about grasping five thousand years of complex cultural history by delivering me my heritage in the language, manner, and skin color of the men who had colonized us for two hundred years and had only just exited around the time my parents were born. The skin-color part I would only realize years later, on reading an essay in the *Atlantic* by writer Shaan Amin. He pointed out how the comics subliminally and overtly valorized the light-skinned, self-sacrificing woman who would set herself on fire on her husband's funeral pyre. The dark-skinned, the lower castes, and the Muslims were, of course, marauders.

Yikes.

But for Shaan Amin and for me and for our generation, here were our heroes, our deities, and our role models as our parents went about their pursuit of modern Indian/diasporic upward mobility, which precluded any deep religious training of their offspring. Thank goodness, but dear god. Of course when I became a mother myself, I also realized how terrifying and age-inappropriate those comics were, with the bludgeoning of baby heads, the trials by fire of women, and the rapes of queens, not to mention the hypersexualized pictures of women's bodies. I wonder if my Indian friends talk to their therapists about the scars sustained from Amar Chitra Katha comics too.

Kamsa. Krishna was born in prison, smuggled out, and given to Yashoda to raise. The babies born to his mother before him had been bludgeoned to death, dashed on the prison floor (I challenge my generation of Indians to erase from their consciousness the comic book visual of baby-head-dashing-on-floor), because King Kamsa had been told that he would be vanquished by one of these babies born to his sister. (Violent uncle for Krishna, violent uncle role model for Gibran, but we will get to that later.)

Yashoda, a woman from a lower caste, had no idea of the divine powers that the baby Krishna was born with. She was handed the smuggled baby to raise and got busy with the job of providing copious amounts of love. She nurtured the baby, sang love songs about this son, forgave him his butter-thieving ways, and, as he grew into a young man, enabled his outrageous flirtations with every young maiden in the village (some of the stories make these flirtations sound more like harassment, so I made a note to do better than Yashoda there).

For all her enabling and privileging, Yashoda raised a feminist ally. How do we know Krishna was a feminist? When Queen Draupadi (from the Hindu epic, the *Mahabharata*) was being sexually assaulted by her brothers-in-law after her five husbands wagered her in a chess match and lost, she damned all of those men in her life and called out to Krishna. The child Krishna had grown into an adult divine power by then, and he was sort of a part-divine-part-human advisor to this gambling-raping family. He showed up as an apparition and draped Draupadi in a never-ending sari. The rapist royals tugged and tugged at the miles of sari until they fell down, exhausted, unable to strip Draupadi naked.

At another point of time in the history of the universe (and in another comic tossed to me when my brother was done), a princess named Rukmini was kidnapped and was being forced into marriage with a king at the wishes of her brother and father to advance their kingdom. Rukmini, who had never met Krishna but had long had a crush on him from the legends she had heard, sent for him through a talking bird. Krishna arrived. She proposed to him. He accepted. They eloped.

May we all find men who, if we so choose, drape us in endless silk or elope with us when we're in a bit of a spot.

My son probably won't be called to exactly such levels of solidarity or divine intervention, and Krishna's own feminism must be scrutinized as a mere flicker of a torchlight in the dark millennia of patriarchal debauchery in Hindu mythology, but it's hard not to see Yashoda's love in Krishna's actions. Her adoption of Krishna in itself was an act of feminist solidarity.

From Yashoda, I learned to love my boy unconditionally.

Yashoda would tell us to love these things about our boys: their plump fists holding our hands to take their first steps; the way they bounce off the walls with a roomful of other kids at a fourth birthday party; the way they hold their necks upright and their faces serious as they disappear under a barber's cape at their first little haircuts; the way they wind their arms around your neck and their legs around your torso because they are afraid in the river or the swimming pool and Mama won't let them go, will she; the way they fall down and cry with all the thunder of the universe over a skinned knee; the way they blink in confusion the first time they are told "boys don't cry"; the way they run up to dogs or run away from geese; the way they look at their hands when they put on their first ever baseball or cricket glove. The way they take up room in the world and say, like an unbludgeoned, full-headed Krishna—*I'm here.*

OK, not all of these notations come from Yashoda. Some of them are mine. And none of these things describes the worlds of boys alone. I want to lean into our love of boys in that space before they are really much different from a girl, a nonbinary space. And I am also hoping and praying for a world that lets our girls take up space in exactly the same way as our boys, because there's enough space for us all, and loving our boys now means teaching them how to move over and make room, *make that safe and fulfilling space*, for our girls.

And I, daughter of Yashoda, could write a whole book about my love for my boy and beat her at being a myth-mom if I put my heart to it because oh, how my heart spills and sploshes with so much love. But, to raise a feminist boy, I had more lessons to learn than simply loving him. Indeed, loving your boy too much, loving him to a fault, is often the problem. The intensity of a mother's love for her son often slips into enabling his trespasses, letting him off the hook on chores, or trusting his word over the word of a daughter. God knows these sons of doting mothers show up among us in dangerous ways. If we loved them into being dangerous, did we love them at all?

And so I learned from Goddess Parvati, who was married to the god Shiva. The love and romance between Parvati and her husband are legendary, technically a myth, but don't you want to believe this really happened: Shiva was the innocent, the trusting, the all-devoted spouse who turned to his wife to guide his life and his decisions. Many young Hindu women fast on Mondays, the day assigned for worship of Shiva, and pray that they may find a husband like Shiva, a true emotionally and sexually satisfying companion for Parvati. I'm not in favor of the fasting, but I totally get the unabashed desire.

The sacred texts say, though, that Parvati was often lonely when her husband set out for days of meditation. On one of Shiva's endless tours, Parvati took the turmeric paste that she rubbed on her skin and mixed it with the clay of the river and the sandalwood of her prayer rituals and created a child. She loved him, sang to him, played with him, taught him well, but most of all, she raised her son to be loyal to her.

One day, when Parvati wanted to soak in a long bath, she told her son to keep guard at the front door. When a man showed up at the door, probably reeking of pot (no kidding, look it up), the boy did not recognize him as Shiva, the father he had never met. The boy refused to let Shiva in. "My mother is bathing," he said. "She deserves her space. You will have to wait for her permission."

Shiva, eager to enter his home and consort with his wife, beheaded the boy, as one does. Naturally, Parvati screamed in outrage and grief. In the manner of men doing a ham-fisted job within the echoes of their shrieking wives, Shiva replaced the boy's head with the head of an elephant. In the wake of this macabre trauma involving child murder and animal cruelty, he thus gave us the elephant-headed god Ganesha, the remover of obstacles. Ganesha was the god I prayed to when I moved with my son to live in America after my first marriage broke down.

From Parvati, I learned to raise my son to be loyal to his mother, to stay by my side, to believe me, to believe women, to let women take up space, and to understand things like the will of a woman. Things like *consent*.

What would Goddess Parvati want us to know today? That we can create our own boys, that we can raise them on our own, that we can have them be our allies, that they can love us deeply and honor our word.

And then I learned from Sita. She married the god Ram, and dutifully followed him when he was a king banished from his kingdom and sent into fourteen years of exile. When they returned, Ram was told to drive her away because she wasn't chaste (she had been abducted and held captive by another king, Ravana, something that probably would not have happened to her if she hadn't had to make the sacrifice of following her man into the woods in the first place).

Sita, pregnant by her husband, took shelter in the ashram of a sage named Valmiki. She gave birth to twin boys—Lav and Kush. For twelve years, Sita and her twin sons lived with Valmiki, where Sita told

Valmiki the story of the life of Ram, and he wrote the epic *Ramayana*. Valmiki taught the boys archery and literature. Sita taught her boys to play the lute and the drum. Valmiki taught them to sing the *Ramayana*.

Many years later, King Ram heard the two boys singing the *Ramayana* in the forest at one of his festivals. He realized that these were his sons. Legend has it that his heart immediately ached and longed for his most-beloved Sita.

Immediately? We're talking twelve human years here. We're talking teenage sons all fed and reared and educated here. Vaccinated, skinned-knees-kissed-and-healed, taken to all scheduled dental appointments. No wonder, then, that when I narrated this part of the story of the *Ramayana* to Gibran (in a completely objective, totally unbiased, free and fair journalistic retelling) as I raised him in Seattle, Gibran sighed and said: "So Sita was a single mom."

Village women in Awadh in the very patriarchal state of Uttar Pradesh sing a harsh critique of Ram and his invasion of Sita's idyllic state in the forest to which he had banished her. Their folk songs say that the boys had identified themselves to their father as the grand-sons of Dashrath and the sons of Sita, and they said they didn't know who their father was. Sita had given them a matrilineal upbringing. (In my interpretation, Valmiki nevertheless sneaking King Ram into the boys' imaginations is an epic example of dudes telling stories of dudes to dudes.)

The women of Awadh also sing folk songs about Ram then going to Sita to ask for her forgiveness. She sat under a tree, combing her hair. To my present-day mind, here was a woman at a retreat, per-forming some much-needed self-care, and now she had to contend with a man's abysmally late apology (and this only when he heard that Sita had begat him sons, ready for the throne and all).

Of course, she forgave him. But after that, yet another person (a man) raised the matter of Sita's chastity. Ram ordered a trial by fire for Sita, as one does. Sita walked through fire, proved her chastity, and then, rather than cozy up with Ram, spurned the universe for disrespecting women and asked her mother, the earth, to swallow her whole.

For banishing his beloved wife to the forest and ordering her to a trial by fire, the god Ram is hailed in some Hindu interpretations as an ideal for manhood. Sita lived to the age of 56. Ram lived for 11,053 years. Oh, and the *Ramayana*—the story of Ram and Sita's life? Valmiki gets all credit for authorship. But I digress.

From Sita, the exiled single mom from Ayodhya, I learned to give my boy a good education. I don't mean an elite education, which my single-, immigrant-mother status couldn't have afforded anyway. I did have some relative privilege, though, in that I was able to move to America and start a life as a single mother with my graduate school education, rather than play a lute in the forest and let a man take credit for my memoir. I sought out for my boy schools that were committed to equity between men and women. I wanted my boy to see women as the possible stewards of his intellect and his emotional development. His middle and high schools had a good number of women and LGBTQ faculty. At the college he attended, the president and the provost (the two highest-ranking administrators) are Black women. Representation matters. Almost all the classes he took for his physics major were taught by women professors.

To be sure, Gibran could have had an excellent education in India. He could have had a *feminist* education in India. He could have been spared the separate but equally egregious forms of misogyny in America. The fact that he could have had more privilege in India as a middle-class male than he had in America is exactly what made it possible for me to shape and reshape his feminist education. Unlike Sita, I *chose* to exile myself from some luxuries and stumble upon other trials.

Sita also raised her boys not to seek glory. Few stories—of ideal manhood or otherwise—make the rounds about Lav and Kush. Sita raised her sons to be ordinary men, not prone to rage or anger or hunger for kingdoms or the status of gods.

Another thing was happening for me in the raising of my boy, something that I would only make sense of later. While I often thought of the motherhoods of Yashoda, Parvati, and Sita, I never dared to imagine the kind of mothering offered by Goddess Kali. As scholars of Hinduism point out, Kali does not lose herself in caring for children. Her devotees are seen as her "children," and prayer-songs are sung in praise of how she negotiates her autonomy and agency and keeps her children aware of her power. She keeps them grateful for her attention.

As it turned out, I would have a lot of Kali in my mothering. I went for self-actualization, not self-sacrifice. I did not hide from my boy the challenges I faced in balancing my career, my single-mothering, my love life/divorce life, and the constant emotional labor of being an "untethered" woman who had to pull off success in order to stay respectable. I was so unlike most of the other Indian immigrant mothers we knew. I certainly wasn't one that fed my boy fresh, rich Indian meals by keeping myself organized in the cycle of fermenting, grinding, kneading, steaming, marinating, spicing, frying, saucing, and garnishing the shit out of my life.

Today, the stories of those goddesses have been appropriated by right-wing Hindu nationalists in India as prescriptive of superior womanhood and female citizenship—women who ought to turn to their duties within the traditional family unit, to eventually raise boys with more agency in their lives than their mothers had. Yet over the years in which I raised my child, I leaned into the better parts of those stories and knew I could do OK because I had an army of goddesses who appeared on the pages of my comics and illustrated to me how to raise a boy. A boy I loved; a boy loyal to me; a boy devoted to learning instead of dominance and glory; a boy appreciative of my efforts.

Some months after that teary appointment in the ultrasound clinic, the wide-open black eyes of an unwanted boy stared at me when he popped out of my womb and was placed on my chest. Those eyes said, "Hi, Mama. It's me. I'm *here*. I'm yours." I felt something crack open deep within, a gash in my soul that isn't meant to heal.

Twenty-seven days after he was born, a Hindu priest performing my boy's naming ceremony said that according to his astrological calculations, we had to pick a name for the baby that started with the letter K. Just for ceremonial purposes, to put down on the holy parchment, he said.

Sure, I replied. Krishna.

TO DO:

- Even in the most patriarchal cultures and situations, there will be stories from which to take inspiration. Take it where you can. Reject some stories, repurpose others as you please.

- Think of an influential story about mothering (or parenting or stepparenting or caring for children generally) from your own childhood. What might you have learned (good and bad) from this tale? What lessons do you want to take away? What do you want to throw out?

Chapter Four

HAS MOTHER GOOSE EVER HEARD OF FEMINISM?

▀▀▀▀▀▀▀▀▀▀▀▀▀▀▀▀▀▀▀▀▀▀▀▀▀▀▀▀▀▀▀▀▀

Once upon a time, there was a girl named Victoria who hated to wear shoes. She lived with her mother and father in their village near a hill. Victoria's feet were always dirty and scratched and bleeding a little from running around with no shoes. Her father worried about the child and her unshod ways. Every morning, he would sit ready with Victoria's shoes, but the girl would give her father the slip and scamper away to her school and then here and there through the cobbled streets and old shops and overgrown meadows. She was forbidden from climbing the hill that she could see from her home. Victoria decided she did not mind waiting until the day the hill would call to her. On that day, she would just go.

"On that day, she would not listen to her parents?"

"Yes, Gibran. On that day, she would disobey her parents and just go."

"Is Victoria a bad girl?"

"No, my *jaan*. She's just an ordinary girl."

Victoria was not a sweet girl. People in her village said that she laughed too much. Others couldn't bear to look at the scratches on her feet. But still others said they liked this child's face because her mouth looked like it was always full of fruit.

"Was it always full of fruit?"

"Only sometimes."

"Was that fruit strawberries?"

"Would you like it to be strawberries?"

"Yes!"

Victoria's mouth looked like it was always filled with strawberries. And it was true that she laughed a lot. She liked laughing more than she liked talking.

One day, news went around the village that a terrible storm was approaching. The village was still recovering from a storm some months ago that had blown trees upon houses and drowned all the crops the farmers grew. Victoria's mother grew wheat, and all of it was gone because of the last storm. People ran helter-skelter readying for the new storm. Cattle were pulled into stables, dogs were locked into homes, bags of sand were placed where bags of sand had to be placed. Prayers were prayed.

Victoria was told to wear her shoes if she wanted to go outside. Then she was told not to go outside. So Victoria sat by her window and stared at the horizon. She was the first to see the storm come slowly in. Victoria was only a little girl, not a sweet girl, an ordinary little girl, but even she could tell that this storm would take every good thing from her village. Before she knew it, Victoria found herself running out the door . . .

"Without her shoes?"

. . . without her shoes, without a plan, without a prayer. Victoria ran and ran and ran until she was on top of the hill.

"The hill!"

On top of the forbidden hill. The storm came rolling in and would meet the hill first, Victoria had seen from her window. Oh, if only you could have seen this child, standing there breathless on top of a hill, her heart beating from disobedience, her face flushed pink against the looming gray of the storm, her red-scratched feet digging into the mud on the hilltop. When the storm came, Victoria looked right in its eye, and do you know what she did?

"She laughed!"

Victoria laughed. She laughed and laughed and laughed at the storm. And the storm, which had never seen such an odd little child and had been forbidden to break down odd things, was startled. The storm was scared. The storm had never been laughed at before. The storm was sad and stung but also so relieved at not having to be a storm anymore. So it turned into a tender rain and rained gently down on Victoria's village and then went its way to be a storm some other day or never at all.

Victoria walked slowly down her hill and no one saw her and no one noticed her coming or her going because everyone was dancing in the streets in the gentle rain.

"Will you tell me this story again tomorrow, Mama?"

"I will tell you this story every single time you ask for it, Gibran."

★★★★★★★★★★★★★★★★★★★★★★★★★★★

"The Girl Who Laughed at the Storm" was the only children's story that I ever made up, a story between my boy and me, never written, only spoken, on a pillow with a mama's head and a boy's head and the story.

I first told it when Gibran was four years old, when we lived in Singapore. Although I was jobless and my marriage was breaking down, we lived what a lot of my friends would consider a beautiful life. My husband was a creative director in a multinational advertising agency. I had quit my job as a chief of the metropolitan bureau for the *Times of India* and had followed Rajat's career, quite happily at first. Then I had found myself freelancing but frustrated. Singapore has a state-controlled press, not quite the free, democratic press tradition that I was steeped in during my journalism career. No one wanted to hire me when they looked at my past clippings filled with investigative stories questioning all sorts of authority.

Rajat worked late. I told myself it gave him the money to buy me jewelry from Tiffany. Rajat traveled. I told myself it gave me the chance to spend mother-son time with Gibran. Rajat went to parties to which he said spouses were not invited. I told myself it gave me the opportunity to hang out with other moms and take our kids to shopping-mall concerts featuring a purple-and-green dinosaur named Barney.

But something else crept into my head during those long afternoons, along with the story of Victoria. A chemical imbalance. A sadness. A depression. A desire to throw myself from the balcony of the tenth-story condominium in which I lived the life of an envied expatriate wife. I imagined myself lying on the ground far below, wearing my Tiffany jewelry, little blue boxes floating on the surface of the swimming pool.

"Will you tell me this story again tomorrow, Mama?"

▼▼▼▼▼▼▼▼▼▼▼▼▼▼▼▼▼▼▼▼▼▼▼▼▼▼

Stories keep us alive. Stories tell us how to live. Stories reverberate through our imagination and reimagining.

The world would give my boy stories of boys and boys and boys. I cooked up for him the story of a girl. A girl with scratches on her feet, not too far from the polio in his mother's leg. I imagined for him an unruly, disobedient child—a girl with agency over her decisions—quite unlike the mother that lay snuggled with him in those curtained afternoons in Singapore and that held onto him for dear life, facing away from the balcony. I imagined for him a laughing girl.

I had started reading to him early. When he was a baby, India's markets had just opened up to economic liberalization, and consumerism was about to be anointed the prince of the land. In Bangalore, a young mother had opened The Baby Store and shipped in baby and toddler products from the United States. She sold these things called bath books. I thought it was the most wondrous thing, a plastic book with pictures of elephants and tortoises and ducks on it to show the baby as you held him in a warm, soapy baby tub.

Gibran's first word was "book." Well, it was "boo," but he was pointing at a book. He was eight months old. Yes, even all these years later, I brag about his early verbal milestone. (He walked late, at fourteen months.)

I must admit I might have ruined some nursery rhymes for Gibran with interruptions like: Why was the *queen* not in the counting house, counting all *her* money (instead of in her parlor eating bread and honey)? Notice that the maid hanging out the clothes was the only one exposed to the elements and so the blackbird bit off *her* nose. Unsafe work conditions!

Thankfully, I'm not the only one. Neuroscientist and writer Dr. Dean Burnett writes about how he read out loud to his son and fixed the rhymes and stories as they went along:

Mary, Mary, quite contrary,

How does your garden grow?

With a carefully planned system of fertilization, soil maintenance, and several other tried and tested agricultural techniques used by professional gardeners.

(So . . . not with pretty maids all in a row.)

Holding your child close and reading to them is arguably the one activity worth all the chaos of the rest of the parenting day. Studies such as one titled "Reading Aloud, Play, and Social-Emotional Development" from 2018 in the journal *Pediatrics* tell us that reading to a child as early as birth to three years old helps develop their brains, calm their behavior, and build closeness in the adult-child relationship. This is also where good human beings are grown. Literature builds empathy and empathy builds solidarity, especially as a toddler boy imagines the wide, wide world and, one day, helps reimagine it.

I asked my son recently if he remembered any of the nursery rhymes I'd taught him as a child.

"Who the hell remembers nursery rhymes?" he said.

Lullabies, then?

I was *asking* for that eye roll.

▪▪▪▪▪▪▪▪▪▪▪▪▪▪▪▪▪▪▪▪▪▪▪▪▪▪

Gibran's probably right. No one remembers nursery rhymes from their childhood, but perhaps we remember them from our parenthood. Isn't it one of the delights of child-rearing, wondering what kind of horrific mental illness drove the farmer's wife to cut off the three blind mice's tails with a carving knife, resulting in the bloodthirsty mice chasing her for eternity? That fish you caught alive . . . which finger did it bite? The adult, mothering me could almost feel a little nip on this little finger on the right. And I could easily forget my last address but I'll be damned if I forget that the muffin man lives on Drury Lane.

Should our hearts be broken that our babies don't remember the scandalous time when the dish ran away with the spoon? Nah. I do believe that what they remember is the love. What their bodies remember is the snuggle. What their voices remember is the singing. What their minds remember is the rhythm of something, the reverence for the word, the width and depth and texture of books. The art. The strangeness of those worlds (where it's OK for old men to play knick-knack on your thumb or little piggies to go to the market or babies to fall with their cradle and all) mingling with the already strange world around them.

In those early years, I read both Indian and Western rhymes and bedtime stories to Gibran, mostly with frustration over gendered roles deeply embedded in our best-known, most-told tales.

I went out in search also for feminist stories that centered girls and women triumphing in the world—for one, the story of Indian warrior princess Rani Lakshmibai, who led her soldiers in battle. I also read him *The Runaway Bunny*; this story of a little bunny who kept running away but whose mother kept finding him brought great comfort to me and helped me sow the idea in Gibran's mind that no matter what, I would always be close.

Contrary to popular understanding, the first fairy tales were written by women and were performed and recited in literary salons and later published in collections. These tales were actually feminist critiques of patriarchy, with heroines who had agency over their own lives, says Melissa Ashley, the author of a novel based on the life of the woman who wrote the first ever fairy tale in the 1600s—Baroness Marie-Catherine d'Aulnoy. The baroness wrote a story about a queen named Félicité, who ruled over a kingdom and showered affection and gifts on her lover, Prince Adolphe. He abandoned her and went seeking fame and glory.

Oh, Félicité, you and I would have been friends in Singapore.

The baroness's tales criticized arranged marriage. In her time, girls were married off at fifteen. (My mother was married off at fifteen. Seventeenth-century France and twentieth-century India would have been friends.)

Where are these stories now? The Brothers Grimm, whose folklore all of us in the English-speaking world know as fairy tales, came along and published their own collections, dismissing the stories of the seventeenth-century women as inauthentic, says Ashley. So in walked the princesses waiting for their princes to find them despite glass slippers and transforming chariots, despite evil stepmothers and wicked queens, despite spells that put them to sleep for a hundred years or forced them to kiss a million frogs.

When I was a girl, these stories had a hold on my imagination so hard, I wanted my brown skin to be white, whiter, whitest, believing that the snowy whiteness of her skin was what gave that girl Snow White such a loving heart. Whiteness was a signal of goodness, of being wanted, of being desired and being worthy of rescue. Cinderella's meekness in cleaning her stepmother's home, her suffering at the hands of the ugly stepsisters, her *victimhood* made her worthy of a fairy godmother. Her silence made her enigmatic. Her beauty and the mystery of her appearance and disappearance from the ball made her worth the pining of a prince. The slimness of her feet made them fit that glass slipper. (My polio made my right foot smaller than my left; would a prince like the limp in my step, that shameful twist in the tale? No.) And Rapunzel would hardly be worthy of notice if she'd had the pageboy haircut my parents made me sport all my girlhood. I wholeheartedly handed my imagination of myself over to these stories that were prescribing looks, poise, behavior, choices, agency, and values.

When it came time to read these stories to little Gibran, I thought I'd be ready with alternative plot twists, but I found myself identifying instead with the wicked witch, with the woman who talked to the mirror from being so lonely, with the stepmother, something I felt I was destined to one day be and that terrified me, because what if aging were to transform me into that kind of *evil*?

I abandoned the Brothers Grimm fairy tales and sought out Karadi Tales. These were homegrown stories from India based on folktales, and they started to be produced in 1996, the year after Gibran was born. The books came with audio cassettes, and the stories were narrated by well-known Indian artists. Stories like *Eyes on the Peacock's Tail*, *Bhasmasura and Bakasura*, and *The Blue Jackal*. Stories about the differences in cultures and the sharing of values. Stories about funny animals and flawed humans.

The old fairy tales will live on and on, yes, but in bringing a feminist lens to them, we can have a whole lot of fun. We can do this on our own, as parents and the village raising our boys, poking fun at the tropes; or we can find alternatives, like I did with the Karadi Tales from my culture; or we can, happily, reach for the retold tales by feminists who have reclaimed the tradition of the mighty literary divas of seventeenth-century France. By the time the humorous modern-day retellings by authors like Gail Carson Levine came around, Gibran had aged out of the wonderland of fairy tales, but it might not be too late for your boy. Go get yourself *Cinderella Liberator* at once. Feminist philosopher Rebecca Solnit finds the heart of the story in the interactions between Cinderella and her fairy godmother and recasts the tale as one of transformation and of women's friendships; she rewrote it for her great-niece. Solnit wanted to keep the wonder and magic of fairy tales but also make the tale more relevant and resonant for the possibilities available to all of us today. The best part of the retold story for me is that it also liberates the prince.

I sneaked into the fairy tale genre recently and found what is now perhaps my favorite book of all time. Which book, you ask? Well, it's called *Princess Sonora and the Long Sleep*, a feminist retelling of "Sleeping Beauty." It's about a princess whose curse is that she is ten times smarter than everyone else. Any guesses why I love this book?

Raphaël Liogier is the author of a book called *Heart of Maleness: An Exploration*, in which he exposes with honesty the male gaze upon a woman's body. In an interview when he was on book tour in Seattle, he told me about the origins of the Sleeping Beauty story.

The original was written by an Italian man named Giambattista Basile, who published a book called *The Tale of Tales* in 1634. In it, the princess is not woken up and swept off her feet—she's raped in her sleep. "A hunter-king comes upon a sleeping woman in a house in a forest," Liogier said. "He 'takes' her. She sleeps through her rape. She becomes pregnant. She sleeps through her pregnancy. She bears twins. She sleeps through childbirth. When her babies are suckling at her breast, they accidentally dislodge the sting that had caused her to sleep. She wakes up and is delighted to see her babies and doesn't question anything that happened before. And the moral of the story, we are told, is that good things can happen to some people even in their sleep." Liogier uses the tale to emphasize the point in his book that shaking off the centuries of storytelling in which women were constructed as the perfect receptacles of male fantasies won't be easy.

In Gail Carson Levine's retelling, Princess Sonora actually has some agency over the spindle and the piercing, and she falls asleep at her own convenience. And whom does she choose as her partner? Not the mighty prince first intended for her but a shepherd, because he has a million questions and Sonora has a million answers. Ahem.

▪▪▪▪▪▪▪▪▪▪▪▪▪▪▪▪▪▪▪▪▪▪▪▪▪▪▪

I checked in with parents of young children to find out what they're reading to their kids these days. My friends Niketa and Abhilash live in Australia and are intentional and dogged in their search for the right stories to share with their two toddler boys whom they want to raise as feminists. Of course they would be. They met while working for a nonprofit organization in India focused on providing microfinance to impoverished women. Niketa's career now takes her around the globe interviewing women in rural villages and urban slums, working with their own wisdom to design programs for their economic benefit.

"We make it a point to find books where girls are the star," says Niketa. A favorite of her family's right now is *RAD Girl Revolution* [pitched as a book for "little girls with big dreams," with pictures of aspiring acrobats, CEOs, farmers, paleontologists, and presidents]. "But we also make it a point to find books in which boys are free to engage in traditionally 'girly' activities, like playing with dolls, and exhibit 'girly' characteristics, such as, well, sensitivity."

It gets harder when you get into nursery rhymes, though. One of their older son's favorites has always been "Ten Little Monkeys Jumping on the Bed." "I've tried and tried, but have failed to find a video version with a female doctor or a daddy monkey," says Niketa. "Perhaps in response, I make it a point to constantly remind my son that his grandmother is a doctor."

Danielle Holland is a feminist podcaster in Seattle with an eight-year-old son. As a cisgender, heterosexual white woman raising a white boy, she feels an urgency to "decolonize her bookshelf." Decolonizing stories is a practice that many are embracing, and it involves actively resisting and rejecting the colonialist domination of narrative, storytelling, and literature that have pervaded the white, Western, and mainly American imagination for centuries. Only 7 percent of children's books published in the US are by Black, Indigenous, or Latinx authors. Stories by white authors about people of color pander to the white gaze. What treasures of wonderment, geography, and representation are we denying all our children?

Holland wants more for her son. "Ever since I read him his first book, I have examined what stories I tell him, what stories I share.

I bring home stories of Palestinian girls, of Black boys in New York City, of princesses who dismantle their worlds and their titles, of Indigenous children, of Latinx girls struggling with identity, of all the ways I want him to be able to see from the lens of, to empathize with, to understand." Curating her son's library is one way to raise a feminist, anti-racist son, Holland says. But a complete censorship of reading material is neither possible nor desirable. "When we read books that push up into territory I don't believe in, we examine it together. I encourage us to push back on it. We read a certain popular Goosebumps book and I asked, 'Why is she being described this way? What do you think it means?' He thinks. He answers."

This kind of critical thinking then extends to other media, Holland says. While watching a new Disney movie recently, her son paused the film, interrupted the story, and said, "This is sexist. This is wrong."

And then Holland witnesses her son reimagining the world, which is the best part. "My son likes to create LEGO creations and then will spend at least the same or double or triple the amount of time telling me about what he created. Yesterday, he built a new LEGO world. And in this world he had created, there were different access points. This is how you enter this world and how you see it if you are a girl; this if you are a boy; this if you are nonbinary." This is how we embed empathy and anti-sexist values in our children, Holland says. And it seems to be working. "So I'll keep doing what I'm doing."

What Holland is practicing with her son is a conscious examination of gender rather than gender-neutrality in the conversation of culture and conditioning. In the book *Raising White Kids*, Jennifer Harvey urges us to practice race-conscious parenting, which she describes as "a broad and proactive way of thinking about how we engage race with our children." Rather than not noticing the race of people around them, which has been the practice of "color blindness" by white people believing themselves to not be racist, Harvey suggests we notice and name race so we can be anti-racist. Rather than shushing your three-year-old who points out to someone's skin as being brown in the grocery store, affirm your child's observation. Similarly, conversations with our boys about gender can acknowledge and affirm differences and, gradually, allow for ways to discuss what those differences mean about how boys and girls or nonbinary or trans people may experience life. Books and stories, I believe, are the best place to do that. Holland's son is discussing the experience of boys, girls, and nonbinary people as different. It gives Holland a space from which to then enter conversations about a reimagined world of equitable joys.

Holland and I both have decentered boys in the stories we brought to our kids. The world will center our boys enough. Holland is aware that the world will center her white boy even more so than it did my brown boy. Staying conscious of these intersections makes a huge difference, which is why creative writing professor Juan Carlos Reyes prioritizes color as much as gender in the books he and his wife, Kandis Reyes, pick for their daughter and son. Juan is Latino and Kandis is Native American. They started out with books for their daughter, who is the elder of the two kids, with stories that would empower her as a girl and as a mixed-race child with a Spanish-sounding last name and as a friend to people of different races and ethnicities. "That said, she also had plenty of board books and early reader comic books that had male protagonists," Juan says. "But her collection definitely swayed toward female protagonists, and I realized how conscious she had become of it when she started pooh-poohing certain kinds of stories—hero stories primarily—that only had male protagonists in them."

Ultimately her little brother inherited her book collection filled with female protagonists, Juan says. Again, curating the books themselves is just one strategy, he points out. "I believe when he was around three years old, I started consciously turning tricks of phrase and wording for some of his old books and some of the books we had received as gifts for him and gifted him ourselves. I started to identify for him how compassion could work for male protagonists."

In order for his son to also feel proud of the gender he most closely associated with, Juan started curating male-centric superhero early reader comic books for him. (Of course, he found tons more of these than female-centric comic books.) His son also began curating for himself books that made a comedy of violence. Juan gently involved his son in conversations about the background of the characters, the consequences of their actions on others who were not on the page, how the characters' decisions were coming from them feeling bad about themselves, how they felt hurt or embarrassed. "He started to welcome explanations about everything else going on in the stories," Juan says.

Again, what Juan is speaking to is a strategy of give-and-take that I, too, had to use with Gibran over the years. I developed an instinct, a vigilance, toward story and story*telling*. We must tell the story, tweak it, nudge our kids toward curiosity, poke fun at some tropes, question stereotypes, course-correct as our kids push back or feel left behind. Juan calls this "a routine of contextualization."

Juan also wants to share with his children stories of formation and family. "Our relatives on both sides are quite the hodgepodge of badasses, male and female alike. There's nothing more empowering and confidence-building for kids than to tell them all about all the stuff their relatives before them have done."

What this all means is that we ourselves commit to a renewed joy of reading and also reading between the lines. It's not enough to be gatekeepers and curators and librarians. We each of us become writers and editors. And we pass on oral history as best we can.

The best thing I did for Gibran in the whole wide sweep of my parenting was give him a love for stories. He went from reading about twinkling little stars to Naipaul to Nietzsche in, like, three days. Or so it seemed. The snuggle of storytelling passed too soon, dear reader. I remember buying him a book in Singapore—*Grover Learns to Read*—in which the Sesame Street character does not want to tell his mother that he has learned to read, because he doesn't want her storytelling to end.

Gibran was no Grover. No such hesitation from him. It was my arms that were left bereft, the expanse from my elbow to my shoulder left cold, my words left hanging mid-sentence. Then one day, he was recommending books to me. Granted, I only pretended to read *Captain Underpants* and never got into the fantasy series *Deltora Quest*, but he did reintroduce me to the work of Indian Nobel laureate Rabindranath Tagore, a man who centered radical feminist women in his stories.

Again, it wasn't exactly the smoothest sailing. In building a world of boy and book, finding the right literature for your child isn't the only challenge you will have to navigate. America, in particular, seems almost to pride itself on an anti-intellectual culture, especially for boys. Not that India doesn't have its categories for men and masculinities, but "the nerd" as a boy with lesser masculinity is a category so deeply reviled and taunted in some sections of American culture, it worried me for years as a mother and it makes the educator in me dig my heels in still.

I encountered this categorization in my first year in the States, when I was in graduate school in Baton Rouge, Louisiana, and Gibran was in second grade. We were at Gibran's soccer game one day. He was running around happily on the soccer field while fathers were cheering their kids on (a bit too heartily, I thought). I was determined to enjoy this afternoon of Americana though, perhaps even assimilate into it if Gibran took to kicking a ball around.

Turns out, he didn't. He missed the ball as he ran around half-heartedly, kept trying to strike up side conversations with the other kids, or simply looked away into the distance. He wasn't miserable. In fact, he looked quite happy to just be there in the midst of the shouts and the shuffles with the other kids, though he was not doing much shouting or shuffling himself. One of the other parents, a father with a Southern drawl, said to me in a friendly voice, "Well, it looks like Gibran isn't going to be an athlete. But he'll still get the girls, because he will be a poet."

I remember laughing then, in the lighthearted manner of the pleasant woman, the immigrant mother just pleased that one of the other parents is talking to her, joking with her, drawing her into this surface form of American camaraderie. Later, though, I was quite bothered. Why were we labeling second-grade boys? Why was my child's lack of athletic skills on display and under scrutiny and available to be commented upon? Would there ever be a contest where Gibran got to win by being a poet and the other boys floundered in a public demonstration of their poetry skills?

I wondered if I was also upset that Gibran wasn't athletic, and I realized with a breaking heart that yes, I was! "The athlete" (later, I would learn that another term for this was "the jock") would be yet another group, another community, in which my boy and I were to be the outsiders, looking in.

It was only a few days later that it caught up with me, the other niggling point that had bothered me about that father's comments. *Get the girls*, he'd said. That man, on the sidelines of a soccer match teeming with seven-year-old boys and girls, was adding another layer of misogyny to his problematic gaze. Although he was talking up a fantasy about my boy's life in a distant future, he was also fantasizing about the girls being the boys' trophies, their conquests, their markers of masculinity. No matter his lesser masculinity, my boy would *get the girls*, the man was reassuring me. Getting the ball wasn't the only point of that afternoon, to his mind. Prowess at the sport would anoint the boys into masculinity; the girls would be the chalice from which they drank, the spoils of their virility. The poet would lie in wait.

By fourth grade, Gibran was concealing his reading habit from his friends. I noticed that he hid his books away when they came for sleepovers. He'd push himself to fit in by signing up for baseball and soccer, which he didn't really enjoy. His grades fell and his teachers said it was because he was bored at school. I took him to see a therapist and she said that when it came time for middle school, I should send Gibran to the kind of school that would nurture his reading and encourage him to develop "his off-the-charts philosophical reasoning." She highly recommended a private school. I struggled with the suggestion and then struggled with the decision (Which decision would make me a bad mother? Was this even about me? What would be better for Gibran? Where would I even find the money?).

The Northwest School was the only private school that offered him financial aid (my worker's visa status at the time did not qualify us for most kinds of financial aid in other institutions). An independent private school, it had the reputation of being for "quirky" kids, which, I later learned, was a word for kids who read, loved the arts, and didn't necessarily want to fit into any of the other categories. They weren't that hot on *competing*.

Because of that school, I found myself less alone in nurturing the love of stories and books in my boy. I came to trust in their curation and their curriculum. When he left for college, Gibran told me that his two favorite teachers had been his middle school humanities teachers, Tamara Bunnell and Jeff Blair. "Speak to Jeff," Gibran said. "He's a feminist man."

Over coffee and a raspberry scone, Jeff told me why the books and stories we give our children, particularly in middle school, matter so much. "At that age, they're still open to influence and shaping. Our job as teachers is to provide exposure and ideas." Jeff has been teaching for thirty-one years, and in recent years, he has doubled down on the idea that schools need to be actively anti-discrimination, pro-fairness, pro-justice, and to present these as universal values, not politicized ones.

For this, Jeff says, we must present young people with stories featuring complex characters of multiple identities. The Northwest School does what it can—it consciously chooses an international curriculum: Chimamanda Ngozi Adichie's *Purple Hibiscus*, Malala Yousafzai's *I Am Malala*, Julia Alvarez's *In the Time of the Butterflies*, and many more. "So in some very mundane ways, we have boys reading stories about, for instance, someone having a period. Girls have that demystified for the boys they go to school with. In our patriarchal, male-celebratory society, the idea is for boys to get as many counter-narratives as possible." The one thing they still struggle with is that most literature presents characters on a gender binary, he says.

Jeff is also quite conscious that good intentions can still lead to things going awry. He recalls a lesson he says was "seared in his brain" while teaching George Orwell's *Burmese Days*. "A student of Sri Lankan heritage pointed out to me that Orwell's characters were two-dimensional at best." The other students in class did not get her critique. The student, says Jeff, rushed out of class in tears. Since that day, he has stayed vigilant to his own prejudices. Students are also speaking out more now, he says. Young people are showing up with an unprecedented level of discourse, drawing from movements like Black Lives Matter, #MeToo, the gay rights movement, and the climate justice movement. The books for this generation are still being written, but they're just around the corner.

Now I realize that the only children's story that I ever dreamed up for Gibran was heavy indeed with some of my own deep-rooted, unseen prejudices and programming. Why had I named the girl Victoria, I wonder after all these years. She must have come from my inability to shed the colonization of my imagination by the British. If Gibran would only ask for the story today ("Will you tell me this story again tomorrow, Mama?"), he'd hear the tale of a disobedient, unruly girl called Vimala.

TO DO:

- Edit the bookshelves: For as long as is developmentally appropriate, find books that give your boy a wide representation of characters with protagonists that (a) don't look like him, in gender, race, ability, et cetera, and with agency over their lives, and (b) that look like him and make good choices. Browse the Resources chapter on page 235 for recommendations.

- Edit the books: Read to your son the stories you loved as a child, but edit and contextualize them as you go along. Enjoy turning things inside out, and switch up male, female, and nonbinary characters.

- Start a conversation: Ask questions like (a) Who needs help or rescue and who is doing the helping or rescuing? (b) Who is outdoors and who is indoors? (c) Who is punished for adventure and who is allowed adventure from the start? (d) Who is working hard to prove they are worthy and who is seen as worthy from the start? (e) And—to question the narrative of why boys must always do the protecting and rescuing—who must fight and rescue? Does it really have to be that way?

- Dr. Judy Y. Chu, a researcher of boys' psychosocial development at Stanford University, encourages us to ask boys what *they* like and dislike about a story. Ask them how they might tell the story differently. Listen to how the kids make meaning. Respond gently.

- Nurture the (feminist) storyteller in you.

Chapter Five

IF IT TAKES A VILLAGE, WHERE'S MY FEMINIST VILLAGE?

▀▀▀▀▀▀▀▀▀▀▀▀▀▀▀▀▀▀▀▀▀▀▀▀▀
▪▪▪▪▪▪▪▪▪▪▪▪▪▪▪▪▪▪▪▪▪▪▪▪▪▪▪▪▪▪▪▪▪▪▪▪

"Is my mommy going to die?"

Gibran was six years old and I was lying bleeding on the side of Highland Road in Baton Rouge, Louisiana. He and I had just been hauled out of the wreckage of our car after a hit-and-run accident on the way to a playdate. It was October 6, 2001, just over three weeks after September 11, 2001. (Gibran told me that for years after that day, when people spoke of "the 9/11 tragedy," he thought they were talking about our accident.)

Scientists say human beings are capable of something called "hysterical strength," which surfaces in a dire emergency like having their child stuck under a car. Child. Car. And those six words: *Is my mommy going to die?* That was the precise cocktail I needed to find the hysterical strength not to fall unconscious.

The people crowded around me said that my leg seemed to be broken. They were pointing not at the right one, which carried the effects of polio, but at the left one, my strong one.

I lay back and let my bones break at will. And still, I kept my eyes open. Oh, how blissful it would be to close my eyes and simply float downstream into my own pool of blood. Under the Louisiana sun of October, my boy's face came into view—he was sitting in the lap of a stranger, a kind-faced, beautiful blond woman among the crowd that had gathered. He was wearing his new gray Old Navy sweatshirt. The tip of a green T-shirt peeped out at his neck. His hair was still damp from the shower I had helped him take that morning.

For just a couple of seconds, I was awash in a peace that I had never felt before nor have felt after, because whatever bones were broken, they were in *my* limbs. All that mattered in that moment of sight and knowledge was that Mama had remembered to buckle her boy's seat belt, and, from follicle on scalp to pinkie toenail, the boy was unbroken, the boy was unbroken, the boy was unbroken.

But he *could* be broken.

He was asking a question, probably the most important question in his six-year-old life, and if you've ever been around a six-year-old, you *know* about their questions. We were alone here, Gibran and I. Rajat was in Singapore.

Rajat had suggested I go get a PhD in the United States, and I had arrived here at Louisiana State University. He had said he would quit his advertising job and follow me from Singapore, that we would immigrate to the US and live together as a family, and perhaps, if we wanted, return to India one day.

I had enrolled Gibran in first grade at Trinity Episcopal Day School with the help of a scholarship set up for us by the dean of the Manship School of Mass Communication at LSU. But when Rajat arrived, I noticed he hadn't brought all his luggage. He said it would arrive in batches. All seemed well at first, but after a couple of weeks, Rajat told me he didn't plan to move after all. He said he would return to Singapore and would visit us in the US every now and then. I was confused. I asked if he wanted me to return with him and he said he preferred to work in Singapore with no distractions. He left.

That day of the hit-and-run accident, as the LSU Tigers readied to play the Florida Gators, my head had been swimming with questions of whether to stay and finish my PhD or to find a way to return to my husband in Singapore and focus on being a good wife and mother.

Is my mommy going to die? I had to give my child an answer. My brain had to wake the fuck up.

Somehow that hysterical strength found its way to a synapse in my head and I asked little Gibran a question of my own: "Look at my face . . . does Mama still look pretty?"

I know I saw the corner of Gibran's little mouth turn up into a smile. As long as his mother was vain, she wasn't dying.

On the way to the ER, he and I lay in twin stretchers in the ambulance. They had strapped me in to keep my spine and neck straight. I swung my eyeballs to the leftmost corners of their sockets so I could watch my boy as he watched me. I could tell he thought this van and all its gadgets were cool and scary at once. "Listen to me, Gibran," I said. "I am not dying."

He couldn't nod. They had strapped him in, too, just in case he had injuries no one could see.

"I will never die," I said. "I will always be here and I will always watch over you. You hear me? I will never die."

▀▀▀▀▀▀▀▀▀▀▀▀▀▀▀▀▀▀▀▀▀▀▀

In the months and years after that day, I would have the time to dwell upon the hysterical nature of my promise. I have since realized that when you make a child a promise not to die, what you are really saying is that you promise to live, to live hard and strong, to keep your eyes open even when your body wants you to be unconscious. To live hysterically.

The weeks following the accident were a blur of trauma surgery, a long stay in a rehab center so I could learn to move again, and, the hardest thing of all—letting people in to help. I was thirty-three years old. In all those years, being raised in India and then living in Singapore, I was steeped in an important cultural norm: present a face to the outside world that says, "I'm all right. I'm winning. My family is shiny and successful and better than yours. They have my back and we have it all." Modernization and liberalization in India had only added a sharper edge to this—we were yuppies, we had walked away from "the village" to form smaller nuclear units, we traveled the globe, and we were living the dream of the glamorous expatriate life.

Letting strangers gather up my pieces from a car crash on Highland Road, letting new friends take Gibran into their home, letting acquaintances set up meal trains and hospital supervision for me until my husband arrived from Singapore felt like a stab of shame even through the haze of OxyContin in my hospital bed.

I had no village in Baton Rouge, Louisiana; I barely had a family. I had a fractured marriage in Singapore. I had a reputation to keep up in India.

The ankle joint in my good leg was mangled in the car crash and lost forever. Surgeons reconstructed things as best they could with plates and rods. (Three years later I would get a fake ankle, an implant.) Rajat arrived to tell me he was in the best years of his career in Singapore and couldn't stay with me to help. "Perhaps you could call your mother? Your sister?"

He left. My mother took time off from her corporate house-keeping business and flew over from India. My mother cleaned my wounds, fed me, and reminded me along with each dosage of medication that I had to save my marriage. When she left, my sister, Suhaani, flew over. She is seven years younger than me. When I was ten and she was three and we were kids in Bombay, she was placed in my charge, and my favorite thing in the world was to walk her to school and pick her up and play with her and tell her she could have anything she ever wanted from all the things I would own, ever. Now, as I lay recovering from the accident, her favorite thing in the world was to get Gibran dressed for school and play with him when he came home. She cooked for me and hid her tears as she awaited phone calls from her new fiancé. He was a British Indian doctor and had given her the most dazzling diamond ring but would keep forgetting to call her at the agreed time from his home in London. When I asked my baby sister if she might be walking headlong into what might be a loveless marriage, my mother called to tell me I was no longer to bring my hopelessness to the family. (And I was to save my marriage.)

Confined to a wheelchair for a few months, I rapidly gained weight. I had hated physiotherapy as a child with polio. Now I spent hours on physiotherapy. Students of kinesiology at LSU helped me find strength in legs that I could barely feel beneath me. One of them, training to be an occupational therapist, asked me about my support system. I said my mother and sister had come and gone but I was managing fine. "I have numbers to call if I need people," I said. "But I'm cooking omelets for Gibran from my wheelchair in the kitchen of my apartment and that makes me feel pretty cool. I'm resilient."

He called his supervisor and they gave me a talking to. "You will have to learn to ask for help. You will have to learn to accept help. You will have to let the world in," they said.

The world came out of the woodwork. The Indian community of Baton Rouge, Louisiana, visited often and sang me my favorite love songs from Bollywood movies. The campus community of LSU brought me books from the library. The faculty helped me keep up with my papers, offering deadline extensions I refused to take. The parent community of Trinity Episcopal Day School took Gibran out on glorious playdates. A young Korean woman in my apartment complex, a PhD candidate like me, drove Gibran to school with her daughter and had him over for meals of delicious ramyeon and kimbap with pickled daikon. A young Indian man, a computer science student, came around to wheel me about the neighborhood in my wheelchair. When girlfriends told me that he might be an admirer, I disbelieved them, so unconvinced was I of my own attractiveness as a woman.

At home, the six-year-old Gibran ran around me as I struggled to put away my walker and take steps on my own. "It's easy, Mama," he said. "Walking is so easy. You just put one foot in front of the other." He would bend down to the ground and hold my feet in his plump little palms to gently tug them forward. And forward they would go, inch by inch.

At night, when he'd hear me whimper from the efforts of the day, he would lie beside me, pat me on my shoulder and say, "It's just pain, Mama. Just pain."

·······························

It took a life-altering car crash to teach me to let the world in. To build a village. Once the village came in, they never left. The village was a concept. It built itself around me in a moment of crisis in the Chateaux Dijon Apartments in Baton Rouge. Thereafter, the village became, for me, a way of being. Where once Virginia Woolf exhorted women to claim a room of one's own, I exhort us to now claim a village of our own.

Those of us that live apart from our families, separated by geography or estranged for whatever reason, have both the burden and the opportunity to reimagine family. To construct a village in which we appoint new elders, new advisors, new aunts and uncles, new cousins and companions.

I did consider returning to the village of my origin. While so many of my friends were raised and educated to emigrate to the United States, I had never dreamed of leaving India. I know even now that I would never have left India for the US. I left *Singapore* for the US. And I only went to Singapore to follow my husband's career. So where in the world did that leave me now?

After I'd healed and was able to get around with less pain, I imagined what life could be like for Gibran and me in India—I could abandon my doctoral studies and go back to work for the *Times of India*, await the return of my husband perhaps one day from Singapore (because Rajat still didn't want us there, offering instead to send us money). I imagined raising Gibran within the axis of my nation's disapproval of my choices—and approval of my state of waiting. I couldn't do it.

I couldn't take my boy back to my country and my family and also build him into the feminist Gibran of my imagination. Over the next few years, this sense of mine—if I had ever second-guessed it—was proven accurate over and over again. For one, I was never quite welcome in my mother's home. When I'd visited with my husband, I was treated like a queen. When I visited as a daughter on the brink of divorce, the visits would start with celebration because I brought with me the golden, beloved male grandchild, but then sour quickly. My brother would be summoned. He would rage at me and physically assault me. If I was lucky, I'd get away with just being physically threatened. My suitcases would be tossed out. And, all through this, somehow, I'd get the sense that my mother still loved me but didn't know how to make the leap to letting me love myself.

The people on the streets of my country had already told me with their taunts what they thought of crippled girls, crippled women. Even as my intellect grew sharper, my body stronger, and my emotions more tender as I rebuilt my life on my own terms in the US, too many in my home country displayed a discomfort, a disdain, for a woman who broke the rules, no matter that I had *wanted* to play by the rules and what was happening to me was not my fault. It wasn't as if India did not have its own towering feminists. In fact, some of the best feminists I know are from my motherland. But in the everyday living, as news stories much more horrific than my own routinely reveal themselves in India, women largely must barter a certain prescribed matrix of respectability in return for protection. To be sure, there are women who don't buy into that. More and more now, women and LGBTQ people are marching in the streets of India, demanding and achieving changes to rape laws and same-sex marriage laws.

My own sister chose to stay in India after her nine-month-long marriage with that British doctor ended in divorce. She chose to keep our brother at a distance and navigate a tumultuous relationship with our mother and father. I still wonder sometimes if I could have done the same, but, while it might have worked for me alone, it did not feel right for Gibran's mother. Without the backing of my family, with the threat of my brother's violence, and with the memories of growing up as a disabled girl in my country, I did not feel whole in my homeland. To raise Gibran to be a feminist, I needed a whole feminist self.

That occupation, that home, that world: they were not built for our well-being in the way we newly existed, my child and I. I felt this now, down to my broken bones.

All right, then. In America, our well-being would come from my diligence. Our prosperity would grow from our minds, which I knew to be strong and fair. I would shelter my child from places where a woman prospered best if she played by the rules. I would raise a man who didn't know these rules and didn't himself prosper by them alone. I would strip him of all his upper-caste, middle-class Brahmanic male privilege. I would strip myself of all sense of lack. We would put our heads down and work for everything we got, and we would hold our heads high and laugh.

With the work ethic whipped into me by the city of Bombay, I earned my doctorate in a swift three years, moved from Baton Rouge to Seattle for a tenure-track professor job, and pulled my body together to its deepest beauty, so the highlights in my hair would distract from the awkward drop of my right foot and the painful gimp of my left. I worked with some focus to ensure that the watermelon-red of my lip gloss, along with the eloquence of my speech, would draw the eye upward from my scars and away from the suggestion of melting muscle, inflexible steel, or wandering screws that lay within my bones. I saved my money and bought stylish clothes and gorgeous boots within which to hide some terrible truths. I fancied myself to be a bit like Frida Kahlo, who, like me, had suffered polio and a tragic vehicle crash. I ignored the fact that she also had oodles of talent that had yet to characterize much of my own work.

But Gibran and I were good at school—we plundered this country's education system, staying away from all kinds of failure and flaw, eschewing both terrorism and the war on terror, and winking at its 50 percent national divorce rate, grateful Gibran wasn't the only child of divorce in his friend circle.

When I arrived in Seattle in July 2003, the only person I knew in the city was the department chair who hired me for the university job. I listed him as my emergency contact (although I was too ashamed to inform him of that). Well, we'd just have to make sure there'd be no more emergencies, wouldn't we? I sat down and made a to-do list: Make friends. Let people in. Find our village.

In this reimagining and reconstructing of my village, I had to give primacy to a feminist village. It was the only kind in which my life and my choices would now fit. Phyllis A. Katz's research and the lived experiences of more and more people around me were making this truer by the day—feminist children are best raised in ways that bend and stretch the notions of family. I am not calling for a rejection of the institution of marriage and traditional family, but research tells us that boys, especially, must see a bending and stretching of the traditional gender roles often played out in the conventional family structure.

In came a new friend named Rachel, who lived upstairs from us. A single mother from a large Catholic family, she'd had her son because abortion was forbidden in Catholicism. She was living a fiercely feminist life with a fabulous job as a Microsoft technical editor, but would deny even today that she was a feminist, such was the peculiar revulsion American women seemed to have for the term. Rachel taught me how to live in Seattle—go to coffee shops, get groceries from Trader Joe's, and definitely make use of the "children eat free" offer at Banjara Cuisine of India, even though the Punjabi auntie there seemed to glare at us, perhaps for laughing too much while never having any husbands along. Rachel also took me and Gibran in as members of her own larger family—parents and sisters and cousins and aunts and uncles with whom to spend Christmas, Easter, Thanksgiving, and the occasional rainy weekend.

In came Mara, a fifty-something professor in my department whose boyfriend was some fifteen years her junior. In an ivory-tower academic world where hierarchies and patriarchies are deeply embedded, Mara used her tenured status to call out colleagues who expected women to do all the work on committees, she challenged administrators who wouldn't hire women in top leadership, and she inspired students to vote in the presidential elections and then threw them a pancake party. She showed me what a give-no-fucks life looked like for American feminists. She doted on Gibran and asked him questions and told him he was one of the smartest young people she had ever met. She told him regularly why he must respect his mother.

In came Shahana, a single woman who had left a violent marriage and a stressful career as an architect and who was steeped in song and philosophy. She taught Gibran to sing Hindustani vocals and taught him to love the parts of himself that reflected a tender Indian masculinity with a voice raised in song.

In came Jen, a young single woman, professor of nursing, who'd take no shit from Gibran. She was the one who'd call him on a sexist remark here and there. She was the one who called out my regression into "sacrificing Indian mother" role-playing when I tried to cook a whole meal for the teenage Gibran while I was sick instead of asking him to cook for me. "Get up, Gibran, and go run errands for your mother."

In came my sister Suhaani again. She now lived, postdivorce, in Mumbai, but we also felt her close to us at all times. She was the classic cool aunt. Suhaani doted on Gibran from the day he was born, and she stayed a constant pillar of strength for me as I left home, first for marriage and then from divorce. She championed me through my ups and downs, even through the ups and downs of her own life and through the heart-wrenching fights we would have as sisters because we were raised into dysfunction, often unable to find our way back to each other for months. When Gibran was a little boy and had to get a shot and was afraid of the needle, Suhaani convinced the nurse to draw her blood so Gibran would see it wasn't so bad. I hold close a photograph of Suhaani and Gibran holding up their arms in solidarity over those shots. She supported Gibran and hosted him in her home in Mumbai at a time in his young adult life when he needed a change of scene from college. She was also one that laid down the law for him. She did all this because she loved me and Gibran and supported my feminist choices unconditionally. She lived most of her life as a single/divorced woman and spoke honestly to Gibran about her own feminist life. She is the Yashoda to my boy's Krishna. To this day, people say Gibran looks more like her than me. If you are an aunt raising a feminist boy, be like Suhaani.

In came Ruth, Jamaican Canadian British globe-trotting immigrant single mom and professor in the Social Work Department at my university. She had refused to marry the father of her daughter and now dated abundantly to satisfy her sexual appetite. One day, when she and a few other friends were over, the ten-year-old Gibran came out of his room and said, "Enough with all this talk about feminist studies. We need masculinist studies! Men need to be heard too!"

As my friends and I laughed raucously, Ruth explained to Gibran: "The world is made up almost entirely of men's opinions and men's histories and men's policies. That's why we have feminist studies— kind of like a whisper in the noise. You're growing up very differently in this home because your mother has surrounded you with loud, opinionated women. You hear us laughing here all the time. You're lucky."

Although Ruth's loving admonishment of Gibran warmed my heart, it also unsteadied me somewhat. Was I going too far? Would I see a backlash from Gibran? And then, deeper down, this question: Would the marked absence of men in my village harm my boy?

In 2005, when Gibran was ten years old, his father and I finally got divorced. Rajat still lived in Singapore and does to this day. A thing I had felt in my gut turned out to be true: even though he was at a distance, Rajat was forced into a more engaged fathering of Gibran than he had shown while we were married. This is perhaps one of the most ineffable and unmeasurable phenomena of divorce and parenting. In the traditional family structure, the mother often becomes the glue, or rather, the *elastic* that allows other members of the family to stretch out and away while still feeling bound to the whole. In our case, Rajat's frequent travels away from us in Bangalore and Singapore had often left me alone with Gibran, even when Rajat's family visited. My being within that family allowed Rajat to be a less present father. When my being with him in that unit was removed, he had to scramble and rise to fatherhood and the presence it demanded. He came through in the best way he could. He rented a studio apartment year-round in Seattle where he'd come to stay for ten days every two months with Gibran, telecommuting to his job in Singapore. It didn't provide a steady fatherly presence, I was aware.

I began to want quite badly for Gibran and me the kind of families I'd see at his soccer games. On Halloween, I'd look past the costumes and see The Family. On Thanksgiving, which really had never meant anything to me before, I'd look past the invitations we'd received for Friendsgivings and yearn to be seated at a table with a family of my own. On any given evening, I'd peer discreetly into windows of families gathered around the dinner table in the flickering warmth of fireplaces, with banter, cheer, and fresh-baked dinner rolls, and I'd feel for Gibran and me a loneliness so intense, I was afraid I'd evaporate into thin air and my boy would be left there standing alone.

In 2005, dating sites like Match.com had an innocence about them. Back then, we weren't jaded by swipes and routine hookups. Online courtships were slower. Alec and I emailed. He sent me a picture of his four-year-old daughter, Beth, making pizza with him. I sent him my résumé.

Alec wasn't the first man I met on Match.com but the second, so let's not say I was too quick to jump into a relationship. The first man was an engineer who said I shouldn't order two desserts at our dinner date, perhaps mistakenly imagining that he was going to be the one to pick up the entire tab, but even so, this made me rule him out instantly.

Alec and I arranged to meet at Caffe Ladro on Queen Anne Hill one day in May. We bumped into each other at the door. I had told friends I doubted that I could fall in love with a white man, but I hadn't contended with that flash of Alec's blue eyes, his warm smile, his open and honest face. In spite of my friends' instructions that dating best practices necessitated that I call the date to a close within two hours, our first date lasted nine hours—coffee, dinner, a drink at the neighborhood bar, and then walking up and down Queen Anne Avenue until 2:30 a.m. (Gibran was at a sleepover.)

I fell madly in love with this man even though he told me he had voted for George W. Bush (yes, even the second time). He fell madly in love with me. Friends joked that Alec and I could be like Mary Matalin, a political consultant for the Republican Party, married to James Carville, a political strategist for the Democratic Party. Everything was so lighthearted back then in the sunshine of this finger-lickingly good love. As we dated, we sparred over politics and made up over his impeccable pancakes. We packed our kids into the car and drove to the tulip fields in La Conner, a couple hours north of Seattle, for my birthday, where Alec surprised me with a birthday cake and the kids laughed as I cut it with my finger because Alec had remembered candles but forgotten a knife. Alec could listen to Gibran talk for hours about this and that while my boy watched this man whip up wood-fired pizza and mouthwateringly delicious saffron risotto and French onion soup and soft South Indian idlis and spanakopita and Turkish garbanzo bean salad. Beth loved to watch Bollywood movies with me.

Alec, for all his conservative politics, was a feminist in some ways (that made me overlook so much else). He spoke with unwavering respect about his women bosses. He'd buy little Beth a shirt that said "A woman's place is in the White House." He'd buy me writing retreats and cheer on my every success and rave about them to our kids and to his friends and family. Once, at a reading event of mine, as I responded to a question from the audience, I caught the look on his face as he sat there in the third row. He looked so profoundly proud and smitten, my breath caught in my throat. Rajat had loved me, but this man, here, was *head over heels*. Rajat used to call me his "diamond in the rough." I never quite polished up, though, did I? This man, here, asked me questions about my life as a journalist in India, about what I'd loved most about my doctoral research, about the books I wanted to write. And he couldn't keep his eyes off me, let alone his hands.

I couldn't help but compare him to the leftist men I'd meet— colleagues, or boyfriends and husbands of friends—who said all the right things and yet did little housework or childcare, "teased" me to bring me down a peg or two, let their hands wander just a bit during hearty hugs of hello, talked over me about politics even though I am a scholar of political communication, and had egos as fragile as the shells of freshly laid eggs. For better or for worse, I threw caution to the wind, and Alec and I began to create an ecosystem of parenting and dating and lovemaking in the packed chaos of our lives.

These were the best years of my life. Within a few years, I had built a feminist village alongside my professional life. I had a bevy of strong friendships and I had a wonderful man in love with me. I earned tenure at my university. Gibran was attending the Northwest School, with its financial aid and its women and people of color and LGBTQ faculty in leadership—the kind of feminist values I held dear.

When we surround a child with the people and values we consider important, they seek out more of the same. And so it was with Gibran. He started to read about feminism and debated with me about its first, second, and third waves.

He fell in love with Virginia Woolf. He fell in love with Rabindranath Tagore, whose work from the turn of the twentieth century is laden with feminist characters like Charulata, a housewife left lonely by her husband (Charulata falls in love with her brother-in-law, who cherishes her intellect; Charulata publishes her own book). Gibran grew more and more inspired by public intellectual Noam Chomsky. He binged the shows of travel documentarian Anthony Bourdain, a rakishly charming yet tender man. In high school, he spent hours after school at the now-shuttered Spine and Crown Books. There, he met Kristofor Minta, the bookstore owner, a straight white man with a wife and children, and a gentle poet, who Gibran counts as one of the big influences in his boyhood. Kris and Gibran left Seattle in the same year, Gibran for Swarthmore College and Kris to study an MFA at Syracuse University, where he now works in the Office of Disability Services. I never met Kris, leaving him and his bookstore to be a space and time that would always belong exclusively to Gibran, but I stay thankful to him for being an invisible (to me) part of my village.

It wasn't a straight and smooth skate around the park, though. Gibran went through his struggles with his place in this village.

Holidays like Christmas and Thanksgiving didn't mean as much to me as they did to him, growing up as he was in America, when his friends would disappear with their families and extended families while all he had was me. We didn't quite fit into the Indian community either—few of them in the Pacific Northwest diaspora had been touched by divorce, and most of them lived the American dream in American suburbs a lengthy drive away from Queen Anne Hill.

America also has a problem with childcare. As a working single mother, especially, I could not afford professional childcare. The inhabitants of my feminist village were, to me, better than any fairy godmother. Their carpools and their quick meals for Gibran saw us through those hard, early years, and I reciprocated. But, although I look back with a rosier lens now, I was often just fucking exhausted.

Friends back in India would say, "I don't know how or why you're doing this. Come back—we have maidservants here!" But what I recalled was an exploitative system of underpaid and often abused, almost always female domestic help. Even though I believed I had been a "lesser exploiter" while in India, I couldn't imagine raising a true male feminist within that web of a classist, casteist, cruelly sexist system. I had hired a nanny from within that system and brought her to help me in my final months in Singapore. That country instituted better pay for domestic help, but class structures prevailed. I still imagine ways in which I could have done better for Brenda Santos, whom I credit with not just Gibran's care but also for keeping me alive during the worst months of my life. In our shared alienation in Singapore, Brenda and I would talk about our favorite places to find plum cake in our hometown Bombay, and sit Gibran down to watch Bollywood films with us. When Gibran and I moved to the US, Brenda returned to India and joined the beauty salon industry; eventually she moved to work in London. We lost touch. Gibran and I often talk about Brenda.

America's own system of childcare is built largely on the backs of underpaid, undocumented women with no health insurance or other benefits. Feminists here speak of their discomfort with benefiting from this system but having few other avenues, as the burden of childcare usually falls on mothers. America's childcare issue is a feminist issue.

Another problem with our village was that Gibran was the only boy of color in his friend group, and in the years he was growing up, liberal white Seattle wasn't yet talking about race. It still has a long way to go, says Ruchika Tulshyan, mother of a four-year-old boy and author of *The Diversity Advantage: Fixing Gender Inequality in the Workplace*. "In Seattle, where you're navigating a white, liberal, well-intentioned but often negatively impactful type of mothering model, it's hugely painful for a brown, feminist mum like myself. I wish I had named clearly—I am looking for a feminist village, people who value intersectional gender equity, who want to raise anti-racist, non-misogynistic children, especially boys." Ruchika is slowly finding the kind of tribe she speaks of, but she says it took a lot of intentionality. It may be particularly hard in a city like Seattle that genuinely believes in and celebrates its liberal, woke status and then is shocked by stories such as one covered in June 2017 by Seattle's local NPR station (KUOW) about an email thread in which parents of white elementary school kids laid bare their racism when teachers and students wore Black Lives Matter shirts to school. In a backlash published by KUOW, white parents from the city's upscale neighborhoods wrote to their principals to say they were displeased. A Black Lives Matter day was too militant, too political, and too confusing for their young kids, they said. Many of them had harsher words.

Azure Savage is an author and activist, and, while still a student at Garfield High School, Savage published *You Failed Us: Students of*

Color Talk Seattle Schools, a memoir and oral history of his and forty other students of color's experiences with racism in the Seattle Public Schools. The book confronts Seattle's education system and shows how programs such as the advanced learning program harm students of color.

This was the Seattle in which Gibran grew up and this is the Seattle in which Ruchika's son is growing up. Both of us worked hard to find our intersectional feminist village, but it took some heartbreak along the way.

▪▪▪▪▪▪▪▪▪▪▪▪▪▪▪▪▪▪▪▪▪▪▪▪▪▪▪▪

As I was writing, I called Gibran to reminisce, and he reminded me of the bumps in his own trajectory.

That admonishment from Ruth? It had made him think. And, he tells me now, it had made him seek that very quality in his girl friends. "Ruth was super knowledgeable, super confident, and even combative. I'm combative when I talk about issues I'm passionate about and I seek that in my friends. I wanted that in my female friends in school and I was stunned when I didn't find it. Girls in my middle and high school would act as if they weren't smart. When I'd ask them why they seemed to be dumbing themselves down, they would say, 'Oh, you're being weird.' I started to have disdain for them. I didn't realize then how I was being anti-feminist."

Fortunately, one of his friends sat him down and educated him. Sienna is one of his closest friends to this day. "She told me about the notion of 'effortless perfection' for girls," Gibran says. "She told me how girls were expected to perform femininity. How they had to do an hour of makeup and yet look natural. How they had to be 'nice' and not 'too forceful' with their knowledge and opinions. It was quite sobering to see how it was for the girls among my peers. And my attitude was contributing to the impossible standard of 'you're damned if you do, you're damned if you don't.'"

I thank the Ruths and the Siennas of my village for being fiercely themselves and letting my boy catch up. When we fill a child's life with a certain set of values, ideas, and people, the child learns to find more of those out there on their own. The village expands beyond our making.

That is how the feminist mother stays hysterically alive. That is how the feminist son lives a better life.

TO DO:

- If you are in a traditional family structure, embrace the comforts and challenge the conventions. Speak to parents of other boys and build a community committed to the cause. Find those unlike yourself. Parents raising LGBTQ children (as well as LGBTQ parents) have experiences and strategies that find pathways beyond the threats of toxic masculinity and oppressive femininity that our heteronormative world places on our kids. If you are a white family, take cues from parents raising boys of color, because we bring intersectional sensitivities to our boys who are already at somewhat of a disadvantage in a world of white male privilege. Don't lay the burden on these parents to share their wisdom, but thank them heartily if they do.

- If you are a single parent or in a partnership with a same-sex parent or in any "unconventional" family structure, find others in the same boat. Give to them the same attention and care you would give to your family. Find your chosen family and nurture it. Find each other and find yourself in each other.

- Vote and lobby for policies and systems that support more than just the traditional notions of family.

- Lobby for childcare systems that don't exploit some women so other women can go to work. Make it everyone's issue, not just a women's issue.

- Enroll our boys in schools that have women in leadership. Rank colleges for the proportion of women and people of color in leadership positions. Our communities and our countries will shift if a whole lot of us heave it in the same direction.

- Meet educators and administrators at schools. Put "the Feminist Boy Project" on every agenda. Find books, exchange strategies, invite speakers and experts for talks and teach-ins. Go ahead—make a commitment to the parents of girls that you are raising good boys.

- Sometimes, as in my case, it takes walking away from one village to build another. Sometimes, like my sister or like Mara, we must stay and question our families, our neighbors, and our institutions.

- Make sure your school-going boy has strong feminist girls and LGBTQ kids among his friends.

Chapter Six

HOW WILL I SHIELD HIM FROM THE MEN AROUND US?

****

As I built my feminist village in my new home, my heart often wandered to those from whom I had walked away. Those men, in particular, from whom I kept my boy apart.

My father is, first and foremost, an officer of the Indian Army. He is a retired major. In fact, this is his strongest identity, so much so that when he got a job after retirement from the army, as an operations manager at the biggest advertising agency in India, everyone there referred to him as Major, as if it were his first name or as if he were leading these ad executives and copywriters into battle.

His signature has the word Major in it. His email ID has it too. If he could have his way, his wife and children would also call him Major.

And although Trump never served in the military and my father is lucky never to have suffered a bone spur, the two men remind me so much of each other. Gibran and I just happen to love one of these men.

My father is terrifyingly like an upper-class white American male. For centuries, his ancestors had been raised to expect the world to order itself to their expectations, and my father just lived out this ancestral reflex, no matter what the evidence. In his natural habitat, the specimen of male that is my father would be surrounded by his own kind, other Maithil Brahmins, considered (by those who are invested in considering such things) the highest within the highest caste of ancient Vedic Brahmins. These people initially settled in and around the state of Bihar, on the banks of the great river Ganges. (The Buddha, too, came from Bihar, but he walked away from this place before teaching them anything. I argue that he *had* to walk away, that he could not have stayed and become the Buddha we know.)

To describe a Maithil Brahmin, a popular line goes: *aj gung ta sang* (along the river Ganges). The Maithil Brahmins are an intensely cohesive community, so cohesive in fact that I still receive LinkedIn requests from strangers across the world with the same last name as mine. I delete these immediately. For a while, the only link to Brahmin that I could bear was the luxury-brand Brahmin alligator purse that my mother purchased at a flight layover and gifted to me. After a friend posted something about this brand name being cultural appropriation, I have let the purse languish in the back of my closet. My dog went and peed on it once.

The Maithil Brahmins have been studied by anthropologists for decades. An anthropologist at California State University, Chico, Dr. Carolyn Brown Heinz, notes the obsessive maintenance of genealogy records in this community. Maithil Brahmin men, through the patri-lineage, gain a kind of immortality, she has observed.

A male infant born into a Maithil Brahmin family will have "a pedigree of known, named ancestors and the assurance of constancy of identity at his unique point in a long, intergenerational chain." There are pundits who chant the names on this genealogy beginning with a "seed man" twenty-four generations ago. These men's names are considered so precious, they get inscribed and reinscribed on parchment every half century, to protect against decay and pests. The books, and the experts who keep them, ensure these Brahmin men's immortality, Dr. Heinz says.

In my generation and in my family, that immortal would be my brother.

And where are my sister and I? Our names, according to the genealogy protocol of the Maithil Brahmins, will never be inscribed, not in my father's line and not in my husband's either (that is, if I had married a Maithil Brahmin; I didn't). My mother's name doesn't exist in any book either, although she, too, is of Brahmin caste. Dr. Heinz tells us that no ancestress is in any book. We are, she says, "anonymous girls among those named and rooted men." The patrilineages of the men in my family go endlessly into the future with their sons, documented and asserted. Dr. Heinz asks us to be curious about how the Maithil Brahmins have used this genealogy and other devices to maintain such thorough-going patriliny.

My sister and I are experts on the devices that maintain such patriliny. In the case of my father's ancestry and his legacy, we have faced the complex and compounded effects of Brahmin patriarchy, aided by class privilege of the zamindars (landowning elite) and the violence of the military.

My paternal grandfather, whom I only met once when I was a baby, was a landowner and also a zamindar, a tax collector from other landowners. He also chose another profession—teaching. People knew him as Pandit Hiralal Jha—the word "pandit" earned for being a Sanskrit scholar and an acclaimed poet.

And yet, these generations of landowners could not but have the highest regard for property. To ensure the right command over property, you had to have command over family ownership. To have command over ownership, you had to maintain command over your women and children—the future inheritors of your property. Your women were to stay pure, chaste, obedient.

▀▀▀▀▀▀▀▀▀▀▀▀▀▀▀▀▀▀▀▀▀▀▀▀▀▀▀▀

My father broke from tradition when he joined the Indian Army. He says he was drawn to the smart olive-green uniform. He left behind his family farmland of more than a hundred acres, left behind his father and his mother—she was the third and only wife of his father who had survived illnesses. She was eleven years old when she married my grandfather, who was then thirty. She bore my grandfather eight sons and three daughters. You will not find this woman's name in that genealogy still being compiled in Bihar, so I will document it here—Bhawani Jha.

I met each of my father's brothers, my seven uncles, at some time or another, but I never met an aunt. Women moved away and devoted themselves to their marital homes and slowly lost close ties to their maternal homes.

My father broke further from tradition when he sent his fifteen-year-old bride, my mother, to high school and then to college. Although theirs was an arranged marriage, my father wanted to live the rest of his family life as a modern, progressive man. None of the women in his family had ever worked outside the home. His three sisters were housewives and his seven brothers were landowners and political scientists and school principals and public prosecutors and politicians and deputy secretaries of finance and the youngest was a veterinarian for racehorses, but none of their wives worked outside the home. My mother did. My father cheered her on to get a job, first as a teacher and then as a career woman in the five-star hotel industry.

He championed his daughters at school and spoke to us about possible careers and said to us, over and over again, "I am not raising you to get married. I am raising you for careers. If you want to get married, treat it as incidental."

My father gets viscerally excited when I achieve and accomplish things in the world. A few years ago, as I stood on stage and spoke during the book launch for my first novel in Mumbai, I caught his eye. In his face was the softness of a man whose wildest dreams have come true.

When I was getting a divorce, my mother wouldn't speak to me, so I called my father. He said, "To hell with marriage. Marriage is for small people. You are too big for marriage."

Feminist writer Jill Filipovic, in her *New York Times* opinion piece titled "Why Men Want to Marry Melanias and Raise Ivankas," talks about how men want their accomplished wives to still maintain a sweetness and traditionalism while true empowerment is reserved for daughters. Fathers finally start to see, on the birth of a daughter, how the world is not set up to see them simply as humans. My father taught me to ride a bike, to swim, and to cook both the softest *lachchedaar paratha* and the quickest weeknight meals so I could focus on work. He taught me to never be ashamed of my polio, to never ask for privileges on account of having a disability (which I now see as a problematic lesson), and to never hesitate to walk into a room as if I owned it.

During this same time period, while he was raising feminist daughters, my father would routinely rain blows on my mother. "She shouldn't have talked back. She shouldn't have provoked me," he would say in his debrief to his children in the aftermath.

The origins of modern-day toxic masculinity are traced to institutionalized violence. In a paper published in 1996, Tracy Karner shared her findings from in-depth interviews with veterans of the

Vietnam War. This was a generation of men drafted into war as an enactment of masculinity, handed down by fathers who fought in World War II (the good war). Military service was presented as a rite of passage.

I remember the summer when I was ten years old, my brother eleven, and our little sister three. Our family lived in Bombay then but we spent that summer at my father's posting in Joshimath, a small army town in the Himalayas. My father had a mock army uniform tailored for my brother.

"No badges and ribbons yet," he said. "Those have to be earned."

My brother spent all summer in that uniform. He spent all his time in the company of young male officers—lieutenants and second lieutenants. He ignored me completely.

My brother had been the coolest thing in my world. Other kids adored and respected him because he was the right mix of charming and mischievous. He was allowed to roam free and I wasn't, but he'd bring me along on his adventures—he'd lead me to the roof-tops of skyscrapers, he'd pick up my favorite comics on his trips to the library, and he'd show me where the crabs hid under the rocks when the tide rose in the Arabian Sea. Something shifted when we returned to Bombay after that summer holiday at the army camp. Our father stayed back at his posting and my brother was now the disciplinarian. He started to beat me up in ways that would not allow me to fight back.

Militaries across the world hold masculine values of discipline during times of peace, protection during times of threat, and attack during times of war. Peace is largely seen as an absence of war. War is defined in masculinity and masculinity is perfected in war. Women, as has been documented over and over across the world and across time, are the collateral victims of war.

In the family, war is imagined as dissent, disobedience. Violence, then, is seen as natural, integral to the disciplinarian, the protector. Often, this calls for punishment, attack. Violence (or the threat of it) becomes integral to fatherhood, brotherhood, manhood.

In the confluence of the patriarchal, Brahminical traditions of his lineage and the brutal disciplinary tools of his trade, my father's boyhood and early adulthood made him both a sitting duck and a hunter. My brother became a natural inheritor.

After twenty years of service, my father wanted more than anything to quit the army and spend more time with his wife and children. When he did, on premature retirement as a major, his marriage was already gasping for breath. Then he physically beat the rest of it to death. The Indian Army had still to imagine a thing called PTSD. Would it have helped? Indian patriarchy would have laughed it off. Sure enough, when I ask my father now if his violence was on account of his being ordered to shoot men down in two wars as a soldier of the artillery division of the Indian Army, my father says, "Why blame the Indian Army for my failings? The army is a terrific institution. It makes men solid."

My failings. My father is close to eighty years old now. In the past twenty-five years or so, he has apologized over and over to me for his violence. My brother hasn't spoken to our father in close to twenty years. None of us women in the family can seem to successfully point out to these men that the very thing my brother inherited from my father is what keeps them apart.

Dr. Judy Y. Chu, the researcher at Stanford University who works on boys' psychosocial development and author of *When Boys Become Boys: Development, Relationships, and Masculinity*, tells me she has met many men from across the world like my father and brother in her role as chair of the Global Men's Health Advisory Committee. "Men who were violent often talk about how they ended up lonely or isolated," she says. They were initiated into toxic patriarchy, which promotes a version of masculinity that is stoic, undesiring of deep connection, and, in its worst form, embraces violence as a solution to dissonance. "Psychologists who work with these men try to get them to change their responses from violence to expressing their feelings. We can't simply say, 'Stop doing this,' so psychologists and clinicians tell them gently, 'Here's another place to land.' They tell them, 'Your children will feel better being around you. You will feel better about yourself.'"

She says that these men often ask: "Am I the only one suffering this way?" They feel shame, Dr. Chu says. It's as if our society sets them up and then makes them feel like they are alone and they are individually responsible. (This kind of work is better done by psychologists and clinicians and not by family members of violent men, though, she cautions.)

Because getting men to a psychologist is often a huge stumbling block, researchers find better luck with getting through to men who go to support groups like those for first-time fathers. "When men feel a tenderness toward their babies, we researchers tell them, 'Other men feel this tenderness too. It's a natural thing.'" Dr. Chu and her mentor Dr. Carol Gilligan were conducting a study with four-year-old boys when they observed fathers who would drop their boys off. "We saw remarkable displays of tenderness as the dads lingered before saying goodbye." When the researchers talked to them, the dads expressed sadness that their boys would soon lose their "real joy," their ability to be vulnerable and be "out there." Dr. Chu and her colleagues encourage fathers to tuck their boys into bed, to talk to them while giving them a bath or driving with them in the car. Ask your boys "What did you think about that?" and then listen without judgment. Don't oversimplify things for them—kids are capable of remarkable nuance and wisdom. Validate their instincts before offering your point of view. "Nobody loves your kid or looks out for them more than you do," Dr. Chu says to young fathers of boys.

This is often easier said than done. Fathers and society in general tend to pass on an initiation into boyhood that gradually dissolves the capacity for emotional presence in relationships and replaces it with the kind of detachment that is expressed eventually as a display of masculinity, such as young men spurning love to prove their manhood in battle.

In many cultures, we rob boys of the range of human emotions and connection, Dr. Chu says. And how are boys often trained in "masculinity"? By distancing themselves from femininity. Dr. Chu says she learned that one of the rules of status among boys was to be mean to girls. Then they learned not to be a mama's boy. "We teach boys to abandon women, and the first woman he must abandon is his mother." The irony, Dr. Chu says, is that the thing they want most is to *fit in*, and to connect, by showing that they don't care for connection. "Stoic" and "aloof" isn't what boys are made of but what they are made *into*, she says.

Connection to self and others is a key attribute for development in boyhood, says Dr. Chu. In a longitudinal study that started in Minnesota and included as many as ninety thousand kids, researchers found that the single best protector against adolescent risk was if a boy had at least one close, bonding relationship. Without these close relationships, boys are more prone to loneliness, opiate use, and suicide.

"Our goal through our studies is to return boys to that *relational social construct*," she says. Dr. Chu and her colleagues want boys to preserve their sense of integrity, authenticity, and honesty. She wants us to stop violating boys' nature. She is haunted by the words of one thirteen-year-old who said, "It would be great if I could be successful and also happy." The two aren't disconnected, Dr. Chu notes. In fact, being present to relationships and showing a tender openness also makes for better professional lives and leadership.

▪▪▪▪▪▪▪▪▪▪▪▪▪▪▪▪▪▪▪▪▪▪▪▪▪▪▪▪▪▪

On a trip that Gibran and I made in 2013, in which I wanted Gibran to reconnect with my family before he left for college, my father told Gibran about one of his fondest memories. "I would drive your grandmother and my three children in our Fiat car around Bombay in the late seventies and early eighties. We would all sing. Do you remember the song, Sonora?"

I did, but I said I didn't.

So, my father sang it. "Manu-bhai, motor chaley pom-pom-pom."

Brother Manu, the motor goes pom-pom-pom.

I remembered those moments vividly. My father would honk the horn of his car in time with the chorus of pom-pom-pom, startling the traffic and pedestrians around us. The five of us would laugh.

And, although my father's favorite memories are of his laughing children, our own lasting memories are of him slamming our mother's head against a bedroom wall. Another memory—our father asking my brother and me to fetch him his hockey stick so he could beat us with it.

"Who, Nana-ji? No way!" Gibran said on the flight home, when I told him of my father's violence toward us. "He's so mellow! *How did he turn it around?*"

My father has done a 180-degree turnaround. His second wife, Sapna, my pretty and doting stepmother, says he has never laid a finger on her. When I asked my father how he did it, turned it all around, he said: "Sapna is a divorce lawyer. She would throw me in jail!"

I was awash in a sad rage when I heard this. So he had it in him all along, the ability to keep his violence in check. My mother just didn't have the same kind of institutional sway over him as my stepmother does. My mother eventually kicked this violent man to the curb and divorced him, but if only the Indian political, legal, and cultural system had had her back, my father would not have gotten away with his years of torment. *She* would have thrown him in jail.

And yet, I am finding it easier and easier to spend time with my once-violent father. Or perhaps I am finding it easier to spend time with Gibran's grandfather. He even helped me with childcare in two hard periods of my life—when I was a busy journalist and Gibran was two years old in Bangalore, and then when I was in a near-suicidal depression in Singapore when Gibran was five. Men like my father have it in them to straighten up, to act with tenderness, and to respond with respect to the generals and brigadiers in their lives. Sometimes, I want to deny him the tenderness of love that Gibran gifts to him. But more than that, I want to break the cycle of estrangement and emotional violence between the men in my family. So I often hit the three-way-call button to Gibran when his grandfather calls me.

▼▼▼▼▼▼▼▼▼▼▼▼▼▼▼▼▼▼▼▼▼▼▼▼▼▼▼

At the age of ten, after that summer in which my brother was conscripted into a grotesque rank of masculinity delivered in olive-green, I did not know that the cells of my body were already thick with intergenerational trauma and were still soaking up new, modern strains of defeat. All I knew was that I wanted my body to be safe one day. I knew I'd have to grow up and marry, but I swore I would marry a nonviolent man and I swore I would never have a son.

At twenty-three, I wrote a matrimonial advertisement on behalf of my parents seeking a groom for me. From the applications and their accompanying photographs, I landed on a man with the gentlest eyes and strongest shoulders I had ever seen. Rajat was from Kerala, a place with one of the only known matrilineal societies. He was not a Brahmin. He was a copywriter and had no plans to join the army. He told me about the feminist public service ads he was writing, about how women didn't get to feel the joy of walking down the street with the wind on their faces at midnight. I fell instantly in love. Three months later, I danced at my glorious wedding, quit my journalism job with that editor who really believed in me, left my splintering family in Bombay, and moved to Bangalore, where Rajat had a new job. At twenty-seven, when I had a son, I swore that no son of mine would ever be within arm's distance of a man who raised his hand on a woman, leave alone aimed a gun at the enemy.

Clearly, taking your boy far, far away from toxic male influences is just one sad, twisted, lonely-making (if effective) way of shielding him. Before I talk about what I may have robbed from Gibran or gained for myself, I will share what a couple of other people have done to shield their boys.

Dr. Flaviane Ferreira is a psychoanalyst who works with young children on Mercer Island, a wealthy suburb of Seattle. She was born and raised in São Paulo, Brazil. She is herself the mother of two boys now in high school, and I am interviewing her about the lives of boys in America, but we turn to talking about machismo in the men from our own countries and how our cultures are so similar despite being continents apart.

Dr. Ferreira speaks of a vivid memory her husband has of his boyhood in São Paulo. "He was playing on the street and got in a fight with another boy and he got punched in the stomach. He went home crying and his father got angry at him and said, 'You go back there and break his arm.' My husband was crushed. He felt he was not understood. He was hurting and he had been punched by a bully, and his father, instead of comforting him, was asking him to go back there and be a bully himself."

Dr. Ferreira remembers her parents telling her brother the same thing. "My husband and I made sure that this was not part of our dialogue in our family as we started to raise our boys." Her husband talked about his boyhood pain in front of his boys. Later, on a trip to Brazil, he talked to his father, who apologized and said he hadn't forgotten and that he was sorry. "Hearing my husband talk about this and their grandfather feel this regret . . . it was implied to our boys to be neither the bully nor a boy who pays back. Be vulnerable, be hurt, find an adult, expect to be comforted and supported. It doesn't make you less of a man."

In speaking in front of his boys about how his father's taunts hurt him, Dr. Ferreira's husband was telling his boys that they don't have to follow that model of masculinity. They are off the hook. *He is breaking the cycle.*

This is a rare thing, according to Dr. Jackson Katz, an educator, filmmaker, and author who studies gender, race, and violence. Writing about the complicity of the policemen who stood by as their fellow cop murdered George Floyd in Minneapolis by kneeling on his neck, Dr. Katz points out that men in cohesive groups like teams, military units, and law enforcement agencies abide by "a boy code, a guy code, or a bro code," which is a set of unwritten rules that govern the behavior of individuals in all-male or male-dominated groups. These rules pervade groups engaged in aggressive competition and sports and politics, and become even more pronounced in military or paramilitary organizations such as the police, Dr. Katz says.

Researchers are telling us that men around us will have to bare their pain. We are here to witness and to catch them.

One such man doing such a thing is Neal Thompson, the author of a fatherhood memoir titled *Kickflip Boys*. Neal tells me his own father was "a distant character" during his childhood in New Jersey.

"I probably started . . . not *distancing* myself from my father but distinguishing myself from him . . . in high school. It's hard to say this and was hard to admit it at the time, but I saw his limits and his flaws and they were glaring to me." Neal's father had started to buy guns, motorcycles, sports cars. "'All these macho toys,' my mother called them. When my brother and I were little we thought they were cool, but later we thought they were obnoxious. He'd spend more money on those things than on providing for his family. I found him to be a selfish person. Not emotive or communicative, not physically affectionate. He was someone who was incapable of saying 'I love you' to his children and his wife. I never wanted to be that way."

Neal's stronger parental influence was his mother, a nurse, who drew him into the care of his sister who had Down syndrome. "I doted on my sister and was physically affectionate toward her." When Neal married and had boys, he and his wife discussed what kind of boys they wanted to raise. The boys would learn from the way their father conducted himself, Neal said. "Right from the start, physical affection with my sons came easily for me, probably because I was allowed to express affection to my sister. My boys are now twenty-one and twenty-three. Every day, when my son comes home from work, I give him a big hug and tell him I love him and he says the same." Neal describes himself as an "easy-to-cry softie." In his book, he writes about his own fallibility as a male and as a father. He writes about forgiveness among men and boys. He writes about skateboarding as a sport and a community that has become a refuge for adolescent boys who don't fit in.

Perhaps what it takes, then, isn't a "shielding" of our boys from the men around us, but, instead, a loving vigilance. Perhaps I could have stayed close to family, stayed close to my father and brother, and watched like a hawk for signs of Gibran emulating his grandfather and uncle. Perhaps I could have stayed in my marriage to Gibran's father, who seemed like the perfect husband on paper when seen through rose-tinted glasses set to a "nonviolent" lens, but who turned out to be emotionally unavailable to me. He stepped up to perform a decent long-distance fatherhood for Gibran, with visits every couple of months, and they developed an affectionate bond over the years, even though our marriage fell apart.

Yet so much can still slip through the cracks. My father no longer beats women, but he makes the nastiest jokes—about fat women, leftist women, famous women, women who are domestic help, my mother, my sister. He's just making jokes, he says. Sort of like Trump's admission about grabbing pussies is just locker-room talk.

Gibran's grandfather may be mellow, but the line between Gibran finding his jokes funny and unfunny? That line is thin. I have interrupted his jokes and often shut him down in Gibran's presence. Sometimes it works, and other times, Gibran has tried to come to his grandfather's defense. I don't want Gibran to think of such humor as "harmless." I don't want to be cast in the role of what feminist scholar Sara Ahmed calls "the feminist killjoy." I ask my father and my son to try harder, to be better at being funny.

And, in other troubles with the men we love, when Gibran would come home from stays with his father, his confidence seemed shot by a put-down or aloofness from the Rajat I well knew. Gibran would let it slip that his father had called him stupid. I'd get to work. I'd point to Gibran's extensive reading, his kindness, his humor. Later, Gibran used this humor to spar with his dad. If they must battle, let them do it with humor.

So when it comes to the men we must have in our boys' lives, we will often have to navigate and negotiate. We will have to talk to these men about boundaries or come in with reinforcements and repairs for our boys. Depending on your own gender, the dynamics of this game may take their toll. A lot of women experience this work as invisible labor and emotional labor. Each family will have to measure how much or how little there is to gain or lose.

▼▼▼▼▼▼▼▼▼▼▼▼▼▼▼▼▼▼▼▼▼▼▼▼▼▼▼▼

So where do we find our sons' role models outside our families?

I went looking in the Boy Scouts of America.

Yes, perhaps this was a subconscious response to my militaristic upbringing. Of course it was. I watched Gibran in his Boy Scouts uniform, watched him collect badges and ribbons, and I thought back to another boy, from my childhood.

At the time though, I had just moved to Seattle, a freshly minted PhD with an eight-year-old boy in tow. Another single mother from among Gibran's school friends told me that scouting would be a good way to get Gibran to be around men and get an American boyhood. A number of new immigrant parents flock to the Boy Scouts. I wonder if the organization recognized itself as a mighty institution of American training.

As we now know, the Boy Scouts went bankrupt after huge sexual abuse lawsuits. Over its years of existence, it also was guilty of homophobia. It insisted girls be kept out and, when they were finally admitted, form their own separate troops. It still required a religious oath while Girl Scouts does not. And yet, what I write here is a love letter to the Boy Scouts of America, Troop 72, Queen Anne, Seattle. Despite my misgivings, we found some wonderful men there— Doug, Jeff, Chris. These were gentle, deeply engaged fathers who took my boy under their wing. They took him white-water rafting in the Deschutes River and sent me pictures of my boy jumping into the rapids. They helped me buy and pack "the ten essentials" for the boys' camping trips. They taught him to shoot bottle rockets. I don't know what that whole bottle rocket thing was for, but perhaps it sowed a seed somewhere for Gibran, who is now a recently graduated physics major.

When I was bound to my bed once, recovering from a third surgery on my ankle, my brother came to stay, to help out in caring for Gibran while working to write a film script. I was deeply moved and imagined a reconciliation of sorts. He offered to take Gibran to the Boy Scouts' Pinewood Derby. Gibran didn't want to build the pinewood derby car, really, which was kind of a requirement. Gibran had (and still has) poor fine motor skills. I took the little piece of wood and the tools and fashioned the sleekest, fastest pinewood derby car. Gibran and my brother came home jubilant—Gibran's car had won second place in the state or something.

We had cheated, but I was thrilled for myself. I was a good Boy Scout!

And then my brother took Gibran on a hike with the Boy Scouts. He returned angry. He said Gibran had been a "sissy," that he'd complained about his hiking shoes, that he wasn't athletic and adventurous like the other boys. Gibran listened. He looked small, red-faced, crushed. I hugged him close and told him his uncle only wanted the best for him.

Soon, my friends started to cautiously, gently point out to me the ways in which my brother was verbally abusive to me. He told me in their company that I was stupid. My friends, who knew me as a brilliant professor and witty, feisty woman, were surprised to see me laugh it off. My brother was also short-tempered with me and then flew into a rage the cells of my body recognized.

"He's been through a rough divorce," I explained to my concerned friends.

"So have you," they whispered.

I saw Gibran shrink away from his uncle. After a particularly violent burst of rage on his part, I asked my brother to leave. He said I was so selfish that I was damaging Gibran's life by taking away a strong male influence. I said I would accept that accusation and I would take that chance. I set boundaries for the sake of Gibran that I hadn't learned (and would not learn for a while longer) to set for my own sake.

I had tried to reconcile with my brother, imagining that he would be different in his role as Gibran's uncle, but it turned out I had been better off with the "uncles" my boy had found even in an institution as problematic as the Boy Scouts.

Wonderful men are all around us. Maybe you are one of them. Part of the work is to question and course-correct the institutions men serve, or change the culture from within. I believe Doug and Jeff and Chris were doing just that within the Boy Scouts of America.

In nurturing my own friendships and calling in the kind of men and masculinity I wanted to model for my boy—building my village—I was modeling for Gibran a way to build his own village. He talks to his friends about *everything*. I have overheard these boys talk about their hearts being broken, about seeing their therapists, about missing their moms.

They talk to each other about the kind of feminists they want to be.

One such friend of Gibran's is Sean, whom Gibran met in college. Sean says the biggest influence in his life has been his grandmother. He credits his feminism to her. He says, "Her family moved from Iran to the US in 1975, when my mother was eleven. Although my grandmother was the top in her class at her school, my great-grandmother forced her to move to Tehran to work as a secretary at the oil company. She had to send money to her family back in Tabriz, eventually being able to send both of her younger brothers to university and support her mother. Her youngest brother became an engineer and her middle brother became a doctor. My great-grandmother was always incredibly proud of her two sons up to her death, but she never showed the same love to my grandmother, who since age eighteen has had to be a caretaker."

Sean talks about his grandmother's life in detail. He narrates dates and places. He narrates emotions. He wants us to feel what he felt. "Seeing my great-grandmother's disregard for her daughter's unrelenting support for the family while giving endless praise to her sons was one of my earlier and more important realizations of the existence of patriarchal structures," Sean says.

The arc of oppression ended with his grandmother's generation. All the women in Sean's family now are scientists or engineers. But here's where the men come in. Not all the men in his family are in step with a feminist agenda, Sean says. "It's just that they've been rendered powerless to perpetuate any misogyny by the strong-willed and empowered women around them." These intergenerational family dynamics have made Sean aware of the kind of males he wants to avoid. "I tend to stay away from guys I find too masculine or self-obsessed or harmful to women. And if I ever find out a friend is harmful to women, I try to warn them [the friends], talk about these ideas, and keep an eye out to make sure they don't end up harming anyone." Sean is majoring in peace and conflict studies.

▀▀▀▀▀▀▀▀▀▀▀▀▀▀▀▀▀▀▀▀▀▀▀▀▀

I am at a point in my life when I see a son in every man. No, I'm not *that* old. What I mean is that I see the boy begging to be raised right. A pliable, wide-eyed, sweet-faced boy. I heard a saying a long time ago that we love our sons and raise our daughters. What if we did both, with all genders? The time is coming when we will take gender out of the equation, when we finally see it as socially constructed, assigned at birth and then followed to a painful "T" by nurture. We are raising our girls to imagine themselves as president, yes, but what would it look like if our men were raised to cry their hearts out, in public, at an injury, at a tragedy, at a moving work of art? What would that look like, if not love?

If I could go back, I would do some things over again with Gibran, take tools from our gender-nonconforming friends and from the parents raising them. When I see the boy in every man, my heart melts. I see the damage done by other men and by everyone who went along with those men. I see the harm these enablers did by not extending to these men the kindness of telling them they were wrong. *I* went along, for a long, long time.

That kind of damage still shows up in my home from time to time, just when I think I can put my feet up and binge-watch *The Mindy Project*. Recently, I was writing an essay, and I told Gibran I was going to refer in it to a time when, at age twenty-one, he was sad and had tears in his eyes. Gibran said to me, "Don't say I *cried*. It makes me sound like a pussy."

Oh, boy. I told Gibran I would quote him on that.

He squealed. He giggled. He complained. He shrieked. He threw a hissy fit. He squawked. He stamped his foot. He fussed. He wailed. He nagged.

How many more gendered ways can I describe his reaction?

The point is, he realized how his words would look in print: sexist, homophobic, misogynistic. And he wanted *no part of that*, at least not publicly. He knew he'd slipped, and neither his mother nor the society he cared for would look kindly upon it.

"That's not how real men talk, honey."

"Yes," he said. "Yes, I know. Thank you for not quoting me. Thank you for not shaming me."

Why I am quoting him on it now is because the context has shifted. What I am representing and highlighting is his retraction, his realization, his hasty retrieval of his words. What I have just described is a skulk as well as a quantum leap. In her book *The Skin We're In*, Dr. Janie Victoria Ward, who studies the moral and psychological development of Black children, offers a thorough four-step program for such instances that need reframing. Her approach—Name it, Read it, Oppose it, Replace it—encourages resistance to damaging social influences throughout the formative years of adolescence.

But for every such "teachable moment" with Gibran, I see losses across the world. Look at the rise of toxic masculine leadership across the globe. We are swept up in a wave of masculine swagger, from Trump in the US to Modi in India to Putin in Russia to Xi in China to Bolsonaro in Brazil. As Dr. Ferreira said, "If you think of our world today, our men are doing exactly what my husband's father told him to do to the boy who bullied him—they're being tyrants, bullies, retaliating instead of using their frontal lobes to reflect and talk."

My son won't be like these men. I know you, too, take some comfort in knowing that you have enough tools, enough vigilance, that your child isn't foolishly going to look at Trump and say, "I want to grow up and be just like him."

But the true concern isn't that our boys want to be exactly like these men. The concern is that they are seeing these men succeed and find seats in the highest offices in the land. In my land and yours and all over the fucking globe. These men are not my son's role models, but he knows they are his leaders. He won't grow up to *be* like them, but he will have to take orders from them.

They make decisions on my son's citizenship. On how much he can speak, which planes he can take to where. Whether he can return to his mother. Whether he would be forced to "go home" to a motherland he didn't grow up in or, worse, stay and fight wars that happened because in this great global dick-swinging era, one of these dicks swung a bit too high. (Or low. I don't know the rules of a dick-swinging match.)

The thought of my son doing his best and still having to take orders from these men rips my heart out. It makes me want to set fire to the world. When I calm down, it makes me want to settle for just changing the world.

TO DO:

- Talk to boys about who their closest friends are. What do they like and dislike about them? How do they feel about themselves when they're with them? Who do they trust, feel comfortable with, talk to? Who knows what they're really like? Who brings out the best and worst in them? Encourage your boy to cultivate intimate friendships.

- Teach boys to reflect critically on what they see in men around them. The goal is not to shield them from the storm but to teach them to weather it. Encourage perspective taking.

- Work to dismantle the problematic messages your boy receives. Employ the steps suggested by Dr. Janie Victoria Ward.

- Give boys and men the permission to care.

- If you are a man, reflect on your own experiences, development, socialization. If you are a father, what is it like to be with your son? What did you lose as you were initiated into boyhood and manhood? Would you want your son to lose that?

- Surround your son with men you trust to do the "cleanup work."

- Focus on the men who are willing to change.

- Try a call-in as opposed to a call-out. Calling-in is the compassionate practice of recognizing that people make mistakes and drawing them back in to try their best and be their best selves.

- This is hard, but set boundaries and go beyond respecting elders to protecting children. If there are men in your boy's life who ignore your call-ins (or call-outs), it's time to set some limits.

- Work to topple militaristic, toxic masculine political and social structures.

Chapter Seven

HOW WILL I SHIELD HIM FROM THE MEDIA?

While I was building my village and bringing in people who would be good role models for Gibran, there was another phenomenal cultural force swirling around us and taking hold of my child's psyche, whether I liked it or not. The media. You know, the thing I studied as a professor and researcher but still couldn't quite pin down as a parent.

And yet, in some ways, the media was working with me. Gibran told me recently about an episode on one of his favorite television shows, *Community*. "One scene was a pivotal moment for me in understanding the pressures on women," he said. (And here I thought *I* was his prime source for a feminist education.)

"Annie is trying to get Joel to join a Glee Club, so she dresses in a sexy Santa costume and does a seductive-little-girl song and dance for him—'Teach Me How to Understand Christmas.' She ends it with just descending into, like, a babble—'boopee-doopee-doop-boop-sex!' The show was making a point about how we infantilize women. It really hit me then what it was like for the girls around me in high school. Have you seen that episode, Mama?"

I hadn't. Although watching television and films had been one of the main activities we did together for years, *Community* was a show to which I left him on his own while I went about my single-mothering, tenure-earning, feminist-researching, book-authoring, dating-for-love ways. To be brutally honest, I recruited the media to be a second mother for Gibran. I plonked him down before the television when I fought off depressive episodes in Singapore. In Baton Rouge, *Yu-Gi-Oh!* and the Game Boy entertained my child as I worked on my doctoral studies. While he watched *Dragon Ball Z*, I read and wrote papers on the impact of media on children; and no, the irony was not lost on me.

I am here to tell you that there is no shielding our boys from the media. I know this as a mother and I know this as a media professor and feminist media scholar. When I first started teaching a course called Media, Society, and the Individual at Seattle University in 2003, I began with an assignment in which students would log their media use for four days. They would come back shocked to find that they tallied up to four hours a day! Today, their tallies are up to sixteen hours a day, which means they are only switched off from the media during their sleeping hours. Some of them report that if they wake up at night, they reach for their phones automatically and scroll their feeds (a concept that did not exist in 2003). I have since dropped that assignment because it feels anachronistic. We are not just awash in media; we are submerged in it, and we are the fish that can no longer describe water.

Our kids are in front of screens and their minds are within screens for most of their waking hours. We no longer live in a time of true parental controls. The only thing we can control to some degree is the conversation. I have found that the media, in fact, can be one of those incredibly useful allies, like an electronic cool aunt or uncle. Invite them in, include them in the family conversation, or let them babysit your kids. Let your kids confide in them and learn from them, and then regroup with you to enjoy it or argue over it all together.

The reason Gibran could read between the lines (or see between the frames?) of that scene in *Community*, the reason he could get the nudge-nudge-wink-wink humor and the sleight-of-hand feminist messaging in it, the reason it stuck years later, the reason it spoke to him, and the reason he spoke about it, is a thing called media literacy. While Gibran and I invited the media into our home like a family member, we also talked over its head and gossiped behind its back.

▀▀▀▀▀▀▀▀▀▀▀▀▀▀▀▀▀▀▀▀▀▀▀▀▀▀▀

Let's begin with a common understanding of the media our boys may either encounter or be steeped in on any given day. We're talking billboards, print newspapers (we should be so lucky) and magazines, television, movies, and the advertising and public relations industries across all of these platforms. We're talking Facebook, Instagram, and Twitter, and TikTok, Snapchat, and WhatsApp. We're talking video games across systems and platforms and levels of privacy. We're talking YouTube and Twitch (currently the world's leading livestreaming platform for gamers). We're talking pornography. We're talking sites like 4chan and 8kun. We're talking dating apps like Tinder. We're talking about music.

Especially in Western nations, media is a profound cultural force not just for telling us who we are but shaping who we can be. I couldn't have known it would all turn out all right for Gibran's intellectual and emotional growth or for my feminist enterprise that I gave him almost unfettered access to all sorts of media. I just kind of knew it in my gut.

Gibran went from watching delightful cartoons like *The Powerpuff Girls* while I worked to watching *Gilmore Girls* with me (we'd settle in front of the TV with our dinner bowls of rice and daal and sing the title song out loud together) to playing video games with his friends to spending hours online on his own, first on his computer and then on his phone. Each medium, each portal, each platform took him further and further away from my eye.

Brace yourself for some startling statistics. A 2019 census of the media use of tweens and teens, conducted by Common Sense Media, an independent nonprofit, found that on average, eight- to twelve-year-olds in America consume just under five hours' worth of entertainment screen media per day and teens an average of just under seven and a half hours' worth—these estimates do not include time spent using screens for school or homework.

Let that sink in.

Also, the medium that parents of Gen Xers and millennials were so worried about—television—is no longer the main actor. By age eleven, a majority (53 percent) of kids have their own smartphone, and by twelve more than two-thirds (69 percent) do, and that's where they're consuming media.

Here's something that tells us why parenting our boys in their use of media may need greater focus. The census found that boys and girls have vastly different tastes in media. (It did not mention what tastes nonbinary kids have. Let's hope these studies start to include all genders in their variables.) Boys enjoy all types of gaming more than girls do: mobile games, computer games, and especially console video games. Video gaming is boys' favorite media activity; for girls, it's one of their least favorite, the census found. Forty-one percent of boys play video games "every day," compared to 9 percent of girls.

Girls' favorite media activity, by far, is listening to music. Overall, girls enjoy music, reading, and television more than boys; and boys are more likely to enjoy video gaming and watching online videos. There continues to be a big difference between boys and girls in terms of enjoyment and use of social media, the research found. Among teens, where social media use is most common, 50 percent of all girls say they enjoy using social media "a lot" compared to about a third (32 percent) of boys. Seventy percent of teen girls say they use social media "every day," compared to 56 percent of boys.

The research asks us to think about both content and context. Two questions to consider: What is lost when shared media time goes away? And how does the shift from watching TV shows with family members to watching online videos alone affect the possible impact of media messages on a child? Children are accessing an array of content, both high and low quality, from celebrity influencer videos to do-it-yourself maker videos to violent or sexual content and everything in between, the research says. More than ever before, we're going to have to pay attention to content even while it is increasingly slipping from our grasp. These electronic lives of our children and ours, too, can exist together (especially in your child's early years, when you are the gatekeeper) or separately, in that one person in a household might be having an entirely different audiovisual, cerebral, or emotional experience in the very same space and time as another family member. With multiple apps and browser upon open browser, regrouping and recalibrating with our children become parallel parenting skills with no precedent in earlier generations.

What do we do about this houseguest of ours who is also with our kids when they're on the bus or at a friend's house or in their rooms when we are asleep? If that sounds creepy, it should. And if it sounds like an opportunity, it should too.

That's what feminist podcaster Danielle Holland is discovering with her eight-year-old son. "Last week, he made himself a TikTok account," she says. "I didn't even know he could do that without me!" Her son started wailing one night right before bed, so she went to him. "He had just seen a TikTok video that depicted a sad and abused pit bull. He was shaking and sad and so lost and was just utterly crying about this dog." But Holland knew there was more going on. Her boy has always loved dogs and other animals, but she sensed a deeper sadness. "I held him for a long time. We breathed together. When he was able to talk, we kind of walked through it all. It was completely more than this one dog. It was all the other shit going on—the protests (for racial justice, in the wake of George Floyd's killing in Minneapolis in May 2020), the police violence he hears me talk about; it was a million things wrapped into one dog video." Holland realized that her boy was processing everything through this one sad video. In it, he found some catharsis. What Holland needed was to understand the context in which the content had landed on her son. "It has made me slow down with him and communicate how I care about everyone, the dogs too, even when my focus has been, as it should, on Black Lives Matter. It was hard for him to understand, but we keep engaging these conversations. I have no strategy other than constant engagement and conversation. I see no other way."

Holland notes one more reason that "shielding" her boy from social media may not be as important as partaking along with him. Given all that is happening in the world with regard to racial injustice, she says, she cannot be the white mom keeping her boy "innocent," while kids of color are forced to deal with harsh realities of videos documenting the uglier parts of our lives.

<hr>

I recall a PTA meeting at Gibran's middle school, where anxious parents discussed social media and how they could keep watch. "You go to this thing called the 'browser history' and do a search," one dad explained. Another parent said, "You just creep in and look on their computer after they leave for school. They sometimes forget to log out of their Facebook. You can see all the people they are friends with and who is saying what."

"Or," I said, "you talk to them about how not to get hurt and how not to hurt people. And you tell them you will never spy on them because you trust them to have values and to come talk to you if something feels wrong."

I got looks. I wondered if I was clueless and dangerously inadequate in my parenting. Or if this was yet another thing I might have missed because of the weak hold my Indian culture had on me and the shaky grasp I had on American culture.

Nope, says Dr. Kishonna Gray, the nation's leading scholar on video games and culture. Dr. Gray believes I did the right thing. She does the same thing with her two boys. Dr. Gray is an interdisciplinary, intersectional digital media scholar whose areas of research include identity, performance and online environments, cultural production, video games, and Black cyberfeminism. And she's an avid gamer and is raising her boys to be feminists through gaming. We talk about *Grand Theft Auto*. I tell her about that time when Gibran was an adolescent and he warned me that *Grand Theft Auto* would be hard for me because "we can kill prostitutes for thrills." I told him to shut it down. He was resentful and said he shouldn't have told me about the game and I would never have known. I backtracked, alarmed at the possibility that my boy could just lie to me if he wanted. It was true, I'd never know. I told Gibran I appreciated his honesty and let him play because he was at least aware, and I didn't want him to lie to me and play it behind my back. I sat down to watch as he played, pretending to be wildly curious. He made the best choices that the game allowed. I wasn't sure I'd made the right call, but when the Gamergate scandal broke in 2015 (misogynist men threatening and abusing women gamers online), my boy spoke out passionately against it among his friends and online.

Dr. Gray says she uses the same tack. "I let my kids play *Grand Theft Auto*, and we talk about how aggressive the police are, so we're able to have conversations. And there's this really sexually inappropriate game called *House Party*. When my kids were on YouTube, the YouTuber they were watching was playing this game, and so I said all right, because I don't want to tell them no. Because I think when I tell them no, that's when I'm gonna lose a connection that we have."

But that game allowed Dr. Gray to have a rich conversation around consent. "It was awful, really, how these men were treating and talking to these women. There were concerns about consent, violations of their bodies. There was one scene where a guy pulls his dick out and so I said, 'OK, kids, you never, ever do that.' And the kids were immediately on board, they were like, 'Oh my gosh why is that guy doing that?' Because I'd watched it together with them, they lost interest in it."

We can try to control the narrative for only so long, she says. "There's going to be a point where they're gonna tune out my voice. I have to equip them with everything they need to be safe in the world, to make sure that other bodies and other people are safe in the world." Such conversations and such training are especially poignant for her in raising her Black boys in America.

Dr. Gray advises us to look for our boys' decision-making processes, to make our boys their own best resources, to have them develop their own literacy, especially digital literacy. Make it intersectional, she says, because, as in the case of the Gamergate issue, oppression in one place will fatten itself into oppression in other places. "Gamergate facilitated the development of a playbook and social connections that then formed the base of the alt-right in both tactics and people," says Dr. Christopher A. Paul, video games scholar and author of the book *The Toxic Meritocracy of Video Games: Why Gaming Culture Is the Worst*. Journalists and scholars have urged lawmakers to investigate how anti-feminist groups such as those that harassed game developer Zoë Quinn and feminist media critic Anita Sarkeesian with doxxing and threats of rape, murder, and bombing (driving Sarkeesian out of her home and forcing the cancellation of her lecture on a college campus due to a mass-shooting threat) have morphed into today's alt-right groups that promote white supremacy.

When it comes to content, we're not just slaying the dragons of inappropriateness. We have to also be vigilant about representation. Dr. Gray wants her boys to be able to see themselves represented in the games they play. Growing up in the nineties, she herself had few options. Stereotypes (like Black characters as DJs and boxers, Brazilian characters as having beastly characteristics, and East Asian characters as mystical) fell short. "When I talk to young folks today, they have Lincoln Clay [the half-Black protagonist] from *Mafia III* to look to. So my boys say, 'The gaming industry isn't racist.' But I really try to urge them to demand more. I'm like, 'A few progressive characters, a little representation won't transform an entire industry that has basically made its money off the fact of stereotyping folks of color.'"

Dr. Gray focuses on avatar creation when questioning representation in video games. You often can't get your avatar to look like you if you're a person of color, such as in *Minecraft*, one of the earliest video games kids learn to play. Other games, like *NBA 2k20*, reflect a range of identities. "I want my boys to know that it took a lot of fighting to get here. And I want them to be aware that they live in an era where companies are responsive, companies are intentionally trying to do better." Companies are also finding out that it often pays well to have more representation. *Mafia III* became the fastest-selling title in 2K Games' history. Which makes me wonder—perhaps we shouldn't be thinking of demanding more from our children in "shielding" them from the media after all. Perhaps we should just get out there and do battle—demand more from media industries. Insist they do better.

To learn more about such possibilities, I talked to those at the heart of the struggle. I interviewed seven feminist video game professionals who work in design, production, and marketing in the gaming industry across the country. They're all lifetime players of a variety of video games. Some of them are single, some are married; at least two are mothers of sons. There are women of color and women from the LGBTQ community. Their names are Shana Bryant, Nellie Hughes, Regina Buenaobra, Ylan Salsbury, Rubi Bayer, Novera King, and Heather Conover. (Note: I am not attributing quotes to specific people here.)

They talk about how there is no feminist video game, but you can shift toward equity by having a variety of games that give you options on character creation, to the type of outfits you can buy, and to how you can develop the stories of characters. The core piece is being able to find yourself in the game.

For parents playing along with their kids, these designers say one trick is to look for the details in the games that are stereotypically gendered. For instance, the game *Animal Crossing* has a royal crown that costs 1.2 million bells, and it looks like the stereotypical king's crown. There's a queen's crown that costs 1 million bells; it is a smaller crown meant for a female head. "They even tell you the price of the goddamn crown as if to recreate the real world in which women are paid less than men!" says a designer.

The problem stems from poor representation among designers and producers in the gaming industry, these professionals say. One of them who has worked in the industry for eighteen years recalls working with hundreds of white women, thousands of white men, but only five Black women, "one of whom is my twin'" she laughs. "I am forty years old and Black and never got to see myself represented on screen until the movie *Black Panther*. Having the smartest person in the Marvel Universe be a young Black sixteen-year-old girl . . .

I can't tell you how that felt." Most game designers in the industry now insist that they have begun to center women. But if and when they do, it's white women, these professionals point out.

Oftentimes the men in these games have a variety of bodies, but the women are of supermodel proportions. In response to such criticism, *Overwatch* by Blizzard Entertainment came up with a wide variety of body types for women. One of the professionals says: "I was so thrilled, I bought the collector's edition even though I don't really play these games. I get my butt kicked in that game," she laughs.

Parents and other adults buying video games for their children should also think about the types of relationships that are represented in games, and drive the gaming industry toward creating better options. "We need to represent gamers that have different dynamics in relationships— female-female relationships, female-male relationships that are not from the gaze of a white cis-hetero male."

The story arc and choices of characters are also important when it comes to creating empathy. One designer says that when she was thirteen, she played a video game that made her cry—*Kingdom Hearts*, in which there's a sweet story about friends who get separated and are linked together by their hearts so they must find each other again. One of the main characters was a girl. There's increasingly a lot of interesting science around the concept of tend-and-befriend as the counterpart to flight-or-fight in video games. These professionals want to see more games like *Stardew Valley* and game apps for our phones that are about self-care.

A lot of these changes in the industry have come about because of the market demanding better content, the women say. *Animal Crossing* looks like it's a game for girls—the colors and characters are cute—but more and more men are playing this de-stressing game.

While they are optimistic, none of these women are gung ho about gaming and our boys. Again, they tell us not to get lax about filtering the games that come into our homes. Pay attention to the ratings—the ones rated M put sixty to seventy hours of mature content into your child compared to two hours at an R-rated movie. "The interactive element of parents talking their kids through their media versus the passive consumption of media is a huge deal when you are talking about someone's personality development and human interaction. Over those hours of gaming, you start to process things differently. Children are embedded in the world. It can be damaging."

The real warning these women have is about live streamers and YouTubers—these days, you don't need to be playing a game. You may not be able to afford a game. But you can watch men play a game on Twitch and make comments. These men are getting more and more right-leaning. "They're celebrities to kids. Be aware of the community of these commentators. They're misogynistic and racist. You don't even have to go that deep—two to three videos in and they're burning crosses."

Here's the core of why some of these online video games may be attractive to our boys—games have been targeted to a fragile male identity, according to these professionals. "These men aren't usually from a marginalized group. They're men who were teased as kids as being nerdy. So they found this place to be empowered as a culture."

One gamer has had the experience over and over again of being pushed out of online games when the other players discover she is a woman. "I have had the experience where when I'm playing an online game, they hear my voice, the tone of the guys changes. You can get kicked out of the room or they laugh or they make comments."

In raising a feminist son who plays video games, he can be an ally, these professionals say. Teach him what bullying sounds like. Get him to keep an eye and ear out for that. If girls and women are being shut down or teased or harassed as they play, ask him to just say, "Hey guys, cut that out!" "In fact, it's hard to be an ally in person; it can be intimidating. But on the internet, there's a new opportunity—if there's ever a perfect playground to be an ally, it's on an online game! As a boy, you have an opportunity to change the conversation. How do you want to use your voice?"

▀▀▀▀▀▀▀▀▀▀▀▀▀▀▀▀▀▀▀▀▀▀▀▀▀

As I write this, an Instagram chat group in New Delhi, India, has been unearthed in which teenage boys in prestigious New Delhi schools shared photos of their underage female classmates, objectifying them and planning "gang rapes." The country is outraged and the boys are being questioned by the police. Celebrities and politicians are calling for setting up codes of engagement with social media, such as suggested in the "online harms" white paper released in April 2019 by the UK government's Department for Digital, Culture, Media, and Sport (DCMS) and Home Office to deal with similar cyberbullying instances in the UK. One survey, by the Teaching and Learning International Survey (TALIS), ranked England the worst place in the world for cyberbullying.

"The impact of harmful content and activity can be particularly damaging for children, and there are growing concerns about the potential impact on their mental health and well-being," said the white paper. Experts in India weighed in and said it is a must that parents discuss sex, sexuality, and gender-related issues with their impressionable young ones.

More than any other media platform, I am often overwhelmed by the unwieldiness of social media. It can be the best channel for bullies, and yet, I also see that it can be the best channel for giving agency. The world before social media would have left us with one version of Monica Lewinsky. But she harnessed Twitter and we now get to have Lewinsky the activist, TED Talk speaker, and contributing editor to *Vanity Fair*. We don't lose her public intellectualism to someone else's version of her story. I watched her live-streamed public lecture at the University of Washington in April 2020. She brought wit and charm to her activism, in which she highlighted how women and other vulnerable people will continue to be slut-shamed, especially through cyberbullying, until we have a public revolution grounded in compassion and empathy.

I wonder once again, as I have wondered over the years, if such discussions might have saved the life of Tyler Clementi, the American student at Rutgers University in New Jersey who jumped to his death from the George Washington Bridge at the age of eighteen. On September 19, 2010, Clementi's roommate, Dharun Ravi, used a webcam on his dorm room computer and secretly filmed Clementi kissing another man. Ravi posted about the webcam incident on Twitter and invited his followers to watch a second tryst between Clementi and his date. Clementi found out and took his own life three days later.

It was one of the first cases that introduced the world to the intensity of cyberbullying. Gibran was fifteen and spending a lot of time online in those days. Ravi was an Indian American boy. I was racked with doubt about Gibran and about his own possible issues of identity and belonging and empathy and love. I know parents across the country may have wondered about this too—could our boys be Clementis or Ravis?

I was right to worry, my friend and colleague Dr. Victor Evans tells me. Dr. Evans is a professor of journalism and media studies and is a gay Black man. "That is actually one of my biggest fears [for young people] especially for the LGBTQ community—the outing that can occur on social media," he says. In a way, the anonymity and clamor of social media seem to facilitate cruelty as much as they can also be a place for empathy and allyship.

Dr. Evans talks about the show *13 Reasons Why*, based on a young adult novel, in which a teen takes her own life out of despair from cyberbullying. The show depicts how we, as parents, may know precious little about our children's social lives lived so deeply online.

So what do we do? I wonder if the solution, too, may lie in media. When we take a deep dive early on and set up patterns of thinking, feeling, navigating, questioning, and conversing with media, perhaps those same patterns go forth with our kids into their online worlds?

Researchers Daniel Anderson and Katherine Hanson tell us in their chapter titled "Screen Media and Parent-Child Interactions" in a book titled *Media Exposure During Infancy and Early Childhood* that co-viewing media with toddlers helps promote their critical and creative thinking. Dr. Evans agrees. He grew up loving television. "My parents didn't allow me to watch TV, and all my friends at school were talking about all these shows. So I cracked the parental code on the cable box and watched secretly. I really wanted my parents to practice what today is known as co-viewing or co-using media which is where parents intentionally watch almost everything with their kids and talk about it, from toddlerhood onward." Dr. Evans's parents eventually watched R-rated films with him and talked him through things like, "This is not how you should behave" and "This only happens in Hollywood." But he wishes he had had that context sooner.

Our media, especially television, have a lot of catching up to do with the realities of our lives. For people like Dr. Evans, these omissions left a lasting impact. Stories like his are important because they tell us where we may need to individually fill in the gaps in the representations and non-representations of our own kids in today's media.

Dr. Evans grew up in Fort Worth, Texas. His grandfather was a Southern Baptist minister. "I grew up hearing my church tell me that homosexuality was a sin," he says. In fact, it was shows like *Dynasty* that allowed him to have conversations around LGBTQ identity with his parents. And yet, television failed him. "Growing up being LGBTQ, most of the images were either comic relief or just quite sad, to be quite honest, just really sad, where they were shown destroying people's families. It was never from the perspective of the individual, but how they were affecting everyone else and how everyone else responded to them. The character on *Dynasty* was 'dishonoring' his family. I think that was extremely negative when I was growing up. It made me feel like by me coming out, I was going to hurt everybody in my family because that's what I saw was happening on television."

Recent representations have been a mixed bag, Dr. Evans says. In *Orange Is the New Black*, Laverne Cox's character is trans and suffers miserably. But characters on *Pose* offer a celebration of LGBTQ identity. "If I could pick something that I'd have loved as a kid growing up where I saw African American LGBTQ people, it would be that show!"

Shows like *Sense8* are makings strides too, with characters across intersectional identities rather than just the white cisgender gay males that dominated LGBTQ representation on television for a long time. *Sense8* is made by the Wachowski sisters, who are both trans women. Representation within the industry and its cultural production leads to representation in content, says Dr. Evans.

He is delighted at how uncontroversial and seamless some of the media consumption of LGBTQ characters has become. "When I was visiting home in Texas for Thanksgiving, my five-year-old niece, who has grown up with an iPad in her hand, was sitting next to me just watching YouTube videos of LGBTQ drag queens. And I was like, 'Why are you watching that?' and she said, 'Oh, it's one of my favorite shows,' and I'm like 'Really!' That really kind of made me feel good because if I was a kid watching that it wouldn't have been nothing, you know?"

I would have loved for Dr. Evans to have had that show growing up. And I would have loved to see myself reflected on Indian television and media with girls and women who were smart and not sexualized or even deified (I grew up imagining that a good woman was one who sacrificed for her family and definitely never spoke of her own needs). I would have liked to see LGBTQ characters who weren't the butt of mockery or the perpetrators of "sin." In America, I would have liked to see boys and girls like my own boy on television. I wish he hadn't grown up laughing along with his white friends at Apu on *The Simpsons*.

<hr />

There is another, more pervasive, almost environmentally embedded media that we hardly ever talk about anymore. Advertising. A whole generation or two of media scholars have studied the impact of advertising on children, adolescents, and adults. Advertisers have that whole business down to a science. From billboards to buses to Super Bowl commercials to our social media feeds, the dancing deity of consumerism isn't just selling us products and services but is actually selling *us* (our information and our profiles) to corporations. Under a capitalist structure, we are seen as consumers more than as whole humans. As that capitalist structure nudges us online, our desires and our purchases—even our idle "(browser) window-shopping"—is easier to track. The most significant data about us, then, is our IP address, which social media hands off to advertisers.

We are beginning to see movements away from social media and toward online privacy. We are beginning to see social media giants like Facebook and its CEO Mark Zuckerberg held to account, to at least reveal the ways in which our demographics and IP addresses are sold to advertisers. These efforts for structural changes are unlikely to bring about an upheaval, though. For most people, convenience trumps fears of invasiveness. Some of us may resist a total immersion, but, for the most part, separating our deepest selves from our consumer selves is like trying to shed skin we can't even see or feel.

So as our lives become more insidiously mass mediated, our boys subliminally learn ideals of masculinity, our girls learn ideals of femininity, and all other genders learn they don't exist in that imagination. In his film *Tough Guise: Violence, Media, and the Crisis in Masculinity* (originally released in 1999/2000, with an update in 2013), educator and cultural theorist Dr. Jackson Katz breaks down the violent, sexist, and homophobic messages boys and young men routinely receive from virtually every corner of culture, from television, movies, video games, and advertising to pornography, sports culture, and US politics. He says that advertising, in particular, sells products by exploiting men's anxieties about not measuring up to "manhood."

Recent campaigns have gone to the heart of this issue and flipped the script. Axe Body Spray has made a series of ads since 2016 that stopped enticing men with the noxious fumes of toxic masculinity. Axe pivoted from telling men that its product would *make* them magnetic to women to telling men that they're *already* attractive. These new ads showed men rocking dance floors in heels, caressing kittens in their beards, and coating their hands in flour to help in the kitchen. In the words of one CNBC journalist, the new ads "Show why fragile masculinity is even more repellent than BO could ever be." In 2017, Axe launched its Find Your Magic campaign, in which ads dealt with men's questions like, "Is it OK to not like sports?" and "Is it OK to experiment with other guys?" and "Is it OK for guys to wear pink?" and "Is it OK to be depressed?" The brand director, Fernando Desouches, says that Axe, once rooted in the notion of attraction being connected to conquest, pivoted to representing "attraction as a game of equals."

Close on its heels came Gillette with its We Believe: The Best Men Can Be campaign after the #MeToo movement took off. The commercial showed examples of women being sexualized or insulted by men and then showed how men could call each other out or encourage boys to be gentler, "because the boys watching today will be the men of tomorrow."

Sure, these brands are tapping into the zeitgeist, getting with the feminist times and all. These are gambles with well-researched and calculated payoffs. But to the extent that we want to pay them off with our consumerism, and to the extent that we still need body sprays, deodorants, and razors, why not put your money into those media and products and services that don't insult or prey on boys' insecurities about masculinity?

While we wait for all media to truly catch up in representing everyone and not sexualizing and sensationalizing the female form or valorizing the male, we can take some measures that fight fire with fire. For your young son, throw in *Dora the Explorer*, *The Powerpuff Girls*, *Molly of Denali*, and *Doc McStuffins* (about a Black girl who plays doctor to her toys and has a stay-at-home dad, a doctor mom, and an adopted sibling) amid the *Yu-Gi-Oh!* and *PAW Patrol*. For your adolescent boy, throw in a sweet film like *Eighth Grade* amid the Jason Bourne series. Play that video game along with your boy, or at least watch as he plays and, as often as you can without losing your mind, keep a conversation going.

The best part of all the change that's coming is that more and more content is being created by a growing cadre of feminist men in the media. One such man is Tom Koshy in Mumbai. On India's Independence Day in 2018, I came across a short film in my social media feed. As I watched the two-and-a-half-minute film, I sat bolt upright. In it, we follow a young woman in a breezy, off-the-shoulder, knee-length yellow dress as she walks through Mumbai at night. She boards a deserted commuter train. She stands by the open doorframe of the train, feeling the wind on her face, and a man comes to stand in front of her. She walks on the railway overhead bridge and four young men whoop it up with each other as she walks by. The streetlights hit red, and a group of men on motorcycles slow down near her and then drive away. On another deserted street, a taxi slows down to pick her up. She falls asleep in the cab. The film is set to the soundtrack of Jawaharlal Nehru, India's first prime minister, giving his iconic speech on the midnight of India's independence from the British in 1947. The film ends with the young woman at home, settling down alone on her sofa. She looks right into the camera. A line runs across the screen: "This is what freedom *should* feel like."

The next morning, I showed the film to my American students and asked them to comment.

"I kept expecting the men to assault her," said one woman student.

"Or at least catcall her," said another.

"Right? With her earphones in! Who *does* that?"

"My heart was beating really fast watching her walk so freely. And then she falls asleep in a taxi? I was scared."

I asked the men in my class what they thought. One of them finally spoke, "I didn't feel any of these things even though I got the sense that's what the film was about. And I had no idea the girls in my class have to think of these things when they walk at night."

"Women!" someone shouted from the back of the class.

"Not just at night," another called out.

And not just in India but also in America, I thought to myself. I went home and looked up the name of the filmmaker. Curious about his feminist influences, I called him recently. Koshy spoke of growing up in the matrilineal heritage of Kerala in India, but also seeing how his father didn't really respect his mother. Koshy's more significant feminist influences came from professional women in Mumbai, where he moved to become a filmmaker. His friend, filmmaker Neha Singh, lives a feminist life, Koshy says. "From her, I learned that it is OK for a woman to make the first move in a relationship. Through her, I met other feminist men." Koshy also learned much from Sofia Ashraf, a rapper and singer-songwriter about whom he went on to make a film. "She was a devout Muslim girl and she used to teach in a madrasa. She became an atheist, took off her burka, defied her conservative Muslim family, and came to Bombay. Her mother wasn't allowed to speak in English because her father didn't speak English. Sofia said this beautiful thing: 'I want to break the cycle of sacrifice. Every woman sacrifices for her daughter so that her daughter may have a better life. And so it goes on. Where is the payoff? I want to take all the sacrifice and end it here so that nobody after me has to sacrifice anymore.' I was blown away by that." When you surround yourself with strong and self-actualized women, a lot of things invisible to men become acutely visible, says Koshy.

And that's how his film about a young woman claiming the streets of Mumbai at night came about. He has followed it up with several other films about women making waves in India with their radical feminism. I plan to screen each of these for my students in America.

▪▪▪▪▪▪▪▪▪▪▪▪▪▪▪▪▪▪▪▪▪▪▪▪▪▪▪

I call Gibran and ask him how it all turned out, our greedy consumption of media and our constant chatter about it all. He says media definitely made him a bit insecure from time to time about his masculinity, but it also rescued him when he looked at it with irony. "I learned how not to be a man from Hollywood movies. I learned of Indian toxic masculinity through watching Bollywood movies and also reading Indian history and Hinduism and even seeing how Nana-ji [his maternal grandfather] and Kaka [his grand-uncle] talk, and even my dad has this . . . although it's toned down . . . there's this internalized patriarchy. These are men who are victims of toxic masculinity."

Gibran credits me as being "the curator of [his] life-influences until [he] was thirteen or fourteen." Beyond that, he says, he went to the internet. "I started reading on the internet, getting into forums like 4chan and Reddit, arguing with people . . ."

This brings me to a key issue. Many of the studies and also the video game professionals I have cited in this book have advised parents to filter and censor video games and social media for our kids. I, similar to Dr. Kishonna Gray, had a more laissez-faire approach. I would say this—so much depends on your own family's circumstance, the language and learning you develop with your child, and your individual child's personality. And your approach can (and should) change as your child matures.

It wasn't as if I was sure my approach was the best. Often, I'd feel terrified that I was doing it all wrong. This would happen mostly when Gibran would inform me about things he'd read online. He'd told me when he read the manifesto of mass shooter Elliot Rodger because he wanted to inform himself about masculinity turned horrifically violent. I remember being shocked that he'd read it. I remember asking him questions and being reassured that he wasn't, in fact, caught up in any sort of morbid fascination with it.

As we speak now, he tells me about the MRM (men's rights movement) and PUAs (Pickup Artists)—precursors to inceldom (a movement that draws teens and men claiming to be "involuntarily celibate" because women won't have sex with them; a movement by which Rodger was hailed as a hero)—and their rantings online, about anger at the family court system, about online trainings for pickup artists (to help "nerds who can't talk to women").

"These guys are involved in removing women from their agency. Their relationship to women has become gamified. They believe they have been scammed by women somehow." Gibran tells me about a man named Stefan Molyneux, a Canadian "public intellectual" who has launched a project to "Make Women Great Again." As Gibran speaks, I go online to check out this man's agenda. I come upon his ideas, such as (a) violence in the world is a result of bad mothers, especially single mothers, and (b) women shouldn't be allowed to wear lipstick at the workplace because it simulates arousal and is akin to "a man showing up to work with a boner."

I can see how all this would be fascinating. I am bothered that all this is fascinating to my boy.

I interrupt him to ask why he goes down that cyber–rabbit hole of misogyny. What did I set into motion, I wonder. Over the course of our conversation, I realize that, in giving him the tools and lenses of feminism, and especially in utilizing the media toward that enterprise, I grew a cultural critic. A scholar of masculinities and media. Not all of them take to academia like this young cultural critic's mother. Some of them go into the world of technology and, as he promises me, work to change the culture of the "tech bros," or "brogrammers," a slang term for the stereotypically masculine programmers who have created a culture that erects barriers to women in technology.

Where did the term emerge? It was allegedly coined by a former Facebook employee, Nick Schrock, who for years ran a "brogramming" page on Facebook. It would appear that Schrock was totally sincere about this trend where men in tech would ask each other to "bro down and write some code." The fact that the term has been appropriated and turned ironic in its use is, to my mind, one of the beauties of what we can do while we dart about, we fish trying to describe water.

During the COVID-19 pandemic, all of us in the electronically connected world became, well and truly, digital natives. Our web-cams became witnesses of our existence. Our screens became our children's teachers. Our children became pixelated projections into spaces we can only fathom in the thirteen inches or so that were allowed into our visions. Our humanity became data, our skin color became distorted in others' view, depending on the light. Our attentions were offered into portals, our minds were allowed distractions upon distractions through browser windows within our shuttered doors. This will forever be a parallel world in which our children breathe, laugh, imagine, plunder, bully, love, and grow.

TO DO:

- Educate yourself on media literacy. Make media work for you rather than against you. Use it to enhance the passing down of your values to your children, especially empathy, inclusion, and allyship.

- Practice co-viewing media early with your kids, especially boys.

- Dr. Chu says that, while we still can, we must limit young boys' use of and exposure to video games and social media and, as they grow, explain the risks. They *want* prescribed limits, she says.

- Dr. Gray encourages us to go ahead and keep watch over their gaming lives. "In our generation, we would get bullied in the school yard and when we came back we wouldn't tell our parents anything. And a lot of the time it was just too late for them to give us the language and tools, and there was no communication around it, we just had to deal with it. I'm just not OK with that, so that's why I really love that gaming puts you right there with them. Find out who they're playing with."

- Encourage your son in calling out sexism and racism on gaming platforms.

- Talk to your boys about cyberbullying. Give them examples of the devastation it can cause. In addition to encouraging their own acts of allyship, encourage them to report cyberbullying before things escalate.

- Ask your boys to educate you on media. Admit to them that you know they will likely be ahead of you in understanding it. Develop a sense of wonder. Keep the conversation open with a healthy mix of argument and acceptance. Whatever you do, don't imagine you can shut it all down, especially with tweens and teens.

- Poke fun at advertisements that sexualize women.

- Actively demand that the media are not in battle with our boys' imaginations. Lobby for media content that passes the Bechdel test, which determines how women are represented. Support the work of organizations like GLAAD (formerly Gay and Lesbian Alliance Against Defamation), which reports every year on LGBTQ representations across different media with their Studio Responsibility Index. Also support the NAACP, which lobbies for accurate representations of people of color in the media. Follow their media ratings and support the media that score well. Put your money into those media and products and services that don't insult and prey on boys' notions of masculinity.

Chapter Eight

DO I REALLY HAVE TO TALK TO HIM ABOUT SEX?

One evening when Gibran was nine years old, we were splashing about at the family swim hour at the public Queen Anne Pool with Gibran and his friends and their parents. A little girl around five or six came running out of the locker room naked. Her mother was running after her, looking mortified at letting her girl out of her grasp to sprint naked for another dip in the pool. People in the pool averted their gaze. Gibran pointed at the girl and shouted, "Where's her penis?"

I hushed Gibran, but he went on. "Is that a vagina? It's better than a penis! It's just like . . . schwoop." He gestured with his hands like a door shutting into itself.

The adults around us suppressed their chuckles.

I said to Gibran: "OK, that's enough."

Now there were *two* mortified mothers at the pool. And there were at least two children who learned that sexual organs and talk about sexuality were inappropriate, shameful, to be hidden, to be silenced.

I regret that response of mine even today. I visualize how I could have smiled and drawn Gibran into a quick and matter-of-fact conversation on the differences of body parts and, yes, how creative his description was.

So the next time Gibran wanted to talk about sex and the body, I was ready. He was in sixth or seventh grade. I had picked him up from school and he was in the back seat of the car. He asked me when a boy and girl could be ready to have sex with one another. (I have also come to think of this as the time that Gibran came out to me as straight. Until then, I had spoken with ease and seamlessness about his sexuality as fluid. "One day, when you find yourself attracted to someone . . .")

I said: "You may be ready before the girl is. She will have a lot of pressure—from society, from culture, from her friends, from boys— to be sexual. But keep in mind that she may or may not really be ready. She may feel bad after. She may want to cry. Or, sure, she may be excited and enthusiastic about it. If you can be her friend through all of this, and you know you both are sure, and you are adults, go for it." Gibran nodded and gazed out of the car window, thoughtful.

In this conversation, I was going by my instincts. I wish I'd combined those with some deeper learning. I felt like so much was left unsaid and unasked. So many aspects of sex and its pleasures, dangers, joys, rules, freedoms fell through the cracks. I was raised in another generation and another culture, where I learned to fear sex, feel shame, stay a virgin until I married, and definitely not get pregnant before marriage. I learned more through sexual assault than sexual exploration. Despite all this, when I became sexually active and found pleasure and joy in sex, it took me by surprise but was still spoken about in secret.

I wanted so much to give Gibran a sex-positive upbringing, but I didn't know where to find such a training. Only recently did I come across the work of Dr. Andrew Smiler, who tells us we must really talk to our boys about sex. A lot. Dr. Smiler, a psychologist in Winston-Salem, North Carolina, and the author of *Challenging Casanova: Beyond the Stereotype of the Promiscuous Young Male* and *Dating and Sex: A Guide for the 21st Century Teen Boy*, has developed the best guide I have found out there for parents talking to their boys about sex.

Sexuality, says Dr. Smiler, deserves as much attention if not more in our children's life lessons as, say, managing money and eating healthy. His research focuses on definitions of masculinity, and he also studies normative aspects of sexual development, such as age and perception of a first kiss, first "serious" relationship, and first intercourse among fifteen- to twenty-five-year-olds.

Dr. Smiler found that only about half of high school seniors or college students say their parents ever talked to them about sex. Even worse, he says in a post on the blog *The Good Men Project*, most of the kids who are lucky enough to have "the talk" had a conversation that lasted less than ten minutes. Things are worse for boys than girls; they're slightly less likely to have any conversation with their parents, and when they do, it's shorter and covers fewer topics.

Dr. Smiler gives us a list. Talk to boys about these fourteen things:

- Your general values about how to treat friends and strangers.
- Sexuality rather than sex.
- The connection between dating and sexuality (e.g. trust and exclusiveness and what message a kiss possibly sends).
- The acceptable age for first sex, based on knowing who your son is.
- The acceptability of hookups and "friends with benefits."
- Consent. ("Make sure he understands that consent is reasonably specific and that he should use terms like 'sex' and not nebulous expressions like 'let's do it.' Frankly, if your son can't explicitly tell his partner that he wants to have sex, then he's probably not ready to have sex with that person.")

- Refusal (coming from either his partner or him).
- Biological basics.
- Reproduction basics.
- Contraception basics.
- Condoms (the only form of contraception guys control).
- How diseases exist.
- Pleasure.
- Porn.

Swoon. Where has Dr. Smiler been my whole life? The truth is, when I read this, I realized once again that although I talked to Gibran a fair amount about sexuality in his adolescent and teen years, I didn't talk as often and as easily as I should have.

We talk to our little girls about sex all the time. When we talk to them about how to sit, dress, or stay safe, we are really talking to them about sex. We caution them not to let someone touch them inappropriately. Unfortunately, it seems we are always talking to them about the dangers of sex, not the pleasures. Boys, on the other hand, commonly learn of sex through pornography, through friends' jokes or challenges, and through societal cues about being the initiators, seekers, and conquerors of sex.

While Gibran and I talked about sexuality in passing, in reference to characters in movies or the appropriateness of some jokes versus others (no rape jokes, ever, thanks son), we deepened that conversation really only when he was away at college. Until Gibran left for college, I had only experienced American campus life as an international student arriving to a PhD program, and then as a professor who taught undergraduates. I had no idea about dorm life and fraternities, dating, hooking up, and parties. It would all be fine, my friends in Seattle who were parents reassured me. (These were mostly parents of boys.) The parents of girls told me that some of their questions were similar to mine and others were dramatically different. Their questions were: What kind of young men would their daughter encounter? Would she be safe from them? Had their parents taught them well? Would she find friends? Would she be loved?

Gibran didn't call often from college, and I was told that was a good thing. It meant he was launched. When he did call, we talked for a long time. We started to have the best conversations we'd ever had. Other parents of college-age offspring talk about this phenomenon. Our kids get really chatty on the phone before they ask for money.

No, of course he didn't want to join a fraternity, he said. Yes, he was dating, and I'd like Katy. Yes, he knew about consent, so could we please not talk about that? Yes, campus rapes were a real thing. Gotta go.

"Wake up," I said in a text message to Gibran one morning. "We need to talk about Aziz Ansari."

It was in early 2018, at the peak of the #MeToo revelations, and Gibran was a junior in college. The website Babe had published an account of a young woman who had gone on a date with popular comedian Aziz Ansari, where she said Ansari kept pressuring her into having sex with him. A cultural storm brewed after the publication of the article. Some said: "It was just a bad date. The woman should have left." Others said: "Well, perhaps it's not so easy to say no after all."

We loved Aziz Ansari, Gibran and I. My boy pointed me to *Master of None* the very day it was released on Netflix. "It's OK, not great, but we should watch it," Gibran said. Of course we should. Ansari is funny, we had already established. And he's somewhat like us, of Indian ethnicity (take that, Hollywood). Also, he is of Indian Muslim origin (take that, Hindu fundamentalists). And Ansari is woke.

When Gibran called me back upon receiving my text, he really didn't want to talk about the whole business with Ansari. "It's cringeworthy," he said.

But mothers of twenty-two-year-old sons must persist through the cringe.

We had talked about the #MeToo movement before. Like many other women, I was highly triggered on the couple of days that followed the birth of the hashtag and the deluge of women's disturbing stories from across the world. I put one of my own stories out there, then called Gibran as he was rushing about his busy day at Swarthmore. I just wanted to hear his voice. I was rewarded with more—his words.

He spoke with a clear and profound outrage at the sexual abuse of women by men across the board. Why spare even Gandhi, we said. And we agreed we would #believeher no matter who the next accused person was (unless, of course, it was our hero, Noam Chomsky; we'd have a hard time dealing with that).

With the Ansari matter, though, the conversation with my boy would be complicated, I knew. That case made us all talk about something beyond sexual assault, abuse, or harassment. We were having a conversation that isn't even really *about* Ansari.

What we really needed to talk about were the cultural conversations that rose up around the Ansari incident. What we needed to talk about is proactively going after the problem and training men to read women the way women have been trained to read men.

What my son must know—and what I addressed directly with him—is that none of this is as difficult as the men around him might be saying it is. It's actually quite easy. Girls are raised into womanhood with a thorough understanding of men's motivations and cues. Through warnings and whispers, through fables and giggles, we are tutored rigorously on what men will want—in the best, nonviolent iterations, they will want your body, they will want your loyalty, they will want your food, they will want you to smile and cheer them on and tell them they make you happy. For generations, we have been lined up—as we apply mehendi on our hands huddled around a fortunate Indian bride, or pose in matching pastel hues of organza around a triumphant American one—and sent forth to laugh heartily at our men's jokes, raise their children, starve our bodies into attractiveness, and fake our orgasms.

Sure, we have also driven change. We have recalibrated ourselves for the "woke" boys—chase your own dreams, be a fun companion, *ooh* over their cooking, *aah* over their shared childcare, smile and cheer them on and tell them they make you happy. But also, girl, *don't push it.*

Women have been trained. Now let's finally, if it's all right with everyone, train boys to know what's going on with girls and women.

▼▼▼▼▼▼▼▼▼▼▼▼▼▼▼▼▼▼▼▼▼▼▼▼

So yes, son, let's cringe our way through the new part of this conversation. But this time, I told myself, it's best I listen.

"We don't need hot takes," Gibran said of the Ansari case. "We need room-temperature, equilibrated, long-term, studied, structural changes. For one, we need pornography that isn't violent or humiliating toward women. Men like Ansari are raised on such porn." (I tried not to think of how much porn my son might be watching.)

His voice drew me back in. "Also, men who refer to the #MeToo campaign as a 'witch hunt' terrify me. This implies they have a huge degree of entitlement and believe that the average-looking guys, the Ansaris of the world, are being unfairly humiliated. We need to watch out for their backlash, Mama."

We do. *We.* With that one word, I will stand steady in the face of any backlash.

As the articles in defense of Aziz Ansari said, though, women do have agency, to leave, to call it all off. Yes, we do. But we don't just show up in our encounters with men with an Uber app on our phones and that glorious word "No" on our lips. We show up awash in the rules and the ruse of patriarchy and its son, rape culture. As comedian and writer Kate Willett posted on her Facebook page:

> Good flirting . . . is paying such deep attention to another person's emotions and body language that you create more intimacy with them. It's a two-way, playful, fun exchange that makes everyone feel good. Sexual harassment is the opposite. It's devoid of empathy, and it's about forcing your will upon another person without having any regard for their desire. You're comparing a paint brush to a wrecking ball.

Sure, yes, our culture is transmuting as we speak; #MeToo, in all its iterations, all its humiliations, and all its chaos and its ebb and flow, is part of the transmutation. But there's so much more to talk about in the years to come—more deeply and with more nuance—with our children and friends and partners.

And so here's what I told Gibran: What the Ansari incident is bringing up for women is that some women gave up their power and silently endured humiliating sex because of self-doubt. Or fear. Some, *like me*, guarded themselves to such a degree to avoid sexual encounters of this kind that we lost out on the joys of flirtation, of mutual seduction, of the pleasures of our own sensuality. We policed ourselves because we knew no one would come to our feeble call. We only partook when we'd checked all our boxes that said "Safe." All of this is rooted in toxic masculinity. All of this is rooted in rape culture.

And yet, when we speak of sexuality and rape, we barely turn our eye on our boys. Even the books that crowd our bookshelves, about raising boys versus girls, frame sexuality as a girl's/woman's problem. Dr. Leonard Sax, a psychologist who lives in suburban Philadelphia not too far from where my boy went to college, is the author of a book titled *Boys Adrift: The Five Factors Driving the Growing Epidemic of Unmotivated Boys and Underachieving Young Men*. The five factors, he says, are video games, teaching methods, prescription drugs, environmental toxins, and the devaluation of masculinity. Dr. Sax has also written a book titled *Girls on the Edge: The Four Factors Driving the New Crisis for Girls*. The four factors he lists are sexual identity, the cyberbubble, obsessions, and environmental toxins. Girls are getting insatiably ambitious and this produces an "obsessive drive," Dr. Sax says. And their obsession with achievement spills over into destructive concerns and behaviors. Dr. Sax believes girls are sexualizing themselves as early as age eight and are presenting their sexuality online, in what he refers to as "the cyberbubble." He suggests that girls need to have contact with responsible women, not just their mothers. He notes the number of such meeting places in the past: "quilting circles, sewing circles, all-female Bible study groups, all-female book groups, Girl Scout troops."

In Dr. Sax's imagination, perhaps there was a golden age in which girls frequented these all-girls-all-women havens and then, un-obsessed and unambitious, went home warm, happy, un-sexualized and un-raped. In *my* reality, eight-year-old girls will be sexualized no matter what unless we start talking about these things with boys and men.

I was eight years old when I was first sexually assaulted, by an army officer in an elevator. I was rushing to catch up with friends out playing, but he stopped the elevator, squeezed my eight-year-old girl nipples and put his fingers inside me before he let me go. After that, I was sexually abused and assaulted multiple times—by strangers and family friends, by doctors (at ten, during physical therapy for my polio), by faith healers (this one also put his fingers inside me, jolting me out of my dream of turning a beautiful sixteen and wearing high heels for the first time if he cured me of polio and my legs and feet grew strong), by family, by others over and over again in my teens, and then in my twenties by the executive editor of my newspaper (who invited me to his hotel room to discuss flexible hours of work for me while I was the lactating mother of a newborn, but also, quite insignificantly, I was a bureau chief of the biggest newspaper in the nation).

It hurts even to write this list, even after all these years. I told no one for years. I was sexually assaulted by so many men that I began to be grateful to men who *wouldn't* molest me. I believed them to be great men. And by "great," I mean Men of Greatness, not as in "George W. Bush would be a great guy to get a beer with."

So although I came to talking to my son a little late about sexuality, because it was hard and triggering and—to borrow Gibran's word—cringeworthy *for me*, I talked about it regularly when he was in college. As it turned out, those years happened to coincide with the years in which all of America was learning of the scale of campus sexual assault for the first time.

Let's take the Ivy Leagues alone. In 2010, new pledges to the Yale fraternity Delta Kappa Epsilon marched through the residential section of Yale's campus. The frat boys, some blindfolded, chanted such revolting phrases as "No means yes! Yes means anal!"

In 2014, Emma Sulkowicz carried around a fifty-pound dorm mattress wherever she went on campus as an art project to represent the painful burden rape victims carry throughout daily life, and in protest of what she described as Columbia University's mishandling of her sexual assault complaint. She said she was raped by another student on that mattress, but the college and the New York police concluded she hadn't. The university settled with her. Emma Sulkowicz and her girlfriends carried that mattress at her graduation ceremony.

In 2015, Brock Turner, a Stanford University freshman at the time, raped an unconscious woman behind a dumpster at a party. He said the woman had consented to his sexual advances and blamed "the party culture and risk-taking behavior" of college for his actions. Turner seemed to know exactly what he was doing, though. He took a picture of the woman's breasts and sent it to his friends on the Stanford swim team. He was looking for their approval; he was bringing home a trophy. A judge sentenced him to a mere six months in prison and was later recalled by California voters for that shockingly lenient sentence. The survivor of the assault, Chanel Miller, revealed her identity in 2019 with the launch of her memoir, titled *Know My Name.*

In her book, Miller has this to say about rape culture: "When a woman is assaulted, one of the first questions people ask is, Did you say no? This question assumes that the answer was always yes, and that it is her job to revoke the agreement. To defuse the bomb she was given. But why are they allowed to touch us until we physically fight them off? Why is the door open until we have to slam it shut?"

I wanted to believe that rape culture was a thing from my past, that I had fled it and that it would never be able to reach over oceans and continents and latch onto my boy's world here in America. And yet, here we are.

So I am going to propose something radical that Dr. Sax will not like and that Dr. Smiler did not suggest: Tell your boy your #MeToo stories. Shift the shame from the abused to the abuser. Normalize the *reporting* of rapes. Expose the staggering extent of it all. Know Chanel Miller's name and know *my* name and know the names of all those millions of women until your boys and men no longer imagine that sexual assault happens only to women who were doing the wrong thing at the wrong place at the wrong time wearing the wrong clothes. Let your boys and men know that survivors of sexual assault (which includes nonbinary people, trans people, cis-hetero boys and men) will no longer be silent in shame.

Remember, Goddess Sita taught me to give my boy a good education. To me, this meant also that I told Gibran about some of my own sexual assaults, at age-appropriate times, after he turned fifteen, without dwelling on details. Little wonder, then, that today's #MeToo revelations from across the world don't leave him reeling the way they do some of his friends. You may be appalled that I chose to make those revelations to my boy. But I urge you once again to think of how much we warn our girls about rape and rapists. Surely they wonder how we're so sure that rape is everywhere and can happen to anyone? Our girls grow up sensing their mothers are speaking from experience and that their fathers, yes, are also speaking from the knowledge of the male gaze and male intent.

But we let our boys go out into the world unscathed, unexposed, unaware, because we can't imagine leaving them disturbed. Daughters, meanwhile, are regimenting their every move, not just disturbed but deadened, unable to imagine the possibility of going through life unbothered and being sexual only when they choose it.

We are saying now that we must turn the attention from teaching girls (and other vulnerable groups) how not to get raped and instead teach our cis-hetero boys *not to rape*. Perhaps it's not such a bad idea to fill them with loathing for the pervasiveness of the toxic male sexuality that left scars on so many of the women in their lives.

Gibran and I had once talked about Elliot Rodger, the twenty-two-year-old who went on a shooting rampage in Isla Vista, California, in 2014. Rodger felt rejected by women and wanted to kill them for denying him sex. He felt rejected by them especially as a young man of color. Today, Rodger is hailed as a hero, a "Supreme Gentleman," by the Incel Rebellion.

I asked Gibran about alienation, anger, rejection, racism, and what it all might feel like for young men of color in America. What Gibran said knocked the breath out of me.

"That's all true about America, so, of course, I sometimes feel alienated," Gibran said. "But I've also always felt loved." He said it casually, and I sensed he had turned away from the phone, to pick something up, or stretch, or something else that implied ease, not intensity, as if feeling loved weren't an increasingly rare thing in our world right now. Then came the nuance: "Mama, this guy's family neglected him—which doesn't excuse his violence, but it explains a part of it."

I want single parents, especially, to take this in for a moment. Gibran was an only child who grew up with a single mother. No matter what the world tells us single parents, don't let them convince you that your child will grow up feeling unloved. The second thing to note—yes, our boys are adrift in a sea of alienation.

"I don't feel that white girls or *any* girls owe me something," Gibran said. "Women don't owe me sex. I mean, seriously—we guys have to get that women are people, and people are ends in themselves. They aren't here as means and devices for our games and our journeys. And I don't need their sexual validation to make me feel better about being brown-skinned."

Have I mentioned yet that my baby's brown skin is luminescent? He gets browner in the sun and his features get stronger, sharper, more beautiful.

"OK, gotta go, Mama. Remember to transfer the money."

For her recent book *Boys & Sex*, journalist Peggy Orenstein interviewed more than one hundred college and college-bound boys and young men of diverse backgrounds between the ages of sixteen and twenty-two. Similar to Dr. Judy Y. Chu's research on boys' yearning to be vulnerable and seek emotional connection, Orenstein found boys talking about an exhaustion with being bombarded by messages of male sexual entitlement and female sexual availability. Boys seemed to think they had to talk about sex in terms that sounded violent rather than pleasurable—"I banged, I pounded, I hammered, I nailed, I hit that, I tapped that." Hookup culture, too, was about status-seeking. A number of these boys and young men craved connection and even talked with tenderness about their partners but then dismissed that as a personal quirk rather than the norm.

Orenstein's research seemed to echo the findings reported by Laurie Halse Anderson in a *Time* magazine article from 2019 titled "I've Talked with Teenage Boys About Sexual Assault for 20 Years. This Is What They Still Don't Know." Anderson, a novelist and poet, lectures at schools and colleges as a sexual assault survivor. She often finds boys who linger after her talk to ask questions in private. Some of these boys are survivors of sexual assault and others half-confess to having raped. Most of these boys' parents had limited their conversations about sex to lectures on "don't get her pregnant." Then the boys learned about sex from friends and from internet porn, which is often about violation and nonconsensual sex. "They don't understand that consent needs to be informed, enthusiastic, sober, ongoing, and freely given," Anderson writes.

▪▪▪▪▪▪▪▪▪▪▪▪▪▪▪▪▪▪▪▪▪▪▪▪▪▪▪▪▪

We don't know if our grown boys are out there hating girls or loving them, feeling lonely or feeling entitled. We can't monitor their online worlds. We can more easily get them to clean their rooms than their chat rooms. So, let's stop trying, shall we? Let's, instead, talk to them, text them, tease them, tease things out of them.

Perhaps we can also give them something to do. An activity. Like, be a part of the solution and change the course of history. Because masculinity has cast them as part of the problem. As *New York Times* columnist Lindy West points out in her book *The Witches Are Coming*, "Sexism is a male invention. White supremacy is a white invention. Transphobia is a cisgender invention." Why, West asks, is fixing sexism women's work?

So how do we heal? How did my son navigate rape culture and have a healthy sexuality? He found friends—men, women, nonbinary friends—who tapped into alternative ways of being on an American campus. They exist, if you will look for them. At my son's institution, Swarthmore College, a student-led group called Organizing for Survivors (O4S) encourages accountability and the role of apology in healing. My son and his friends were moved especially by the stories that six students posted online about their experiences with sexual assault. It helped in an interesting and profound way: the students turned the shame onto the offenders rather than the survivors. My boy and his friends talked about how one day, perhaps, survivors would no longer have to share their stories for campus communities to pay attention.

We, as college administrators and educators, haven't exactly made it easy for these lovely beings placed in our care. Although one in five college women reports sexual violence during her time in college and 43 percent of dating women report experiencing violent and abusive dating behaviors, too many universities have been accused of mishandling sexual assault complaints and violating Title IX rules. Universities, until recently and perhaps even now, focus their sexual assault orientation materials on potential victims, dishing out tips to young women on how not to get raped by limiting their own behaviors, their dress, and their mobility. Our institutions are afraid of a public relations nightmare and most still ask the victim to approach the institution rather than the police.

How do we get boys and young men to take this on, especially when the pressure is on them to grin and fit in?

Help is on the way. The conversation is finally shifting to the potential assaulters and *how and why not to rape.* The "Consent. Ask for It." campaign consists of on-campus events at over one hundred colleges around the country, complete with an activist toolkit, posters, giveaways, and free condoms (the Trojan condom company is a partner). Student advocates plan campaigns around the country to talk about consent. Columbia University is engaged in a massive ethnographic study—the Sexual Health Initiative to Foster Transformation (SHIFT). They invite students to describe their experiences about dating, sex, friendships, partying, academics, peer pressure, and more. SHIFT is trying to meet young people where they are to promote sexual well-being and prevent sexual assault. The goal is to foster sexuality in a spirit of respect, perhaps romance, and a climate in which healthy relationships can be sustained.

And that's the key difference between talking to our boys about sexuality versus talking to them only about sex. A person's sexuality includes everything from their biological sex, gender identity, and sexual orientation to pregnancy and reproduction. Not everyone will experience every aspect of these. Sexuality is influenced by the interaction of biological, psychological, social, economic, political, cultural, ethical, legal, historical, religious, and spiritual factors. When we talk to our children only about the sexual act (and in most of society, we perhaps only speak of heterosexual sex), we leave out so much of the wonder of humanity. We must speak of sexual health, for instance, which includes things like personal hygiene, healthy relationships, sexuality, and consent.

What would our boys' sexuality look like if we talked to them early and often about it? If we could remove the stigma, take away the shame, teach boys about the pervasiveness of sexual assault and harassment, teach them to see sex as a site of mutual pleasure, not as a project or prize?

We could free them up to talk about their bodies, to talk about their sexuality, to fantasize, to fall in love, to have safe sex for recreation or romance, to love themselves, to love across gender. And to pick up the phone and call home to tell us at least a little about it.

TO DO:

- Talk to your boy about sex! Use Dr. Andrew Smiler's list on pages 133–134 as a guide.

- Psychologist Dr. Karen Weisbard says to create a culture in your family in which you talk about emotions, pleasure of different kinds, body autonomy, and consent. Start early so it doesn't feel overwhelming or embarrassing later.

- Tell your children, especially your son, your #MeToo stories at an age-appropriate time, when you are able to help them process it. Seek advice from a counselor on how to go about it.

Chapter Nine

IS FEMINISM GOOD FOR HIS BODY AS WELL AS HIS MIND?

My earliest anxieties about Gibran's body began even before he was born. I was convinced I would pass on my polio to him somehow. My ob-gyn assured me the virus wasn't passed on genetically. But I distrusted science and imagined that if they could have given me a vaccine that failed on my body, somehow my body would succeed in its betrayal of me and infect the little fetus.

I didn't share these anxieties with anyone in my family, not even with Rajat. I was afraid I would be considered unworthy of carrying a child. I was afraid of being considered a woman with a diseased womb. I wondered if a boy with polio would suffer its stigma worse than I had as a girl.

I am struck by the realization now, as I write this, that it has always been the stigma, the shame of disability, that's cut me deeper than the disability itself. I am fortunate in a way, to have had a milder atrophy of my muscles, a lesser limp than most people with polio, and some decent compensations from the rest of my body to keep me upright. But the shame that comes from the gaze, the questions of others, the having to drone out a quick medical history in my response, it walks in lockstep with me every moment of my life.

So the possibility of a disability in my baby was one of the first reckonings I had with the masculinity of my child. When I discovered his sex, I had wept, for myself. But this new fear was a fear for *him* about his relationship to masculinity.

Gibran's healthy baby body, then, was a source of primal maternal pleasure for me. The world over, we count a newborn's fingers and toes. I counted his fingers and toes and measured his limbs in the spans of my thumbs and forefingers, massaging baby fat and baby muscle. I marked in bold pen the dates on the calendar when his vaccines were due. Measles, mumps, rubella, polio, smallpox, chicken pox. None of them would get a flick of their tongue at my baby.

They don't have a vaccine for the ills of masculinity, though. And those ills first crawled out as germs within my own brain: A girl with a limp could be considered less beautiful, but also perhaps my fragility is what drew the attention—good and bad—of men wanting to protect me or harm me. A boy with a limp would be considered weak and could never be perceived as a protector.

Gibran's Apgar score was low at birth. So he'd be a "sickly boy" then? I've mentioned that as a toddler in Bangalore, he started to talk at eight months old but walked "late" in comparison to my friends' babies (and you know that first year is all about comparisons). Every cell of my polio-racked being strained in anticipation of my baby's first steps. When he finally took them at fourteen months of age, I felt as if some superhuman strength had entered my own limbs. I hadn't birthed a "sickly boy" after all.

On his fourth birthday in Singapore, he didn't bounce off the walls as much as the other boys. He moved slowly even though his mind was a wondrous and wondering thing. His fine motor skills were impeded by his large daydreaming skills. In the process of tying his shoelaces, he'd fall into a Byronesque middle-distance stare and tell me that it was important that I never forget that in Pokémon, Charmander evolves into Charmeleon, who then becomes Charizard.

Gibran's cousin Samir, the son of Rajat's brother and sister-in-law, came to visit us in Singapore. Samir was a few months younger than Gibran. As I showed their family around the parks and malls of Singapore, Samir dashed about, hiding under park benches, running up escalators, throwing himself like a *toofan*, a hurricane, into the swimming pool of our condo. His father chuckled and called him a little monkey. In the next instant, he called Gibran a philosopher.

The monkey and the philosopher. These comparisons, these gauges, these titles we place on our boys, within their hearing or at a distance, they measure and prescribe the way their bodies move in the world.

I had to coax my philosopher into the swimming pool. I spent a vacation in Goa with Rajat and Gibran quietly miserable because my child would run away from the tiny waves of the Arabian Sea that crept toward our feet on the shore. This was the singular most pleasurable thing my body and soul had experienced on our planet and my child was going to find pleasure in it, goddammit. Back in Singapore, I hired a swimming instructor. His methodology was to push a child into the pool and let them sputter and almost drown until the fear of water was knocked out of them.

That's when I came to my senses. Watching my child's panicked face, his beautiful big eyes widening in terror as they disappeared into the water—that's what it took to knock my sexism out of me. We hear fathers speak of how they realize the pressures on women only when they have daughters. I realized the pressures on men as I stood there, complicit in—no, commissioning and *leading*—this assault of masculinity upon my child.

I dove into the water and pulled my child into my arms. The way Gibran locked his legs around my torso and his arms around my neck and placed a slippery wet kiss on my cheek is a memory that still hits me like a tidal wave carrying its debris of emotions. I held my five-year-old like a mother shaped from water and I danced around the pool with his body clenched on mine, day after day, holding, dancing, hugging, kissing, singing in the pool no matter how much people stared, until one day Gibran slackened his grip and swam by my side.

For the rest of his childhood, I'd navigate the riptides of masculinity as they came for my son. We took it one tide at a time. Yes to soccer as long as he liked kicking a ball around. No to baseball because he didn't like the way the other boys laughed when he ducked from the ball instead of running to it with outstretched arm. Yes, at first, to Bollywood dance class, because I wanted so much for my son to dance like Shah Rukh Khan, but OK, no, when he stood fuming down at me from the stage and refused to shimmy his shoulders. Yes to camping but no to expecting him to be the one setting up the tent. Yes to theater until his teachers said he was so good at acting he should do more of it, and he said no, he didn't like the pressure. Yes to Ultimate Frisbee. Yes to snowboarding, which I never got to see because I couldn't navigate snow with my bad ankles, but, with my good imagination, I could see my boy enjoying the winter air on his face as his body flew down ski slopes.

Yes, as he grew older and developed a rich inner life, to contemplative solitude. No to those who said he should "be handy" around the house because he was now the man of the house. Yes to him doing our laundry since the age of eleven. No to him messing with hand and electrical tools (those fine motor skills just never came around).

The one thing that stayed a yes for Gibran's body for almost all the years was swimming. When we settled into Queen Anne Hill in Seattle, we went to the public pool and my boy and his little buddies swam and played, and then protested every time they had to leave. When I started to date Alec and we brought our kids together, the four of us would go to family hour at the pool. We devised the White Whale Daddy game. Alec was a White Whale Daddy and he would have me anchor onto his back, with Gibran on my back and Beth on Gibran's. The White Whale Daddy then would carry his whale family in a long, smooth glide round and round in the pool. People would watch us, jaws asunder, unable to explain what they were looking at. But we knew. We knew we were whales.

▼▼▼▼▼▼▼▼▼▼▼▼▼▼▼▼▼▼▼▼▼▼▼▼▼

At the end of Gibran's sophomore year in high school, something changed. Gibran's class was invited to an end-of-year pool party in the home of one of the wealthy parents who had a pool. Gibran left for the party and I noticed he'd forgotten to bring his swimming trunks with him. I grabbed them and ran after him.

"Aren't you glad I caught up with you?" I said. "You would have missed out on the swimming!"

"I don't need the trunks," Gibran said. "I won't be swimming."

"Are you cold? Planning to go somewhere else instead of the party?"

"No. Just don't want to swim."

I won't detail my systematic interrogation here but will cut to the chase and tell you that right as his friend's car pulled up, I discovered that Gibran didn't want to swim because he felt chubby and the other boys had washboard abs. As he jumped into a car with his friends and left, I stood there, his swimming trunks in my hand, still trying to frame a coherent sentence.

While I had been looking the other way, chastising my boy over the years for saying things like "Scarlett Johansson is chunky," and teaching media literacy to my students with documentaries like *Miss*

Representation and *Tough Guise*, something slimy rose up like Jason in *Friday the 13th* and took my boy's love for water down with it. Boys, not just girls, were worried about being seen as fat. My boy was skinny, though, I argued with myself. He wasn't chubby, but OK, he just didn't have the kind of abs that his white male friends did. He has a different body type. Couldn't toxic masculinity just get some fucking nuance?

Feminism asks that we chip away at gender roles. When we chip away at those, we chip away at the expectations of how bodies are supposed to move in space. We disempower the way sound and scent and touch invade or evade the gendered body. We change the spaces; we change the objects in our children's orbit— bringing dolls when Gibran asks for one as a two-year-old; bringing fruit-scented bubble-baths because he loves those at nineteen.

We disempower gender. We empower humans.

I am here for all that empowers my body. I am here for all that empowers my son's body.

In thinking about how society comes after our boys' bodies, let's get subtler than subtle. Let's not even go into the demands made on their sinews (which at best offer their strength and at their most toxic flex in violence upon women) or the jokes made about their size (it may feel fair, this kind of body-shaming, because women have to endure so much more, but we must understand that it comes from the same place, of shaming, of shame, that drives so much of the pain we push on each other). Instead, let's dwell upon the eyes.

When Gibran was a baby and I was visiting my mother's home in Mumbai with him, I once met a girl of about nine years in the elevator. She looked at Gibran in the stroller and said, "She's so pretty."

I smiled. "Thank you. But why do you think the baby is a 'she'? He's a boy."

"That can't be! Look at her eyes!"

I looked at my baby's eyes, the thick black lashes and the gorgeous round shape. I saw what the child had seen and I grinned. Over the years, as Gibran grew, I would often get glimpses of what that elevator child had seen, but I also watched as a certain sardonicism gathered around the edges and a learned brevity of the gaze took hold. Gibran's eyes and the way he looked through them became masculinized. I could never have explained it to anyone. You'd have had to see it for yourself, through the eyes of the elevator child and the young mother she addressed.

In the beautiful and unusual illustrated novel *She of the Mountains*, author Vivek Shraya tells the story of a young man exploring his sexuality and gender juxtaposed with a reimagining of the mythology of Hindu deities. In one scene, the protagonist says to his high school crush, Kevin Wheeler, "I can't figure out why everyone keeps calling me gay."

"*It's the way you use your eyes*, Kevin responded, shrugging his shoulders as though the answer was obvious," Shraya writes.

One more eye story: my dear friend Siddharth Dube was in Seattle to read from his book *An Indefinite Sentence: A Personal History of Outlawed Love and Sex*, about the multiple possibilities of gender and sexual desire. At his reading at the Elliott Bay Book Company, Dube told the story of his older brother, who had always been a supporter and ally, telling a group of friends when they were teens, "my brother shapes his eyebrows."

"It broke my heart," Dube told his audience. "I said 'No, I don't!' My eyebrows were naturally arched. But something about them seemed less masculine to my brother and his announcement to our friends felt to me like a betrayal. Why hadn't he asked me if I shaped my eyebrows?"

The reason I tell these stories here is that in their simplicity and subtlety, we encounter the daily assaults our boys face on their bodies and their psyches. Neither my baby in his stroller nor the lovestruck boy in Shraya's story nor my friend Siddharth were *doing* anything with their eyes. It's our gaze that ascribed gender, prescribed behavior, circumscribed intent. The cisgender heterosexual boy, the homosexual boy, the transgender woman or man could all just be babies riding in elevators, but even a nine-year-old child and a twenty-seven-year-old mother will make an elevator pitch on assumed or assigned gender.

In her 2018 book *Looking at Men: Art, Anatomy, and the Modern Male Body*, Australian artist and scholar of visual culture Anthea Callen explains the modern-day idea of the desirable male body. She says that from the 1800s to the 1920s, the intimately linked professions of art and medicine gave us an image of the idealized, virile manhood. Naturally, most of these men were white. And, even as these images sometimes gave us homoerotic views of male bodies swimming, rowing, wrestling, or boxing, male artists and medics leaned heavily toward a gladiatorial ideal that embodied signs of dominant power and signaled differences of race, class, gender, and sexuality. The popularity of the Greco-Roman male body—white and virile—also signaled "otherness," and the undesirability of an "inadequate physiology," as shadowed, as "a threat of loss, of a Darwinian 'degeneration' that required vigilant intervention to secure the health of nations." In other words, these images contributed to present-day racism, homophobia, and classism. They contributed to the social construction of these oppressive things.

And what have these idealized images from art done to the current gaze on masculinity? Such narrow notions of the perfect male body show up in all of global visual culture today, Callen suggests. The science-fictional idea of the cyborg (humans augmented with mechanical, superhuman powers) and the increasingly muscular, "war-ready" popular depictions of superheroes like Iron Man, Superman, or the bioengineered RoboCop have normalized a striving among boys and men for pushing their bodies beyond limits of endurance. "With testosterone-driven politics, we are now witnessing global male posturing on a dangerously megalomanic scale," Callen says.

A storm is coming, warns Dr. Flaviane Ferreira, the psychologist on Mercer Island. She is working with school counselors to counter an epidemic of anxiety among Generation Z children. "They're unhappy with their bodies. We used to see this in girls but now we increasingly find boys who say they are fat. Body dysmorphia is rampant. Boys are cutting themselves."

Dr. Judy Chu, the Stanford researcher who works with boys as young as four years old, also asks parents to keep an eye out for body dysmorphia in boys. More and more, they are showing anxiety about their musculature and height, she says. They're working out too much and guzzling protein shakes. All around them, they see a narrow image of masculinity. We must talk to our boys about this, Dr. Chu says. She advises us to ask them why they are exercising—to grow strong or to look attractive? Is that to look for approval? Is it to feel worthy or valuable? Wouldn't they be happier if they could enjoy feeling comfortable with their bodies instead of dissatisfied?

When I remark at how these are the very same questions we'd pose to girls and women who starved themselves into skinniness or surgically implanted curves in spaces deemed desirable, Dr. Chu sighs and riffs on a famous quote—"We must now say that 'feminism is the radical notion that men are human beings too.'"

What does our rapidly narrowing ideal for the male body mean for the disabled male body? Disabled bodies are made invisible, says my friend Amelia, whose son has serious disabilities, including an inability to articulate his pain. Although parenting her son means navigating a complex ecosystem of doctors, nurses, specialists, therapists, care teams, social workers, paraeducators, and in-home providers, nothing feels more brutal than the kind of exclusion that happened with her son's first grade class.

Amelia speaks about an incident when she saw a sign for a musical that her son's class was to be in. When she inquired excitedly about it, her son's music teacher said that it wasn't for kids in the special ed class because "these kids just can't learn the songs." The expectation of the school even for first graders—that the songs and music be performed perfectly—was another way that Amelia and her son experienced a rejection of anything that didn't seem to measure up. "Patriarchal (and white-supremacist) values about what is 'normal' and 'beautiful' not only entrench and enforce gender norms, but also make people uncomfortable with bodies that do not conform to gendered and abled expectations. This leads them to want to remove, put far, far away so they don't need to see it, the thing that is causing the discomfort—namely, my son and others like him," Amelia writes.

"Our son's favorite thing in the world is music," she continues. "Somehow this particular experience of exclusion, out of the many that have happened, was the worst. I felt different putting my son on the bus the next day."

Amelia didn't want to let this one go, so she and her husband shared their distress with their son's teacher and principal, who were receptive. Her son and his friends from special ed were included in the second-grade concert. "It gave us great joy to see him and his classmates up on the stage with all the second graders, included in a music concert for the very first time at that school. Yes, my son was tired and slept through some of it, but he was happy," Amelia remembers.

Now her son's class has a buddy class in general education. All kids will benefit from inclusive education practices, and so will the world they take leadership in as adults, says Amelia. But getting to that point is not ever going to be easy. Amelia speaks with a deep honesty and self-awareness about how she had to overcome her own socialization and experience around gender, which, as was the case with me too, made her afraid of having her boy. Added to that was the way she was socialized around disability and how it influenced her capacity to understand what it would mean to parent a child with disabilities. "Intersectional feminism, along with the disability justice movement, helps me continue to understand and work on this," Amelia says. "And though I would like to say I am doing this for myself, I am not." Amelia is a professor and scholar of social work, and she is working for her own liberation and that of others, she says, in order to even have the possibility of a world where her son can have a rich life in which he is celebrated.

"After eight years of being his mother, I can't even imagine not having a son. And I can't imagine not having a son with disabilities. I can't imagine not having my son exactly how he is. I don't even want to try. When you ask what I want for his future—it is simply this: I want the world to view him as I do. And embrace him for the fullness of who he is, exactly as he is."

▀▀▀▀▀▀▀▀▀▀▀▀▀▀▀▀▀▀▀▀▀▀▀▀▀▀

I can't help but think of what such a feminism and such a world that Amelia is working toward would have meant for me as a girl with polio. I try but I can't imagine a childhood in which I was included in playground games, let alone sports. I can't imagine a self-esteem that wasn't eroded by aunts whispering to my mother in the kitchen that my family would have to pay a high dowry to get their disabled girl married. I can't imagine what it would have been like to reclaim those years between ages fifteen and twenty-nine when I stopped getting into a bathing suit because I was ashamed of the asymmetry of my legs. At twenty-nine, I got into the swimming pool again so

Gibran could splash around. When Gibran was fifteen, he stopped swimming. He rarely, if ever, swims today. The intersectional feminism Amelia speaks of cannot arrive fast enough.

Instead, right now, we police bodies and we police what those bodies touch, what they listen to, what they taste, what they see, whom they love, where they go, and what sounds they make. We do this in staggeringly violent ways and we do it in insidiously subtle ways. In her essay "The Gender of Sound," Anne Carson writes about some of the historical meanings invested in the sounds made by women versus those made by men. She says: "It is in large part according to the sounds people make that we judge them sane or insane, male or female, good, evil, trustworthy, depressive, marriageable, moribund, likely or unlikely to make war on us, little better than animals, inspired by God." Carson writes about women's shrieking or certain kinds of laughter as being considered distasteful, as well as certain voices, such as Margaret Thatcher's. Women, she says, are perceived as making a disorderly or uncontrolled outflow of sound. When a man lets his current emotions come up to his mouth and out through his tongue, he is perceived as losing some sort of control and is thereby feminized, she says. In the Greek notion of sophrosyne, she points out, a man must control the sounds he makes. He must control his pitch. And yet, as a society, we have decided that some sounds in a high pitch are seen as inherently male domain. Whistling, for instance, is considered male domain, say scholars of gender studies.

When Gibran was readying to leave for college, I'd watch him around the house and feel an ache for how much I was going to miss his physical presence in this room or that room. One day, I was in the kitchen and I listened to him whistling as he showered. I broke down in sobs. His whistle. His perfect whistling is what I would miss the most.

If I'd had a daughter, what of her would I miss the most? Would I miss her whistling?

When we demand a feminist world, we let women's bodies be. When our boys encounter women's bodies *being*, when our boys demand that women's bodies just be and that women have ownership over who or what gets to be in their body (a lover, an embryo), our boys can let their own bodies just be. Consider the things we deny boys and men because we see their bodies as a threat.

In India, men walk in the streets holding hands. Gay and straight men. They easily throw their arms around one another's shoulders and walk around holding that partial embrace. Naturally, when I lived in India, I did not see this as odd. Later, after years of living in America, when I took my American students on a study abroad to Mumbai in 2008, we were walking along Marine Drive, Mumbai's beautiful seaside promenade, and one of my students remarked on this public display of affection among men. The student who spoke up was a young white gay man. I saw such awe, such admiration, such *longing* on his face. To his mind, I imagined, this was some version of paradise, where gay men could so openly express their affection in mainstream public. I told him that the men were not necessarily gay. The young man seemed even more pleased. While my student's gaze was celebratory of this phenomenon, I wondered how long it would be before, as with more and more things in this global media world of ours, Indian men would feel the West's homophobic gaze upon something so organic and their arms would fall away from each other's shoulders. American homophobia denies same-sex affectionate physical contact to its heterosexual men. I haven't seen the teenage or adult Gibran and his friends in Seattle throw their arms around each other or hold hands.

Pardon me if I misled you for a moment to imagine India as some sort of feminist haven. For a reality check, I want to now tell you the story of an Indian boy who is not my son. For the first few years of his life, this boy was raised as a girl. His parents had two sons before him, both of whom died in childhood. So, to protect their third son from the evil eye, they dressed him in girls' clothes and adorned him with a nose ring, a marker of femininity. What they couldn't do, though, was change what the people around them believed about women (this wasn't their intention in any case). When the boy grew up to be a man, he one day took a gun and shot a man named Mahatma Gandhi three times at point-blank range as Gandhi was walking to a prayer meeting in New Delhi.

This man—Nathuram Godse—who made no attempt to run away, later said in court that he was sickened with Gandhi's "womanly politics" and the way Gandhi was emasculating a Hindu nation and pandering to Muslims. Godse's years disguised as a female did not make him empathetic to the female condition; they filled him with self-loathing.

The fault did not lie in the nose ring. The fault lay in the beast that rises just as strong and rabid today as it did back in Gandhi's 1948 to eat my child and yours. We are talking about the beast called misogyny. The hatred and fear of the female form and of feminine ways, of peaceful politics over brutal force, is a pandemic that runs over the globe and across centuries.

In France, it showed up for author Raphaël Liogier in his right-wing Catholic bourgeois family and what he calls his redneck countryside peers. When I met him in Seattle, we walked from his hotel to a restaurant for our interview, and I saw women throw quick glances at this handsome, well-dressed man. During the interview, Liogier told me he grew up with severe body image issues and even today has terrible phobias. "I was beaten by my father and bullied at school. My father would knock me out. I would pass out from the beatings and he would feel bad, so he would do it even more. He thought I was acting. He wanted me to toughen up. Now I am a hypochondriac, I am scared of flying, I have to fight against my fears every day."

During his childhood, Liogier began to be convinced he was a woman. "I thought my waist was too small, so I would hurt myself because I would try to lift my ribs and stretch them, extend them, because I thought men had to be wide. Boys around me were doing bodybuilding, getting bigger and bigger. I thought my legs were too long and too thin. I thought I was weak and I was a woman, that's why I was beaten. I would do push-ups. I thought my voice was too feminine."

We pause to consider what he is saying: to be beaten was a fate that befell women, and Liogier didn't want any part of it. Precious little has changed since his childhood, he says. "Even in the so-called gentle French masculinity, men will assert traditional notions of masculinity through irony. Even President Emmanuel Macron was dismissed as gay because he's with a woman so much older than him. Of course, they think he is gay because he isn't signing on to what I call the 'symbolic economy' of sexuality, where women are treated like commodities that indicate a man's masculinity."

To be beaten and to be bartered is a fate that befalls women. And yet, we have boys beaten on playgrounds, boys beaten in schoolyard fights, boys beaten and raped in locker rooms, boys beaten and raped in their homes, boys beaten and raped in the military, boys beaten and murdered by the police . . . what have I missed? Fill in the blank for boys beaten and murdered and raped at _____.

It is in this twisted misogynistic moment, dear reader, that we bring our boys to feminism. In allying with women to free girls' and women's bodies, our boys not only become more human, they also get to stay alive in their own very human bodies. No one knows this better than my friend Siddharth, who recounts his harrowing experiences as a boy at the Doon School, an elite boarding school in India, where he became the target of male desire manifested as sexual abuse. He tells me, "If boys and men are made comfortable about feeling human, about feeling 'gentle' as a human quality and not a feminine quality . . . and we see this in some Adivasi communities and among Buddhist communities . . . then they will not feel the need to express and internalize toxic masculinity. They will not feel the need to resort to sexual violence."

Not all invasions on our boys' bodies are overtly violent. Max Delsohn, a twenty-seven-year-old writer and comedian who is transgender, tells me about what they miss most about presenting as a woman. "I used to be able to walk up to babies in strollers and play with them. Now I realize that parents look at me differently because [for them] I'm a man walking up to their baby. I miss being able to walk up to babies."

In the violence of our strictly gendered ways, the man who is afforded the pleasure of whistling a tune into the winds is also the man denied the pleasure of tickling the toe of a stranger's baby as the baby gurgles.

▀▀▀▀▀▀▀▀▀▀▀▀▀▀▀▀▀▀▀▀▀▀▀▀▀▀▀

Psychologist Dr. Karen Weisbard urges us to take a deep breath and then take small steps. "We can get boys to think about their bodies without making a big deal of it. We can ask them to link physical sensations and emotions. Ask, 'When you run, how do you feel?' Name the feeling—exhilaration. 'When you are anxious, what do you feel in your body?' Name the sensation—a stomachache. 'When you imbibe alcohol?' A lessening of control. 'When you kiss someone you like?' Pleasure." Connecting the body and emotions, Dr. Weisbard says, will equip our boys to understand body autonomy and consent. They don't have to consent to a grandparent's insistence on a kiss. They don't have to sit on an uncle's lap. They can check in with their bodies and their emotions and say, "No, I don't feel like it right now." This way, we may coach boys to understand consent and perhaps later manage their own sensations and emotions of rejection.

Intimate conversations such as these in recent years have made things easier for younger parents. Danielle Holland, the feminist podcaster whose son is eight years old, says, "As a mother to a boy, as a mother who wants to raise a feminist boy, as a mother who has been raped and assaulted, these conversations had to be had from the beginning. When my boy was a toddler, I started communicating to him about 'my body' and introducing the language of consent. To begin to understand that my body wasn't *his*, because it sure felt like it was, from his point of view, when I was nursing. I started to tell him, 'This is mommy's body, and you need to ask.'" Holland says she was lucky also to find a naturopathic physician for her boy who made consent and ownership of one's own body part of her regular language.

Dr. Chu found herself needing to turn such conversations about consent and bodily autonomy onto her extended family because her son has a neurological condition that makes him sensitive to touch. "It made me realize how much we touch children. Even I had to monitor myself," she says.

Younger parents today believe it is never too early for kids to learn about bodily autonomy. I was struck by a Facebook post by my friend Michael. Michael and his husband have a two-year-old. I reproduce the post here with Michael's permission:

> This child has an amazing inchoate sense of his own bodily autonomy. He loves giving and getting hugs, getting tickled, etc. But when he does not want these things, he simply says 'no' or 'stop it.' Let's hope that once he begins to understand

reciprocity he can learn how to expand and extend this attitude into an ethic of consent applicable to all relationships with other people! (Side note: It's simultaneously awe-inspiring, anxiety-inducing, and weird that it is my job to teach him these things.)

In my years of sadness in Singapore, I devised a game called the Mama Clinch. In this game, I would hold Gibran in a tight embrace. The rule was that he would kiss me on the cheeks and with every passing kiss, my arms would grow weaker and weaker, until they slackened and he was able to escape my grasp. My body can still feel my little boy, and my cheeks can feel his kisses and his giggles. By the time he was around seven years old and we lived in Baton Rouge, he had become too grown up to play the Mama Clinch. I learned to read his signal when I'd say "Get ready for the Mama Clinch!" and he didn't immediately jump into my arms, couldn't tear himself away from the video game or the book at hand.

Much as I was disappointed, I stopped playing the game. I read and respected his signal in the way I so wish men had read and respected mine.

As the world went through a pandemic that made us reevaluate our touch and our breath, I wanted more than anything to see Gibran right before my eyes, not through a FaceTime screen in his first-ever apartment in Boston, where he'd moved for his first full-time job. I wanted more than anything to hug and be hugged by him. The world got painfully attuned to the body—where we are in space and in distance relative to each other, where our hands are and when we last washed them for twenty seconds while singing "Happy Birthday" twice, whether that cough we just coughed was dry or wet, whether we are old or young, whether we love our families after all when we are forced into isolation with them—hours and hours on end with them—whether the single, solitary ones among us will survive the virus or the loneliness. Whether we will die alone.

In all these hours alone, I am learning to whistle. If and when I see my boy again, and if the contagion warnings have been lifted, I will first hold him in the Mama Clinch. And then I will whistle a tune and watch his eyes widen.

TO DO:

- Stop your own body-negative language and actions. Do not let your boy hear you saying anything negative about your own, his, or anyone else's bodies.

- Tell and show your boy that your love is unconditional, and that your love will stay steady for him no matter what his body looks like or what it is able to do.

- Respect your child's bodily autonomy and boundaries. Speak about your own body autonomy, ask your child's physician to speak to them, teach your child to say no, and speak to family and friends about why it's important to respect that, for everyone. For the most part, issues of health and safety aside, *they* get to decide who touches their bodies and how.

- Use tickling games as an opportunity to practice consent with very young children. Ask if you may tickle them (no, it won't "ruin the fun"). Listen when they say to stop.

- Help your boy practice these rules with his friends, and make sure your family and caregivers are on board as well. He doesn't have to hug or kiss anyone he doesn't want to.

- Encourage embodiment and bodily awareness. Dr. Chu recommends talking to boys about why they may be working out too much (or feeling ashamed of not having a gym-toned body). Get to the emotions behind the image.

- Work toward a world in which all bodies are respected, accommodated, and cherished. Like Amelia, speak to schools, push for political action, and demand a feminism that intersects with disability rights.

Chapter Ten

WHAT IF HE SLIPS UP?

I think a lot about this one afternoon in the summer of 2009, when Alec and I took our kids—my Gibran and his Beth—on a day trip to Soap Lake, Washington. We had been dating for around four years and this was one of the things we did: build a date with our kids. We loved our own kids, of course, and we loved our time together, and we were growing to love one another's kids, although the kids themselves had still to hit their stride with each other. Some weekends were better than others.

Dating as a single parent is hard enough. Dating as single parents trying to blend their families together is even harder. Dating as people from two different cultures, different countries, and different politics is insanity. Add to that the fact that these two kids of ours were different genders and different ages—on the day that our little troupe arrived in Soap Lake, Gibran was fourteen and Beth nine.

Despite all these differences, though, when the four of us got into Alec's car and headed out of the city, we became a unit. In the smaller towns of Washington, where we'd stop for a potty break or for pancakes, we would often get open stares. A blond-haired white man and a blond-haired white girl; a black-haired, brown-skinned woman and a black-haired, brown-skinned boy. People tried to make sense of us. Years later, Gibran would tell me that he always noticed those stares, *felt* them on him. "I don't know if I thought of them as racist, really, but I felt like people peered for longer because they would try to make out if I was biracial. It's a special kind of stare, you know?"

On that day in Soap Lake, we were all in good form. Brown and white, we were there for all to stare at, in our bathing suits, leaving behind the damp clouds of Seattle and straining toward the sunshine as we waded into the lake. It rarely gets warm enough to be in water in Washington, except when you drive over the mountains to the eastern part of the state. The little strip of beach around Soap Lake was no Juhu Beach from my childhood, but it would do.

"They say the peat at the bottom of the lake has medicinal properties," Alec informed us. "We could cure your polio."

The kids laughed. I liked this kind of humor because it made the kids laugh.

We waded and swam and caked our bodies with globs of the peat that we dug up from the bottom of the lake. Alec took photographs. I still have a picture of me with my face covered in a mask of black peat, standing with a mock menacing expression behind Gibran with his crooked-toothed smile, electric blue braces.

After we cleaned up, we all walked around the little town of Soap Lake, each of us craving different foods—Alec a burger, me fish tacos, Beth pizza, and Gibran Thai red curry, as if all our other differences weren't enough. The kids decided on ice cream. As we looked for ice cream among the touristy shops and restaurants on the main strip, Beth tried to draw Gibran into a conversation.

"When I grow up I'm going to be a singer like Taylor Swift," she said, skipping up to him.

"Uh-huh," Gibran said. Then he added, "That's a ridiculous plan, but whatever."

Beth stopped skipping but now walked fast to keep up with Gibran. "Why? I can sing like Taylor Swift! Do you want me to show you?"

"No, thanks. Please don't. I just think it's ridiculous because (a) Taylor Swift sucks, (b) you will probably not even be half as good as her even though she sucks, and . . ."

A note here: Before he even got to "C," I saw for the first time the little piece-of-shit mansplainer that I had raised to the age of fourteen. The term "mansplaining" wouldn't be coined for another few years, inspired by feminist philosopher Rebecca Solnit's 2008 essay titled "Men Explain Things to Me," but we all have known the phenomenon for centuries, and my little darling was doing it right then with his ABCs.

". . . (c) the music industry doesn't usually let people break in so easily."

Beth slowed down and Gibran kept walking without breaking his pace, trying to catch up with Alec, who was busy looking for an ice cream shop. I looked at Beth's face. Tears were flowing down her reddened cheeks and she was trying to dry them quickly.

I asked if I could give her a hug. She shook her head. I asked to hold her hand. She gave it to me. Then I said to her: "We don't cry when boys are mean to us. Gibran is not an expert on the music industry; he is not a music producer or a music critic. He is not an expert on how to follow your dreams. And he definitely is not a good singer. Why should you give him the power to make you cry with his meaningless opinion?"

Beth smiled.

I called out to Gibran and asked him to wait for us. He hesitated and then, turning around and spotting the look on my face, he shuffled to a stop.

Holding Beth's hand, I said to him: "You are not allowed to throw around an uneducated opinion and hurt someone's feelings. You need to apologize."

"What? No way! I didn't do anything wrong! I'm allowed to have an opinion on Taylor Swift's singing!"

"Sure. But you used your random opinion to put Beth down, not to draw her into a conversation . . ."

"I was just trying to save her the disappointment . . ."

"Worse, you didn't listen. You had the opportunity and the gift to listen to someone's dream and you chose to try and crush it instead."

"It's OK," Beth said. "He doesn't need to say sorry."

"That's kind of you, Beth, to not expect an apology from him," I said. "But he still needs to apologize. And you don't need to forgive him."

"I'll apologize but I won't mean it," Gibran said.

I wanted to grab him by the scruff of his neck and shake him. I took a deep breath and said: "Let's hear that apology."

"I'm sorry I didn't listen to your dreams, Beth," he said in the mocking tone of a fourteen-year-old boy whose voice is beginning to crack (arguably the most annoying tone known to humanity). He threw a quick glance at me, and, not seeing satisfaction there, he added, "And I'm sorry I said you couldn't be as great as Taylor Swift."

For his shitty, conditional apology, Gibran did not get ice cream that afternoon.

<hr/>

In the summer of 2019, I sat in the audience listening to Eve Ensler, the bestselling author of *The Vagina Monologues*, at the launch of her latest book, *The Apology*. Her onstage interviewer read out loud the book's dedication—"For every woman still waiting for an apology." A collective sigh went up in the hall.

Gibran was not a fully formed feminist at the age of fourteen, and he isn't one even now as he turns twenty-five. At fourteen, he was straining toward a sense of his masculinity. Society told him he needed to have opinions and to assert them. At twenty-five, society tells him to find his feet, be a breadwinner, build heft into his claim to manhood. Part of the hubris and the curse of masculinity is that it must always be the fount of knowledge, opinion, decision. Get it right. Don't be a loser. Win.

Trying to insert the notion of error, of wrongness, of *failure* into the cocksureness demanded from young men is like asking a bull to sit down to a tea party after waving a red cape in its face. Dr. Judy Y. Chu's research says that boys are often taught to base their identity and sense of worth on maintaining an appearance of "masculine" confidence, competence, and control. These boys then tend to struggle and feel shame when faced with setbacks. To counter such shame, they may act dismissive or be disruptive.

So what are the ways in which a feminist boy might slip up in his growing years? He may use his fists on the playground. He may say to a buddy, "That's so gay!" He may push a girl off a swing. He may tease his sister for her games and toys and sports and ways of being in the world that society whispers in his ear are "less than." He may bully his peers. He may call a classmate a slut. He may join his friends in rating their female peers based on their faces and bodies. He may try to coerce girls into sex as a conquest. He may try to shut a girl down when she's smarter than him. He may try to lash out at a girl when she laughs at him. He may try to talk a girl down when she shares her dreams.

Teaching a boy to expect to make mistakes and to expect to be held accountable when he makes mistakes is the key. Teaching a boy to be able to laugh at himself . . . sigh . . . wouldn't that be such a gift? Teaching him to hurt at his folly, cry, feel empathy, feel shame, feel remorse, and *to apologize*, perhaps without demanding forgiveness, is an essential part of a feminist upbringing. Over the years, often with a sick feeling in my stomach, I realized that I was not going to be able to raise a perfect feminist. I couldn't fashion a boy or man who was wholly alert and engaged in the scrutiny, study, and practice of dismantling an immutable structure that offered him a paradise of privileges for having a penis and taunted him as a "pussy" when he tried to so much as move a single spoke of said structure. What I could do was teach him to see when he'd slipped up, to hear someone when they said he'd slipped up, and to then just fucking apologize. A tender, sincere apology, please.

Your boy *will* slip up. For your boy, becoming a feminist is a gargantuan enterprise. We are asking boys and men to do confusing and difficult work that we haven't even agreed as a society is good for them. Recall the story of the blind men and the elephant. The men are asked to feel only one part of the elephant with their hands and describe what they are touching. Each one has a different description—it's a rope, says the man feeling the tail; it's a tree, says the man feeling the trunk—and none of them knows it's an elephant. Feminism is an elephant. Its tail and its trunk will only really grow out when we have true and lasting equity. Meanwhile, we are all blinded by the flash of the glass ceiling, and we're asking our boys to feel this elephant with hands that are often curled up into fists. (If I haven't already pushed that metaphor to its edge, let me add that the elephant never wanted all this groping anyway.)

As a university professor, I am required to explain assignments to students with a clarity and coherence that was hardly required from previous generations of faculty. When I sit down to grade assignments, I have to go past the attitude of "I'll know an A paper when I see it." So I labor over clear assignment descriptions. I hand out grading rubrics to students, clearly tabulated and categorized. I list and explain "learning outcomes" on the syllabus. The Gen Z students would have me fired if I didn't.

But the assignment of feminist practice that we are now handing out to boys and men has no real description (except a dream and a nightingale's song), no rubrics, no clear outcomes, no grades, no trophies (except the vague promise of a longer life, filled with everlasting peace, love, and solidarity). Boys and men would be quite justified in throwing at us that old whine, "What is it that you *want*?"

The best of them will jump right in, unafraid to flounder, even *expecting* to fall and to work invisibly with no congratulations (no, we won't thank you for "babysitting" your own kids). And, yes, even the best of these boys and men will slip up. If you set out only to ensure that he never slips up, or if you call it quits when he does so over and over again, the feminist enterprise is lost. Focus instead on teaching him to recognize, apologize, reflect. I cannot emphasize this enough.

Eve Ensler was faced with the prospect of going her whole life without a sorely necessary apology from her father, so she ripped a whole book out of her aching heart and her wild imagination in the form of a letter written to her by her deceased father. In this imagined letter, Ensler's father apologizes to her by recounting in detail the sexual, physical, and psychological abuse he inflicted on her from the ages of five to ten, and acknowledges the lasting effects on her life. He holds himself accountable and asks for absolution. For an apology to be effective and sincere, the apologizer must get into detail, Ensler said to her interviewer that night on stage.

After Ensler's reading in Seattle, my friends and I went to dinner to catch our breath and share our own stories of hurt and healing by men in our families. They were stunned when I told them that a few years earlier, my father had apologized to me for the violence and abuse he inflicted on me, my siblings, and our mother for most of our lives lived with him. My father said he was suffering because of what he did. "I tore our family apart. I was violent because I felt inadequate as a man. I am not saying it was an excuse, but in those years, I was struggling to provide for my family as an army officer, and around me in Bombay, other men were prospering. I took my anger out on you all. Now my son hasn't talked to me for years, my daughters keep their distance, and I will never have the friendship of your mother even all these years after our divorce."

I reflect on what psychologist Dr. Flaviane Ferreira told me about how her husband had carried the pain for years of his father shouting at him to go back and beat up a boy who had pushed him around during his childhood in São Paulo, Brazil. We had talked about how we didn't expect men from our fathers' generation, especially in cultures of patriarchy and machismo such as Brazil and India, to apologize. That they did is a sign that we can expect more.

When I think of my father's apology, I think of these things and I heal—he didn't ask for my forgiveness (perhaps afraid I wouldn't forgive him); he made the apology in front of his current wife, my loving stepmother; he made the apology in front of Gibran.

Studies in psychology and in business, such as one conducted by researchers at Ohio State University's Fisher College of Business and published in 2016 in the journal *Negotiation and Conflict Management Research* tell us that there are six parts to the structure of an apology:

1. Expression of regret

2. Explanation of what went wrong

3. Acknowledgment of responsibility

4. Declaration of repentance

5. Offer of repair

6. Request for forgiveness

I'd add a bit of nuance to that last one, that in the request for forgiveness there be no demand or expectation of forgiveness. I recall a little girl on the sidewalk in Soap Lake saying, "It's OK. He doesn't need to say sorry." Girls are taught very early to be sweet, to be likable, to be compassionate, to get along, to forgive, to not demand anything. Often, we do this automatically before we even know how we feel about the harm done to us.

I recall when I was the chair of my department at my university and a white male faculty member—a feminist man—had shouted at me loudly and violently in public when I asked him in a quiet conversation to pull his weight at work. I was shaken. The advice I got from a woman in upper administration to whom I reported the incident? "He probably regrets it. Draw upon your compassion. Reach out to him and work it out." Obediently, I wrote to the man who had left me triggered and feeling threatened from his shouting. I offered to take him out to coffee to discuss the whole thing. He didn't even bother to respond. He was allowed to set a boundary. I was asked to overcome my feelings of physical and psychological safety and to once again put myself in harm's way.

I prefer, then, what psychologist Dr. Karen Weisbard told me about the notion of "rupture and repair" and how she uses it with her sons so she can model it for them to use in their own life. "If I hurt them, I say: 'I made a mistake and I know I hurt you. I am sorry. I am not going to go out of my way to compensate for it or try to fix it in some way that only serves me. I don't need you to forgive me. But I want to say that I am here to stand in the discomfort of what I did and I am here to repair our relationship.'"

▀▀▀▀▀▀▀▀▀▀▀▀▀▀▀▀▀▀▀▀▀▀▀▀▀▀▀

When Gibran turned eighteen, the summer before he left for college, I was desperate for him to connect deeply with my family. I was estranged from them, hurt, cautious. But, I thought, if Gibran was now launched and increasingly independent of me, would he think of them, *feel* them, as family? I wanted him to have them independently of me. It pinched a little to think I would no longer be their way "in" to the joys of Gibran, but I also just want my boy to have as many people loving him across the world as possible. People across the world to call if he needs something. People across the world in whose arms to fall into a hug.

So I prepared myself for a difficult trip and an even more difficult journey. The hardest part was going to be the prospect of meeting my brother. The last time we'd met, he'd chased me down in front of his wedding guests with the full intention of physically assaulting me. He was enraged by something I'd said about not yelling at our mother. He'd said: "You come back here from America like a 'visiting professor' and poke your nose into our lives." I'd retorted, "What is it that really bothers you? That I made it to America and you couldn't?" (Even today, some believe I deserved a good beating for provoking my brother with my sharp tongue.)

It was only years later that I realized that it was the fifth time in a row in our adult lives that he'd raised his hand on me to throw me out of either my mother's home or my motherland. At that wedding incident, however, something broke inside me. Indeed, it wasn't just the fact that, for years, my body had flinched in the presence of my brother. It was that my heart ached at the silence of the enablers. I could not ignore that not one of the wedding guests walked out in protest. They danced the night away.

My sister offered to leave the wedding with me, outraged for us both, but our mother pleaded with us to quiet down, get dressed, and join in the celebrations. Not only was I not allowed to feel my own pain and rage, I was expected to smile for the camera. And I did. Among my people, those worshippers of the angry goddess Kali, I was prohibited from feeling even human. In her book *Rage Becomes Her: The Power of Women's Anger*, author Soraya Chemaly says that in cultures across the world, women are expected to turn their anger inward, while there are always excuses for men who turn theirs outward. My mother wanted all her three children together for this wedding. My family aches for togetherness. We want so badly to have a wedding that dazzles followed by a marriage that lasts. Well, my brother was offering this opportunity to us. Not me, not my sister, but my brother—whose first wife left him because of domestic abuse.

So three years after the wedding incident, on that "healing and reconnecting" trip with Gibran, I had no desire to connect with my brother. I'd get out of the way so he could connect with Gibran, I told myself. As it turned out, that did not happen. Gibran's uncle did not make any plans to spend time with him.

At the end of the trip, as I put Gibran on a flight to visit his father in Singapore, I told him I was sorry he didn't get to see his uncle. "The family wants me to forgive him for his violence toward me," I said to Gibran. "I guess I'm being too harsh. I should try and forgive."

"Has he *asked* for your forgiveness, Mama?" Gibran said.

I was silent, stunned. No one did such things in my world. And no one asked such questions.

"Has he apologized?" Gibran said.

I shook my head. Gibran shrugged. "Then the ball isn't even in your court yet, right? Not that it should be. You don't owe him forgiveness, but he owes you an unconditional apology."

As I stood there in the Mumbai airport, my mind swirled and spun back a few years and a few continents to land on a boy and a girl and a woman standing on the sidewalk in Soap Lake, Washington.

Now the electric blue braces on the boy were gone and he stood here before me on the brink of manhood, a growing, grinning feminist.

This solidarity, this allyship from Gibran, that went beyond the questions and answers my feminist instruction had provided, have left me in tears of relief often. The time he gently stood up to my mother who said I'd lied about my abuse. The time he asked me not to apologize to *him* for someone else's insensitivity. The time he told me not to ask questions like "Is that a man or woman?" but to just see "a person."

As Gibran boarded the plane to Singapore, I had no one to whom to shout out his feminism. I'll write a book about all this someday, I said to myself.

▾▾▾▾▾▾▾▾▾▾▾▾▾▾▾▾▾▾▾▾▾▾▾▾▾▾▾▾

Let us be clear that when I dwell on the question "What if he slips up?" I am not referring to the ways in which the average man slips up, here, there, and freakin' everywhere. Those ways are a million, and they may or may not be forgivable, or may be, as it seems at this point in time the case with my brother, beyond repair. I am talking specifically about the ways in which *feminist* boys and men slip up. I place these into the following three main categories:

The Predatory Feminist: These men declare themselves feminists but they're really, scarily not. The declaration of feminism is predatory. A perfect and perfectly abhorrent example of this would be Eric Schneiderman, the New York State attorney general who was hailed as a champion of women's rights, an investigator into charges against Harvey Weinstein, and a vocal advocate for reproductive freedom, among other absolutely dreamy feminist things. Then *The New Yorker* published a story in 2018 detailing the many ways in which he had abused and exploited women, including choking his sexual partners, while writing a bill specifically to punish the same kind of strangulation.

Feminist writer Jill Filipovic examined this kind of feminist man in a *New York Times* op-ed on May 8, 2018, titled "The Problem with 'Feminist' Men." She wrote: "He seems to have used his feminist-minded political work to advance his own career, to ingratiate himself with the women he would go on to harm, and to cover up his cruelties." A bit further down on this spectrum of feminist men we can do without is comedian Louis C. K., accused of sexual misconduct—masturbating in front of women who worked for him—while also writing feminist-allied sketches on his show. Coming up not too far behind is comedian Aziz Ansari, who, as my boy and I had discussed, was accused of pressuring a woman to have sex on a date, while also being a vocal critic of the ways in which women are undermined in dating culture. These two comedians were exposed in the height of the #MeToo revelations but bounced back soon enough (Louis C. K. to a standing ovation in a New York comedy club; Aziz Ansari to a successful comeback tour and Netflix special). These men made feminism their schtick. They used it to draw women and audiences and money. And their apologies were either nonexistent or so awful (Ansari said on his comeback show: "I just felt terrible that this person felt this way.") that I almost wished women would just stop asking for apologies already.

The Performative Feminist: We all know this guy. He's read the literature, calls out the way movies he loves don't pass the Bechdel test, speaks a bit too often and perhaps a bit too loudly of the ways in which his girlfriend or his female colleague are sexual assault survivors or have been overlooked for a promotion, and he may even ask for enthusiastic consent on a good day. This guy declares himself a feminist because it's cool to be a feminist. But he hasn't thought it through and so he doesn't actually intervene when a woman colleague is being overlooked for a promotion because "it wasn't the right moment or forum to speak." He sometimes may explain feminism to women or ask combative questions because he "wants to understand." You know, play the devil's advocate. He's what we can call "a feminist, but . . ."

The Partner Feminist: This is your son and mine. Black author and activist Ibram X. Kendi says that it's not enough to be "not a racist" (avoiding stereotypes and examining one's own implicit biases), but that we must actively work to be anti-racist (proactively dismantling structural racism and building a society that is truly equitable). I am here to say that it's not enough for our boy to simply be a feminist who states an academic conviction in the full humanity of women. He must be anti-misogyny, anti-patriarchy, anti-racist, anti-ableist, anti-homophobia, and anti-systems-of-capitalist-heteronormativity that aid and abet the dehumanizing of women. As Filipovic points out in her op-ed, we can scrutinize the male feminist's relationship to power by asking sharp questions, among which is this: "When they're pushing for women's rights, what's more important to them: the result or the recognition?"

One of the best examples I have seen of a partner feminist is in the work of Raphaël Liogier. He told a packed audience at Seattle's Town Hall in February 2020 that he wrote his book as an apology. A woman friend of his had accused him of mansplaining to her in the wake of the #MeToo movement. "She asked me if I had even read the tweets of the women making the #MeToo accusations. I said I had, but really, I hadn't." Later, Liogier read the tweets and found himself moved to write an essay confronting the conditioning and socialization that promote a man's twisted gaze on a woman's body. "I apologized to my friend. And the thing is—it felt like a relief to apologize. I want men to know that a genuine, heartfelt apology with no expectations just feels *so good*."

Your boy and mine must grow up to be this partner feminist. He must speak, cry, shout, join his voice in ours when his voice is needed, shut up and be quiet when it's not, and he will know the difference because he has actively and unobtrusively asked us over and over, in times of battle and times of peace. He recognizes, checks, and refuses his privilege. He calls his buddies out on it, he calls his bosses out on it, he calls himself out on it.

He buys a round-trip plane ticket to NYC, shows up at the comedy club, and heckles the fuck out of Louis C. K.

Tall order, but hey, high rewards. Ice cream, perhaps.

TO DO:

- Dr. Chu's research on boys' psychosocial behavior shows that they want to feel connected and vulnerable. Encourage such tenderness in your boy so they may also have empathy for others' emotions. "If they are self-aware and self-accepting, they will learn to forgive themselves and tend to others," she says.

- Model apologies. Utilize the rupture and repair model.

- Call your boy out (or call him in) when he slips up in his feminism.

- Follow up after the situation, in a less fraught moment, to debrief on what happened, what he could do differently in the future, and assess if there are further repairs or amends that still need to be made. Listen and engage thoughtfully.

Chapter Eleven

WILL MY BOY OF COLOR FEEL TOO BURDENED? WILL MY WHITE SON FEEL TOO GUILTY?

While I was asking Gibran to apologize, to listen, to step aside, another thing was happening. He was growing up.

More specifically (and the specificity is where the ghost lives), he was growing from a brown-skinned boy into a brown-skinned man in America. The first time I noticed that my boy was a man was when I was forced to see it not through my own eyes but through the eyes of an angry white man. This little fact breaks my heart every time I think of it.

It was September 2011. Alec and I were married a month before, at the prettiest wedding ever. I wore a peach-pink gold-embroidered sari and Alec wore a royal-blue silk kurta. Gibran wore a red-and-gold churidar-kurta and a wide smile. Beth wore a gold lehenga and was one of my bridesmaids, along with my sister, Suhaani, and one of my closest friends, Rachel. Our sweet blended family moved into a rented house on Queen Anne Hill in Seattle. We had flowers in the backyard, we had laughter in the living room, and we took hours to decide on what movies we would all watch together. I had everything I could want from America, in hues of gold.

On that September day in question, a month or so after our wedding, Alec and I were driving to pick Beth up from a festival at her school in Wallingford. I got a phone call from Gibran, who had turned sixteen that summer.

"Mama, I don't know what to do," he said.

My heart heard his voice and flew out of my chest to the skies so it could scan the earth and find him and swoop down.

He had forgotten his keys at home, he said, and when he got back from school with his friend Gabe, they decided to climb in through the open bathroom window. Oh, OK, I thought. He's stuck in a window and he doesn't know what to do. That's funny.

"The neighbor just called the cops," he said.

The neighbor just called the cops, I repeated to Alec, who was driving.

Gibran said on the phone, "I heard the neighbor shouting into the phone that he was reporting a burglary in progress. He was looking from his front door right at me. I went over to talk to him and I said, 'Sir, I'm not a burglar, I live here with my parents,' but he saw me coming and slammed the door shut in my face. So now the cops are on their way and I don't know what to do."

I was confused. But Alec wasn't. He told me calmly yet with urgency to tell Gibran and Gabe to take off their jackets and sit on the front porch with their hands exposed. "No hoodies. Hands fully exposed."

This was 2011. I didn't quite understand, but I repeated the instructions.

We picked Beth up and then drove home as fast as we could. On the way, I got a phone call from a policeman. "Ma'am, how are you related to a Mr. Gibran?"

"He's my son," I said with a voice that didn't sound like mine. He's my son and he's not a "Mr.," he's a child, I wanted to say, but didn't.

By the time we got home, the cops had finished with questioning the boys and left. A single police car was parked a little way down the street.

"They swooped down and burst in with their guns aimed!" Gibran said, his wide eyes wider. "One of them was screaming to the others to surround the house, run to the back of the house so no one could escape. We sat on the porch with our hands exposed. They asked us some questions and then called you and then hung around for a while. We asked them if we could go back inside and play video games."

For a time, I imagined that that last question must have been the clincher for the police in determining that my brown child was not the armed and dangerous invader of their imagination. (I believed that until October 2019, when Atatiana Jefferson, a Black woman in Fort Worth, Texas, was shot dead by police while playing video games in her bedroom with her eight-year-old nephew.) Or maybe it was that Gibran was accompanied by a perfectly respectable-looking white boy named Gabe. Or maybe, as Gibran pointed out, the police left because they got another call on their wireless of some other break-in somewhere. But yes, the police had left. I was still confused by it all.

But you know who was not confused? Alec. He had known exactly what the boys should do. He had known what America's police would have seen and what they would be looking for, what they were looking at. He had known what the next-door neighbor saw. He had known what the next-door neighbor hadn't seen for the month or so that we'd lived in that house. The next-door neighbor had seen a white man and white girl but he hadn't *seen* the brown woman and brown boy, or if he had, he'd imagined them as occasional guests, not the residents of this fine house. Not citizens. Intruders.

"That man is a racist and we never have to speak to him," Alec said to me. I nodded gratefully. I looked at my boy and I squinted to see what the racist man had seen. I had to squint hard to see the grown and dangerous man that America saw in my sixteen-year-old son.

Five months later, on February 26, 2012, Trayvon Martin, seventeen years old, would be shot dead by a man who followed the boy as he walked home and assaulted him even though the police he called to falsely report the boy as a burglar told him to leave the boy alone. It would take a few days before that story would trickle from Black media to the national media. When it did, I would no longer be confused about what had happened with Gibran.

I followed the Trayvon Martin story like a fiend. He was shot by a white-presenting Latino man with a gun. I was married to a white man with guns. He was killed on Alec's birthday. He was wearing a hoodie. He had Skittles in his pocket. I sat in bed and wept and told Alec that the specifics were what kept breaking my heart.

"That case had nothing to do with race and guns," Alec said.

Now I was confused again. I quoted articles and found my voice getting louder, more desperate, more scared. I asked Alec how, because he loved my son, he could declare our neighbor a racist but couldn't see that . . .

"Why are we letting the death of some boy in Florida cause so much tension in our marriage?" Alec said.

"His name is Trayvon Martin," I said. "Could you please use his name?"

Alec never used his name. Days went by. Alec never said Trayvon's name. Five months later, after seven sessions with a marriage counselor, on the day I left that white home of ours with my brown skin and my brown son, I asked Alec once again if he could understand. He said I was being ridiculous asking for a divorce just because some boy in Florida was dead.

Our marriage didn't even make it to the first anniversary. I wondered if our friends who had pointed out our differences for years may have said to each other "I give it a year" and were now going to rake in money.

President Barack Obama said, "If I had a son, he would look like Trayvon."

Over the next few months, as Gibran began his senior year at high school, I wept into a beige couch in a small hot apartment into which I'd moved the two of us, just a mother and son, not the family of four I'd wanted so badly. I avoided phone calls, especially from friends who disregarded their husbands' "foibles" and stayed, settled, threw themselves into work or social life, ran marathons, dieted themselves down to skin and bone, kept up appearances "for the kids' sake," told themselves—and me—that this is just how men can be sometimes.

I wasn't as concerned with how men could be as I was by how women could be.

I dusted myself off and bought a condo with the money I earned from selling a piece of land I owned in Bangalore. (The parts of my parents that were feminist had advised me to buy an apartment in Mumbai when I was twenty-one; I'd since sold that apartment and bought land in Bangalore on which I'd dreamed of building a home with Rajat. The land had lain abandoned for years.)

For better or for worse, although I was divorcing an American, here I was, wedded to America. I was laying down roots here now, in sickness and in health, and America was really sick. Within that sickness, though, I saw the spectrum of privilege in which my son and I, as South Asians, as members of a "model minority," were further removed from the danger posed by white America, with its history of violence upon Black and Native American bodies. We were further removed, but we weren't insulated. We weren't protected, no matter how white-adjacent and assimilated we tried to become. We were still brown-skinned intruders climbing in through the window.

If a Black child wasn't safe here, my child wasn't safe here. If Black and brown boys weren't safe here, Black and brown girls weren't safe here. If these children weren't safe, their mothers weren't safe, their fathers weren't safe, LGBTQ people weren't safe, even white women weren't safe. In the early 2010s, white supremacy was still a wolf snarling at the edges of our collective honesty, but we had seen the trails of blood left in the night.

I was a woman raised with blows on her body. I carried violence in my cells. And every fiber of my being told me once again to raise my boy here rather than let him ride on the privileges of Brahmanic patriarchy (upper-caste patriarchy, not too different from white supremacist patriarchy) in India, because I knew in my gut that I could raise a loving human here among the oppressed *but not from among the oppressors*. A child of color in America—especially boys as they turn to men and begin to be feared—must carry the burden of uprooting misogyny because it will lay bare the deeper rot.

Dismantling patriarchy and snuffing out misogyny is both a burden and an embrace into which boys of color must lean.

As I write this, I wonder if Gibran has come to feel the same way or whether I am too quick to explain away the mess I put him through (because, yes, there were racist moments for him before that day in 2011, and after). I write Gibran to ask him—has it been easier or harder for him to be a feminist, given all the things he went through as a boy of color?

"Easier," he writes back immediately. "Feeling marginalized even in fairly minor ways just kinda tunes you in to other people's suffering.

Also, I think it helped that I wasn't steeped in any particular cultural milieu that told me to look at women one way or another. All I had in terms of a culture or a value was empathy."

Whew.

But was being a feminist as a boy of color a burden? "No," says Gibran. "It made things easier. It can't even be a choice." He got busy then and never quite explained, but I will tell you what I think my boy means.

In September 2015, I would meet Trayvon's mother, Sybrina Fulton. She was at my university to deliver a talk. As I rode up the elevator with her and some university administrators and Black activists, I wanted to say something to her, to tell her something about how my story connected with hers, but I instead found myself just thanking her for being there. I realized that so many people must have tried to tell her the same thing—that their story somehow connected to hers—not to appropriate her pain but because so many of us felt in solidarity with it in some way, because this was such an American story. What could I say to her—I, as the mother of a live son—that she, as the mother of a dead son hadn't already heard? I decided to just shut up and listen to the thunderous talk she gave. "My son was profiled, followed, and murdered by George Zimmerman, and there was nothing accidental about that," she said.

There was nothing accidental about the killing of Michael Brown in Missouri in 2014, the year before Fulton said those words. There was nothing accidental about the killing of Philando Castile in Minnesota in 2016, the year after.

Gibran called me from college when he watched the Facebook Live video of Castile dying after being shot by a policeman. Gibran was sobbing so hard, I could barely understand his words. I tried to keep a calm voice. I asked him if he was scared. Not for myself, he said, I am relatively privileged.

He had his eyes open. In spite of working his way into scholarships to attend an almost–Ivy League college, he wasn't getting co-opted. He could see his privilege. He could weep, he could feel outrage, he could agitate. He could call me. And he called friends to cry to, to cry with. That was feminism at work for my son. *It made things easier.*

Writing about the summer when her son Jonathan was turning from a teenager into a man, Audre Lorde said in an essay titled "Man Child: A Black Lesbian Feminist's Response": "And our sons must become men—such men as we hope our daughters, born and unborn, will be pleased to live among." Lorde wrote about how sons of lesbians have to make their own definitions of self as men and that this is both power and vulnerability.

This vulnerable masculinity was the biggest gift I assembled for my child in my years of wandering confused from home to home. I was heartbroken to find I had married a white man who couldn't see alongside me. I was heartened to find I had raised a brown man who would see beyond my seeing.

A feminist life and a feminist lens—a feminist way of breathing, a feminist way of sobbing—is more comfort than burden for my son.

▪▪▪▪▪▪▪▪▪▪▪▪▪▪▪▪▪▪▪▪▪▪▪▪▪▪

So do we give up on white men and white boys? No. Each of us must encounter the social construct that is race—people across the spectrum of color and, yes, also white people. We tend to think of race only when we think of people of color, but ultimately, race is about whiteness. Racism, racial identity, racial injustice, race all exist because whiteness exists and whiteness defines and whiteness *normalizes.*

White people, particularly white men, benefit so hugely from racialized structures, and yet, I wonder if we can also see how white boys and white men are trapped by whiteness and its brother, racism.

Joanna Schroeder, media critic and mother of white sons, tweeted her experience with the way her teens were being seduced online by social media thought leaders and vloggers who were laying the groundwork in white teens to grow them into white supremacists. She documented how they start with memes making "innocent" jokes about women, people of color, Jews, and queer folk. When the boys are called out at school for sharing such jokes, they are drawn into a network that pits them against the "snowflakes." The rise of white male terrorism in the United States is often directly linked to their acts of misogynistic violence prior to mass shootings.

"These boys are being set up—they're placed like baseballs on a tee and hit right out of the park," says Schroeder. She doesn't want her boys to be fools, she says, and she believes in direct intervention. "Look through his Instagram Explore screen with him," she says. "Explain what's underlying those memes. Explain why 'triggered' isn't a joke . . . evoke empathy without shaming him."

Shame and guilt are the two things that trigger boys (especially white boys, if I may). How do we skirt past those and hold our white boys close, close, close, in a hug that lasts forever?

In her book *Raising White Kids: Bringing Up Children in a Racially Unjust America*, Jennifer Harvey asks us to think about how white kids are being racialized every bit as much as kids of color. Even factoring in things like class and other intersectionalities, white kids are generally elevated, fast-tracked, told they can dream and the world will support their dreams. There is no privilege without underprivilege, Harvey points out. Systemic and structural racism will tutor your child quite quickly, as early as age three, she says. The only way toward equity is to talk the heck out of the mess.

Remember the college admissions scandal? In 2019, thirty-three parents of college applicants were accused of paying more than $25 million between 2011 and 2018 to a man named William Rick Singer, who used part of the money to fraudulently inflate entrance exam test scores and bribe college officials. The list of parents included celebrity actors Lori Loughlin, Felicity Huffman, and William H. Macy. Psychologists and social scientists talked about the deep harm to the rich white kids who lose face, lose self-esteem, and learn that their parents don't believe in their ability to make it on their own. (Let alone what it laid bare about disadvantaging kids from lower income families.)

I recall how many of my white students were so deeply troubled by what that scandal revealed. Some of them confided in me that they had confronted their own parents in outrage and asked if they had paid bribes to have them accepted into colleges. These kids were facing a crisis of confidence. As more and more structural privilege becomes apparent, our white kids are asking to get off that train. They want to feel proud of their own merit. How beautiful is that?

Gibran, too, called me to ask if I'd paid Swarthmore to get him in. I laughed out loud and then realized he was serious.

"Not in money," I said.

"Eww," he replied and hung up.

Jokes aside, I'm just here to say that if we parents of brown and Black boys are pushing them to feminism, we do hope that parents of white boys are coming along to meet us at the intersections of race and gender. Yes, we are, says writer Anastasia Higginbotham, a white woman who wrote a children's book titled *Not My Idea: A Book About Whiteness*. It's a book asking white children to be tough enough to feel painful feelings about racism without being overwhelmed by guilt. In a video about her book, she centers white boys reading sections aloud. "You can be white without signing on to whiteness," one adolescent boy says.

To my mind, one of the best depictions of white male privilege and white male allyship that I have seen comes from Mindy Kaling in her show *The Mindy Project*: season 5, episode 12. I tell everyone to watch that episode. I recently told the white male dean of my college to watch it. In it, the Indian American Dr. Mindy Lahiri, a highly qualified ob-gyn who keeps getting passed up for promotions in favor of white men, goes to bed one night wishing she were a white man. She wakes up the next morning with her wish granted. She goes through the day in the body of a white male ob-gyn, watching taxi drivers pull up for him, coworkers laugh hard at his jokes, and all-male interview panelists offer him the job even though he blows the interview. Realizing that another woman of color is more qualified than him, the white male Mindy now pushes to get that coworker to be offered the promotion. The white male Mindy thinks to himself about white maleness—"Your life is so carefree, you start wondering why other people don't just help themselves. Because you think life is just as easy for everyone else." The episode ends with the idea of how white men don't realize just how much they could accomplish as good allies.

▼▼▼▼▼▼▼▼▼▼▼▼▼▼▼▼▼▼▼▼▼▼▼▼▼▼

Let us turn to the matter of guilt. As so many books and activists on race and anti-racist work will tell you, guilt can leave you frozen. What I have come to realize is that we are going to make mistakes. All we can hope to do is self-correct. When I first arrived in America, I refused to even see racism. I so badly wanted to believe I had arrived at a better place than what I had left behind. I still trip up at the intersections. To raise a feminist son, though, I have to endure my own discomfort and stand at the crossroads. When I stand here, people draw me close, teach me, forgive me, lead me and my boy into love.

Let me tell you about the time when I was the walking, talking cliché of the anti-Black South Asian racist (yes, that's a problem, and we "model minority" folks need to talk about it). When Gibran was in second grade, he won the spelling bee in Trinity Episcopal Day School in Baton Rouge, Louisiana. All the little children cheered wildly, and some of them carried Gibran on their shoulders and ran around the room and then fell down in a tumble together and laughed. You know who was silent? All the parents. And when they spoke, none of them turned to me. They turned to each other and said these words that I couldn't understand at the time: "Can you believe it?"

When I walked up to the second-grade teacher, Mrs. Graham, to thank her for teaching Gibran good spelling, she turned to me, and, before she could take in who I was, that I was the immigrant brown-skinned mother of the immigrant brown-skinned boy, she said, "Can you believe it?"

I wondered if this was an American phrase, a silence-filler people said to each other, like, "How're you doing?" or "Good to see you!"

"No," said my friend Cleo, who was in the PhD program along with me. A native Louisianian for generations, she now teaches at a historically Black college in New Orleans. "What they're saying is that they didn't expect a brown boy to win the spelling bee," she said, arriving at the doorstep of my graduate student housing with a hamper of gifts for Gibran because "we must celebrate our boys of color when they succeed in white-dominated schools."

Do you know what I said to Cleo? I said she was exaggerating a bit. I told Cleo I didn't expect America's racism would be directed toward us South Asians. Cleo cocked an eyebrow at me, drew deep on her cigarette, and laughed.

Ten years later, a few days after the incident with the neighbor in Seattle, I called Cleo and apologized for the racial gaslighting (although that term wasn't common in 2011). Cleo said she didn't recall me doing that and would have forgiven me anyway because I was new to America. I consider it one of my top five fortunes in life that I was forgiven for such an unthinking act of pure and simple racism.

Cleo was also the one back then who told me the story of Emmett Till. Although my education and my work as a journalist in India had given me knowledge of the genocide of Native Americans, slavery, and anti-Black racism in America, I had somehow never heard of Emmett Till until I arrived in America's Deep South to work on my PhD in media and politics. I was haunted and still am by the story that gets to the heart of why #MeToo and Black Lives Matter must have a reckoning. White women have the power to have men of color, especially Black men, thrown battered and dead into a river.

"Emmett Till's story is the story of the Black experience," Cleo says to me when I call her now to talk about her boys. "What I didn't realize, though, was that my boys would have a different view of America compared to mine. I went to all-Black schools and didn't interact much with white people. But my boys went to integrated schools. They came to believe they lived in a post-racial society, even before Barack [Obama]. They pooh-poohed me when I tried to warn them. Now they're in their late twenties and are getting to see. And they hear me remind them that women get paid eighty cents to a dollar compared to white men and Black women get paid sixty cents to a dollar. I tell my sons to have better aspirations for America."

My friend Anastacia-Reneé, a queer Black poet and educator in Seattle, says she invited the burden of raising Black boys upon herself. "I prayed to God to give me boys. I said, 'Please God, give me boys so I can mold and shape humans of the kind I haven't seen.' I wanted to raise children who think all genders are equal; I wanted to raise loving children; I wanted to raise children who are perceived as boys who can have their opinions heard without raising their voice."

But, of course, the world didn't agree with everything she was teaching them, Anastacia-Reneé says. And yet, the teaching is what saves them. "Both of my kids are queer—my oldest is queer as in they are attracted to all genders and my youngest is a trans woman. They get pushback from the world. I feel that all the teaching I did for them was just in time."

Yes, it's a burden, but boys of color do not have the luxury of checking out of feminism, Anastacia says. "If you are a white sixteen-year-old male feminist, you can still walk into a department store and no one's going to follow you around in the store. If you are a brown boy, you gotta deal with everyone assuming you're bad. You don't start off with a clean slate. And then we tell them that also they need to stand up for women. And also, I need to teach about gender roles. I do think it's a large burden to bear. But they don't get to take a break. None of us get to hang up our gender or color. My children don't get to hang up their skin color. I feel guilty about the burden, yes. But I'd feel guiltier if I didn't explain to them why it's important to be extraordinary."

Extraordinary. Anastacia-Reneé frames her quest of raising her children to be feminist as raising them to be extraordinary because, yes, that's what it takes. "They need to know about the people who are their predecessors, those who don't get mentioned. I sometimes feel tired of having these talks. But can you imagine if Harriet Tubman said, 'Fuck that, I'm tired. I don't want to be the go-to person'? Half of us wouldn't be here! My kids need to have the knowledge, and people under twenty-five these days don't have the gut instinct to find out about history. Part of being the mother of boys is that we have to be the archivist. We say, 'This is how something that happened in 1850 applies to you now.' It's my job to help them connect the dots."

Unlike Cleo and Anastacia-Reneé, because I didn't grow up in a deeply segregated America, it took me longer to feel its gaze, its imagination, upon my own skin. But Gibran? Gibran was out there having his own experiences in this nation, things that I didn't know about. My boy is an introvert, but he has cultivated a small, loyal group of friends. He probably hid a number of unpleasant racist experiences from me to avoid heartbreak upon heartbreak for his mother. Our lives together and his life outside of me and my influence led him to socialism. In high school, he volunteered to work on the campaign of Socialist Alternative candidate Kshama Sawant, to elect her to the Washington State House of Representatives. This was before Sawant—fellow Mumbai girl and now my friend—became the woman to take down Amazon in the city council elections and became known as "the most dangerous woman in America." Gibran found in her a hero. For Gibran, socialism, anti-racism, and feminism are in a deep embrace.

I thought of Audre Lorde's wish for her son: "I wish to raise a Black man who will not be destroyed by, nor settle for, those corruptions called *power* by the white fathers who mean his destruction as surely as they mean mine. I wish to raise a Black man who will recognize that the legitimate objects of his hostility are not women, but the particulars of a structure that programs him to fear and despise women as well as his own Black self."

▰▰▰▰▰▰▰▰▰▰▰▰▰▰▰▰▰▰▰▰▰▰▰▰▰

It wasn't until I met Kimberlé Crenshaw, the public intellectual who gave us the term "intersectionality," that I encountered another reason why I, as a woman, a mother, and an educator, must stand at the crossroads for as long as it takes. Crenshaw is an American lawyer, a civil rights advocate, a philosopher, and a leading scholar of critical race theory. I met her during a writing residency at Hedgebrook, a women's writing community, in February 2017, barely two weeks after the first Women's March, in which an estimated 4.8 million people across the world marched to protest Trump being sworn in as president of the United States. Crenshaw was one of the organizers and speakers of the Women's March in Washington, DC.

During a conversation at the dinner table, I said something about Black mothers losing their sons. She asked me why I didn't mention Black mothers losing their daughters. Or Black women losing their own lives. She meant it as a nudge, an act of intellectual kindness from one professor to another, one feminist to another. It crushed me at first and then I let it educate me. I went and read up about Crenshaw's #SayHerName campaign. Then I read up about missing and murdered Indigenous women. I haven't stopped reading and I haven't stopped talking to Gibran about what I read.

I read now the work of activist and writer Rochaun Meadows-Fernandez, who tells us in a *New York Times* essay titled "Why Won't Society Let Black Girls Be Children?" about how her teacher labeled her as "manipulative and intentionally disruptive" at the age of three years old. "I was experiencing what academics call 'adultification,' in which teachers, law enforcement officials and even parents view black girls as less innocent and more adult-like than their white peers," she says. She points at a report from the National Women's Law Center titled "Dress Coded: Black Girls, Bodies, and Bias in D.C. Schools," which documents how schools enforce a dress code policy that is harsher on black girls and polices everything from their hair to their clothes and their bodies.

My Black women friends tell me they have lived this phenomenon as girls. They are sexualized sooner than other girls; they are deemed more violent than other girls and women. If you have seen the video where a Texas state trooper pulls Sandra Bland over for a minor traffic infraction and then totally loses it just because she asked him why she was pulled over, you see the intersections of race and gender, you see the white gaze, you see white male rage.

You see the work our boys must do.

▀▀▀▀▀▀▀▀▀▀▀▀▀▀▀▀▀▀▀▀▀▀▀▀▀▀▀

I want to tell you now about an incident that took place a couple of years after Alec and I got divorced. We had started dating again, partly because he said he wanted to do better, partly because I believed I could change his mind about race and guns, and partly because I still, back then, craved a semblance of a "full" family. It would be another couple of years before I said goodbye forever.

Gibran was twenty years old and Beth was fifteen. The kids still related to one another as stepsiblings. It was summertime and Gibran was home from college. I am an academic, so I, too, was home from college. Each day was rolling into the other in that delicious way of summer that makes academics stay in the job for low pay. On this particular day, I was driving the kids from thing to thing and they were both whining and complaining about all of it.

I drove them up to a building in an upscale part of the Ravenna neighborhood where Beth got math tutoring from the daughter of a friend of mine. Gibran was antsy to get the drop-off over with so I could take him to get the gyros I'd promised him. Beth jumped out of the car at the building and was waiting outside for her tutor to come downstairs and let her in. I couldn't find parking but I didn't want to drive away until she was inside. Beth had come directly from a yoga class and was wearing a midriff-baring tank top with spandex yoga pants. She looked lovely, but #YesAllWomen, so I didn't want to drive away. I asked Gibran to get out of the car and stand on the sidewalk and keep an eye out for her until the tutor came downstairs.

"Ugggghhhh, why? I'm hungry! She'll be fine."

I gave him a look. He looked over at Beth and saw with the lens that I had tutored him to see with when necessary. He groaned again, but he got out of the car. I drove around the block, and when I returned, I saw a middle-aged white man standing not far from Gibran, his hands crossed on his chest, glaring at my boy. Gibran was turned away from him, oblivious to the target on his back.

I saw, once again, through the white man's gaze. What he was seeing was a brown-skinned young man watching a blond white girl in yoga pants. What he was imagining was so far from the truth. He didn't see a reluctant young man ordered to watch over his former stepsister. He couldn't have known that these two people had grown up together and linked their limbs together as they swam on their stepparents' backs in the Queen Anne Pool, had been punished for fights, and had faced the heartbreak of their parents' divorces together, that the girl still texted her former stepbrother about her high school crushes and that he sent her eye-roll emojis. I could forgive the man his angry gaze upon my son because of #YesAllWomen, but I couldn't ignore the way he stood over my son, because this man also stood in the shadow of Emmett Till's murder. He stood in the echo of the bullets that men still shoot into Emmett Till's memorial plaque.

He couldn't have known these stepsiblings' truth, but he should have questioned his own. The cross of his arms had a righteousness this country affords its white men. His feet standing his ground had the reassurance of an alliance with law enforcement, always just a phone call away.

I saw my boy looking out for his white sister as I'd ordered and I saw a white man looming behind him with a single story.

As I write this, I am at a DIY writing retreat with my friend, writer Novera Alim King, a Black Muslim woman. Outside our Airbnb in Gig Harbor, the sun has broken through the rain clouds and a deer family has come out to nibble on the grass growing thickest green under a white picket fence. We smear Nutella on our afternoon toast and watch the deer as I tell her about that day with Gibran and the cops and how Alec knew that the boys should sit on the porch with their hands exposed. And a question uncurls itself cold inside me for the first time. If Alec knew how the police would look at my son, why hadn't he turned the car around? Why had we kept driving to pick up Beth first? Why hadn't we called her school and told them we would be late because of an emergency?

Novera says, "Alec knew what the cops would see but he didn't feel the danger from the other side. A Black man would have known. A Black father would have called the uncles and aunties, and he would have called another white neighbor to go sit with the boys. He would have driven like a madman to Gibran."

Alec's bluest eye was limited to the white gaze of a policing America. I had no such luxury. I saw the dangers for Beth and I saw the dangers for my son.

In later years, as we'd dated again, Alec had laughed at the idea that America could have a rape culture. That only exists in India and Africa, he said. In the end, Alec lost me[3] because he refused to see the danger. He refused to even listen to stories of the danger. He refused my invitation to see, to imagine beyond white imagination, to feel the fear and then face it. He refused to be the madman I needed.

---

3. Did you notice that I used the phrase "Alec *lost* me"? Losing me is not easy to do, because I don't easily quit on things. I don't easily walk away. And losing me is a big fucking loss.

So I gave to my boy the gift of knowing the danger and relishing survival. I gave him the stories of laughing into the eye of a storm and standing in solidarity with a village. I raised him to be a madman.

America, my love, I have given you a madman who will watch out for your daughters. You will watch out for my son, right?

TO DO:

- Educate your boy about race and intersectionality, starting from when he is very young (see the Resources chapter on page 235).

- Teach your white boy about our world that privileges whiteness in the same way boys of color are taught about staying safe in that world.

- Celebrate the accomplishments of your boy of color.

- Help your boy of color see the structures of oppression, and to view their own oppression as a lens to develop empathy with other oppressed peoples.

- Model an anti-racist life for your children.

Chapter Twelve

WHAT IF *I* SLIP UP?

▄▄▄▄▄▄▄▄▄▄▄▄▄▄▄▄▄▄▄▄▄▄▄▄▄

"Please check the mailbox every few minutes. And when the letter arrives, just text me the word 'accepted' or 'rejected,'" Gibran said.

"I will never, ever, under any circumstance, at any point in our lives, text you the word 'rejected,'" I replied.

The date was February 14, 2013, a Valentine's Day when I had no plans for the first time in my life since I was twenty-two; except, of course, the plan to check the mailbox every few minutes for Gibran's admission letter from Swarthmore College. He couldn't do it himself because he would be in class in high school. So, naturally, I decided to take a day off from my full-time job as a journalism professor to go up and down the elevator of our building in my pajamas, waiting for the mail delivery.

If you have led the life most human beings live, I don't have to tell you about the agony of waiting for a message whose contents can be interpreted as either "accepted" or "rejected." In fact, most of life, one may argue, slip-slides ridiculously between just those two words.

Gibran was no stranger to this dichotomy—I had raised him alone on both ends of it (oh, how much we had accepted and rejected!) and told him we were doing it just to build character and learn words like "dichotomy"—but this time, we really, really just wanted him to be accepted. A few months earlier, he had left our two-bedroom condo in Seattle to go check out Swarthmore, all by himself. He had slept in a dorm room with a Swattie (I wanted him to forgo this particular college because they referred to their students as "Swatties," but Gibran didn't think it was a solid enough reason to knock this institution off his already thinning list), he had attended a class or two on the school tour, and he had sat through admissions and financial aid presentations. What he hadn't done was answer his cell phone when he saw a call from his good mother in Seattle, so she could know he had arrived safely on the Swarthmore campus in Pennsylvania. Naturally, I called their director of admissions, who went to the cafeteria and traced my boy as he was holding forth to potential future classmates about the argument made against materialistic orthodoxy in David Chalmers's *The Conscious Mind*. The director of admissions told him to call his mom.

Any frustration my boy felt with me in that moment had clearly melted by the time he flew home, his big black eyes shining and taking up even more space on his boy-turning-to-man face; his mismatched clothes wrinkled on his lanky, long-legged frame; his mess of unwashed thick black hair looking like he was about to declare a physics major, all of which told me he was now madly in love with one of the most prestigious and most expensive private liberal arts colleges in the country. "I have found my people," he said.

I had wanted nothing more, in all the years that I had raised my son away from our people, than for him to find his people.

<hr>

I had left my family, I had left two husbands, and I had left a country of a billion people so I could raise one good man. But who were our people? Who were *his*? How would he know to find them?

And so it was that I came to stand with all these questions in my head at the mailbox within seconds of the mail van pulling away from the curb outside my building. In one swift move of key within keyhole and one clumsy grab, a thin envelope with a beautiful archaic red emblem was in my hands. A Pottery Barn catalog was in my hands too, but we'll get to that, perhaps, later.

A thin envelope doesn't mean anything these days, Gibran had told me. Still, my country had trained my heart to sink at everything. I ripped the envelope open. My eyes fell upon the first word: "Congratulations." Then, a little lower down in the letter—"Class of 2017." The rest of the words went blurry.

In that moment, with those three little words, on that Valentine's Day, it truly hit me for the first time since we had begun our journey, that this child of mine, the only family I had on this continent, was leaving my home. Leaving to heed the lure of the glorious red emblem, to answer the call of the year 2017.

▀▀▀▀▀▀▀▀▀▀▀▀▀▀▀▀▀▀▀▀▀▀▀▀▀

I would be alone. My divorce from Alec was to come through twenty-eight days from that Valentine's Day. I would file my taxes as "head of household" for the second time in my life. I would have to find someone to be my emergency contact. And on top of that, now, my child would pack all his things into the two suitcases we owned, he would hug me at the airport's security check, and then his head of black hair would disappear down the line of mostly brown and yellow hair. Six hours later, a piece of my heart would beat, for years, far away in a small town in Pennsylvania.

I wouldn't have someone to help me change from DVD mode to cable mode. I wouldn't get text messages asking me what was for dinner, and I wouldn't have to hurry home for anyone after late evenings at work.

I steadied my hand to call his cell phone, recognizing a moment of irresponsible parenting on my part in case he was in the middle of class. He answered on the first ring, whispering into the phone, "So?"

"Hello, sweetie," I said, whispering at my end too, for some reason.

"Hi, Mama. Anything?" he asked.

"Hello, Swattie."

<hr>

And then, it began, my unhinging. It had been a hard year for both of us, but I hadn't come unhinged yet. (In my defense, I might have been due for an unhinging.)

The night before my second divorce was finalized, as I stood in the living room of the new condo I had bought, frozen, wondering if I was making a big mistake in letting go of a second good man, Gibran said to me: "Some people are not meant to be married. I don't think it's in your nature to be a wife." He was smiling, kindly, with a look that said that he sort of admired this thing about me, this inability to stick with a marriage.

My heart sank. Was this the legacy I was passing on to him? If I hadn't given him a model for a lasting relationship, was he condemned to suffer, crying into his pillow in the dorm room of his $62,000-a-year East Coast liberal arts college, listening to Maroon 5 on his headphones? Had he inherited a gene that rendered him unable to attach to love, or let love attach to him?

Get a grip, I told myself. He hates Maroon 5.

OK, so I hadn't given him a model for lasting love. What else had I failed at as I set about living a feminist life and raising a boy within that lived feminism? I was possessed by some of the most important questions I had ever asked myself: What kind of man was I sending out into the world? Had I raised a feminist? Had I taught him to love? Would he be loved?

I spent the next few days listening to Maroon 5. On one evening, the volume was up too loud and Gibran heard it playing in the living room during a pause in his own playlist running in his room. He came out and asked me what the heck was going on with me.

"I'm worried about you," I said, sliding into a chair at our dining table, beckoning to him to sit in the chair opposite mine.

"You're the one listening to Adam Levine and you're worried about *me*?" he said. He was not smiling kindly and was not looking like he admired this thing about his mother.

"I'm worried about the man I'm sending out into the world," I said, gesturing again at the chair. "I'm worried if he will . . . you know . . . find and give love."

Yes, we should have this conversation. This is where it would begin, my quest, my atonement.

"Well," he said, turning away from me and walking slowly back toward his room, "I don't expect much from any of it. It's not like I have any training."

I thought I heard it wrong, for just a second, and then I knew I'd heard it right.

"You . . . did you just . . . you don't have any training?"

His bedroom had a sliding door. It was made of thin, large sheets of cedar and glass placed asymmetrically within its frame, to achieve a fragile Japanese aesthetic. It had cost me good money. I knew he wouldn't slam it behind him.

He paused outside that door, sighed, and glanced at me over his shoulder. "*Do* I?"

I blinked. "*Don't* you?"

He shrugged. "I suppose things could only get better in that regard."

The dining table at which I was sitting was a thick slab of steel atop a dark oak frame, purchased at West Elm on sale, a solid investment, along with our stylish bamboo bookcases, pieces of furniture that pulled this small condo together into the kind of home I had long desired for us—a home where a family ate and read and talked about fine matters. I gripped the edges of this cold steel table before me and widened my eyes. I was waiting to see my boy's face burst into a smile to tell me he was just joking, but it didn't.

Instead, he said, "Things have been sort of dissociative around here. I guess we didn't have the time to train for love?"

I blame the books. He had read one too many. For once, I wished he would be a normal teenager and let me off with a roll of the eyes.

"It's been a good life, though?" I said. "A fortunate one?"

He shook his head, not in disagreement, but in the manner of a philosopher signaling to himself dissuasion from a line of conversation that he believed would meet with indifferent success in the company of the solipsist with whom he cohabited. He'd wandered closer, though, and he was browsing the bookcases, picking out one book after another, putting some carefully back, setting others into a neat pile. I watched him and felt a rush of articulations in my head, of all the things I would say to the things he might say.

After a few minutes, he picked up his pile of books and walked into his room without a backward glance. As he slid his door shut, he mumbled, "Good night, Mama. Love you."

I sat there, staring at the space in which he had been standing.

Dissociative. What did he mean?

I could ask him. I could look it up. I think I knew.

I looked down at the yellow notepad before me, bright against the gray slab of steel, and I made a list of the ways I had slipped up, as a feminist and as a mother:

1. **I may not have modeled love.** If he looks at me, this boy of mine, and wonders, "Whom does my mother love?" what answer would he get? He already knows I love *him*. But has he seen me truly love anyone else? Gibran has seen relationships. He has seen encounters of love, during visits and through stories and in the recent yearlong marriage of his mother's. But he hasn't witnessed the kind of unremarkable, fattened, lazy love that is in the staying, not in the upping and leaving.

2. **I haven't taught him to cook.** I haven't taught him to sew. I always thought this was OK, because I was rushing about and had no time. I thought it was OK because it's not like he had a sister who was doing these things while he was exempt. Besides, both his father and stepfather were good cooks. Why didn't *they* teach him to cook? The result is, he could be *that guy* who expects his woman to cook. One of the quickest things that people think of when you ask them to imagine a feminist male is "He cooks and cleans!" Gibran doesn't. A friend reassures me he will get to it. But boy, how did I slip up on *that* one?

3. **I often let him mansplain to me.** He was a smart, well-read boy and he's grown to be a smart, well-educated young man. He has a good brain. I often forget that *so have I*. I was raised to expect men to be smarter than me. I deferred to Gibran's father's smarts even when I was a high-ranking journalist in India. I hesitated to file my stories and film reviews before he had looked them over. When Gibran was an adolescent, I began to nod a bit too deeply when he held forth. My child has that self-assuredness we generally encounter in assholes.

4. **I told him my #MeToo stories in moments of anguish instead of in calm.** I thought a feminist teenager should know about sexual assault and rape culture, so I used my own experiences

with it as examples. Yes, I did it at age-appropriate times, and, yes, I edited things down, but I told him in moments of distress. I should have done it in moments of calm, with the help of therapists. Gibran says that although he was fifteen, he felt traumatized, disturbed about our safety in society. Because this was before the #MeToo movement, before we saw how pervasive it all was, my boy felt my trauma and felt we were alone. I could have protected him from that. Or perhaps all of society could have protected him from feeling we were alone.

5. **I talked too much about my weight.** I never cut back on eating gulab jamun or Safeway strawberry-vanilla shortcake, and Gibran and I fought and giggled over bags of Flamin' Hot Cheetos, but I was always talking about being "on a diet." I should have had my cake and eaten it too.

6. **I should have done more gender-neutral parenting.** Gibran was born in Bangalore, India, in 1995. We assigned him "boy" when the ob-gyn saw a penis on the embryo in my womb. I would become aware of gender-neutral parenting around 2015, some twenty years after he was born, by which time the world and I had lain all forms of masculinities upon Gibran's being. Yes, sure, I bought him that Barbie doll that he wanted so badly when he was two years old, and yes, I glared at his pediatrician who scolded me for dressing the infant Gibran in a mauve frock, but if I could go back in time, I would replace gendered terms like "Smart boy!" with "Smart kid!" and ask him often about what made him feel scared or vulnerable in the world. I should have combined this with the conversations that must be had, of course, conversations that I was having with him on how one gender is privileged over others.

7. **I should have told him he was handsome.** I didn't because I thought I wanted him not to care about looks, especially in girls and women. But I didn't know then what I know now about the way boys of color—especially Asian/South Asian boys—are judged harshly on the meter of masculinity. Research shows they are the least likely among heterosexual men to get a positive swipe on dating apps in America. In my own colonized imagination and despite my academic focus on media, perhaps I, too, judged my boy's darker-skinned, non-angular face and physique as lesser? (Even Bollywood movie stars started to aspire to a brawny, chiseled masculinity from the 1990s on. Our very own favorite—Shah Rukh Khan—now modeled for a skin-lightening cream called Fair and Handsome, a "brother" cosmetic to the abhorrent Fair and Lovely marketed to South Asian girls and women for decades.) I should have told Gibran he was handsome and then I could have followed it up with why that shouldn't matter.

8. **I raised him away from my family and our country.** Was it a self-serving act, raising him alone in America? Would my family have been as toxic for him as they were for me? Should I have returned to stay close to my sister? Should I have returned for my mother? Did I abandon them both in my mighty feminist quest? Could I have stayed back and healed my family? Could I have done some journalism that gave voice to my country's women? Could I have raised a feminist son in India, with the influence of the brilliant, fierce, and kind feminists who thrive there? Could I have raised a feminist son a different way? Could I have raised *a more feminist son*?

I could go on with the list. I could go on slipping up. In raising a feminist son, I did too little and I did too much. But in moments when I am kinder to myself, I stop the agonizing. I recognize that perhaps a woman's most feminist act is to forgive herself.

As I suggest in Chapter Ten, perhaps some of our slipups call for an apology. I have apologized to Gibran for a few of my listed mistakes. I haven't burdened him by asking for forgiveness, though. He responded to some of these with a nod, others with a hug, and at least one with laughter.

In talking to other parents about slipups, I am reassured that everyone feels like they're often fucking up. My friend Cleo says she regrets that she didn't talk often enough to her two Black boys about how they don't live in a post-racial society. "I raised good men, but if they believed race didn't impact them, maybe we didn't talk enough about the status of women either."

My friends Yancy and Emily, who are white parents of a seven-year-old boy, worry that sometimes it all feels a bit distant and abstract, this raising of a feminist son. Yancy says, "We read books or talk about gender and racial justice, but in our daily lives he doesn't see me doing very much about any of that. I make sure he knows that I'm the one who usually cooks and who usually cleans the bathroom, but when we're out watching men's soccer or at a happy hour with our mostly white friends, I worry that he'll catch me out. More work to do."

Yancy also wonders about the best way to intervene when his boy acts out with his mother. "There are days when he can be a real jerk to her, and again it worries me that while we might be making some progress on the intellectual level, the level of lived experience and emotion risks perpetuating the sort of BS that women still have to deal with from white males. We're looking into family counseling, but of course there are waiting lists. And the last couple of weeks have been better—fingers crossed it sticks."

The last couple of weeks. Yes, the raising of a child changes week by week. And what of us, the parents living our lives alongside, with our multiple identities, tossed about and trampled on or raised on pedestals or knocked down when rugs are pulled from under our feet? Even a homemaker dedicated to that oldest of unpaid professions (no, not sex work, that's usually paid) does not simply clock in and out, but brings their whole self to the job and can never really leave work. There's no one skill set, no hack for parenting a feminist child. And then there are things like intergenerational trauma.

Seattle family therapist Dr. Karen Weisbard tells me: "We all have to deal with our own traumas. So we have to be able to be reflective of how we became the gendered people that we are, and how did we decide on some level what were the appropriate expressions of us, of our masculinities, of our femininities." We are constantly constructing our identities, Dr. Weisbard says, and raising a feminist son is an enterprise that will brush up against our imagination and reimagination of these identities. She notes that plurality is key.

Perhaps the best way to move on from the slipups and forgive ourselves is to embrace the Buddhist notion of loving our regrets. It takes an ethical being to feel regret. It takes a growing being to value the lesson.

Yes, says my friend Sharon Suh, a scholar and professor of Buddhism and gender studies. Sharon runs workshops on mindfulness. "Forgiving ourselves is a feminist practice," she says. "We have to acknowledge our conditioning and all the cultural and political pressures that lead to some of our actions." Women's relationship with food is one such ground where we need to exercise compassion for ourselves. In her workshops, Sharon works with women who are culturally conditioned to glorify abstention when it comes to eating. "We are raised in a diet culture in which we say, 'If I don't eat cake for thirty days, I will be thin and so I will be happy.' Then we crack and eat the cake and hate ourselves for it."

Single parents, in particular, may carry the guilt of not giving their children a traditional family. "One thing I really love about Buddhism is that guilt is not a Buddhist virtue. If you feel guilt toward another person, it becomes impossible to move on. You end up centering yourself as opposed to working through something that may be meaningful to the other person. Instead, exercise self-compassion," Sharon says.

She recalls a time when she was on a retreat for people of color. "This beautiful thing happened. On the third or fourth night, there was a forgiveness meditation. You were asked to allow yourself to feel your own sorrow and regret and the recognition that you have hurt yourself, either *knowingly or unknowingly*, through pain or anger. You acknowledge how you abandoned yourself, hurt yourself, harmed yourself by your own action; you ask for forgiveness from yourself; and you allow yourself to repeat—'for the way in which I have hurt myself through action or inaction, from pain, anger, guilt, fear, confusion . . . I extend heartfelt forgiveness. I forgive myself.'"

The next step was harder, she says. You were asked to extend forgiveness to those who have hurt you. You don't have to forgive your rapist, she says, but instead see the practice as a release to the extent that the harm constricts your heart. "And you can always change your mind. You can be, like, 'There's no fucking way!' It's about liberating yourself, not re-traumatizing yourself."

Part of letting Gibran go out into the world would mean letting go of my regrets and forgiving myself. Yes, Gibran was right, perhaps it had been a dissociative life. I hoped that if not from me, from somewhere or someone along the way, he will pick up the skill to *associate*. I hope he will associate so hard that somewhere out there, in college and after that on his own, wherever in the world he'll have a kitchen, that my boy will cook. That he will build a family, a large family. Or a small one, whatever. That he will invite me and I'll bring a new boyfriend, or at least my dog. That he'll ask the women in his family, perhaps a partner or a daughter, to explain something to him that he doesn't know. That he'll be on the phone and I'll ask who was that? "It was Naani [his maternal grandmother; my mother]. She says to tell you hi," he'll say, passing me the bowl of Flamin' Hot Cheetos.

TO DO:

- Make a list of your regrets.

- Forgive yourself for each one.

Chapter Thirteen

HOW WILL I KNOW IF I'VE SUCCEEDED IN RAISING A FEMINIST SON?

....

Ghosts

My mother's earliest memory is of being given baths by her mother. She also remembers that her mother forbade her and her little sister and their five brothers from running out into the scorching afternoon sun in their village in Bikramganj, Bihar. Exasperated with my mother's rebellious forays into the great outside, my grandmother told her that between noon and 1:00 p.m., ghosts came out in Bikramganj village, collecting little children to be haunted and killed.

My grandmother is, perhaps, the only human in the world that managed to scare her little children with stories of daytime outdoor paranormal activity. Would you blame the woman? She had seven children. Allow her a ghost ruse or two.

Even though my mother stops running around in the afternoon sun of Bikramganj, she is not really learning to cook like the other girls in the village, nor hand-washing and drying the family's clothes like them, nor waking up early and praying. Because this is Bihar and the summers are hot and the winters cold, the other girls are also knitting wool sweaters and scarves. The best of them are learning to embroider. "I didn't want to learn any of that. My mother was good at making food, and I was good at eating it," my mother says. She learns to cook no more than two or three dishes from her mother. (Among these is a fried whole wheat and jaggery biscuit that will delight the older of her two daughters—me—for years to come.)

Her childhood is soon to be interrupted with an offer of marriage, arranged by her relatives. But she is getting so good at climbing guava trees and mango trees. If you were sitting under one of the three hundred mango trees owned by her father, Dr. Rameshwar Jha[4], in Bikramganj in the summer of 1963, you would see a fourteen-year-old girl waiting for the strong gust of wind that blew just before the monsoon. You would see her whoop for joy as the first lightning and thunder shook the trees, and the children stood still because the mangoes would fall from the trees on their own, no need to pick them. "We would pick up one mango from the ground and another would fall right next to us."

In this summer of 1963, my mother knows little about men and she knows even less about cities. She has been to Patna, the capital city of Bihar, because her brother studied at Patna College. Her family would go during the festivals of Dussehra and Diwali, and the children would get new clothes and new shoes and maybe even be treated to a movie. In her own village, she was only allowed to watch films about Hindu mythology. For this or even to buy a packet of biscuits, she was to be accompanied by a male: her father, brother, or a trusted servant. She dreams of a life in Patna, where girls wear school uniforms of white and blue. Her sister, just four years younger, would benefit from the dramatic changes of the 1960s when

---

4. Yes, my mother had the same last name and caste as my father before marriage.

all-girls schools began to make an appearance. But for my mother, the route to education—and to the movies—is through a twenty-year-old army second lieutenant whose marriage proposal has arrived at her father's home.

The young man and his family arrive to "see" her in February 1964. (The young man and girl are not allowed to actually see each other that day. My father sees a girl with her head covered by her sari's *ghoonghat*. My mother gets a glimpse of my father's military uniform.) The groom speaks English, she is told. These two things make her fall instantly in love.

They are married on June 4, 1964. When the bride raises the *ghoonghat*, the veil of her wedding sari, so the groom can line the parting of her hair with *sindoor*, he catches his first glimpse of his wife. She is tall and beautiful, he thinks to himself. In keeping with tradition, the bride and groom separate for three days after the wedding. On the fourth day, when her groom comes to fetch her, he speaks to her for the first time. To his utter shock, she cannot speak a word of English or Hindi. Only the local dialect, Bhojpuri. This will not do for the wife of an officer in the Indian Army. He vows to put her through college and teach her English.

She can tell her husband is disappointed in her because he tells her that she is a *dehati*, a bumpkin. He tells her she is lucky to have married him. She agrees. She enjoys the times they go to the movies. He takes her to see her first "adult" film. The movie, *Sangam*, stars her favorite actor, Raj Kapoor. It is an adult film because the heroine is featured in a bathing suit.

Then her husband tells her that if she doesn't speak to him exclusively in English, he will not respond. One morning, when they are guests in his cousin's home, a man arrives to sell eggs and hot bread. My father asks my mother to fetch a basket. She looks at him and doesn't know what he is asking of her. She has seen a servant fetch a basket from the kitchen every day for the bread and eggs, so she goes to the kitchen and fetches one. Her husband cheers with joy and she realizes that what she holds in her hands is a "basket."

"The first word I learned in English was 'basket.'"

▀▀▀▀▀▀▀▀▀▀▀▀▀▀▀▀▀▀▀▀▀▀▀▀▀▀▀▀▀

I never knew any of these details about my mother's life. She may have shared some stories with us, her children, in our growing years. But the stories didn't stick, perhaps because she told them hurriedly in the overwhelm of her life as a young working mother, or perhaps because of the self-absorption of her children.

I heard these stories because Gibran did an interview with her for a research assignment. He learned all this and much more about his grandmother on a phone call from Seattle to Mumbai. Later, when my mother is chatting with me about her experience of being interviewed by Gibran, she laughs a lot. She is delighted by the experience. She says, "When I told him I was married off at fourteen-and-a-half, he asked me, 'Were you scared, Naani?' I was taken aback. Nobody has ever asked me if I was scared. Nobody asked how I felt. Yes, I remember I was scared."

You will know you have raised a feminist son when he asks women questions about their feelings.

Girls

I never got to know Sienna very well in the years that she and Gibran were close friends in school. It is one of my bigger parenting regrets. Was I too busy? Or was it just that high school friendships find themselves spending time more outside the home than inside? She wasn't one of the lined-up-in-sleeping-bags friends from middle school, but Sienna Hiller, a straight, white, cisgender young woman is, to this day, one of Gibran's closest friends.

"We got close at an emotional level in eighth grade," she tells me now over a Zoom interview. "I remember it was specifically on a day when I didn't want to go to a pool party because I was self-conscious of my body. I remember he said to me, 'Yeah, I know what you mean. All my fat goes to my belly.' I was so surprised to hear a boy say something like that. So super-specific. Even if [cis-hetero] guys feel it, they rarely say such things, especially to girls!"

Sienna strikes me, even on Zoom but especially from the years of hearing Gibran talk about her, as a very serious young woman. She worked as a server in a restaurant for a few years after high school and then at a marijuana store and then with a nonprofit in their development office. Now she's back in school to get a criminal justice degree so she can work with a nonprofit in restorative justice.

I thank Sienna for something that Gibran told me recently. "You told him about the pressures on girls to be perfect but not so perfect that they intimidate the boys," I say. "Thank you for making him a better feminist."

Sienna smiles as she recalls that conversation with Gibran. She tells me about another time when she had to nudge Gibran to be a little more sensitive. "We were hanging out with friends one time and he said about another girl, 'Well, technically, she is more attractive than you,' and I had to tell him that while he could be right, he could also be insensitive. He totally got it and admitted that he was so into his opinion that he hadn't considered how it might hurt my feelings."

I ask her to be honest with me about something that worries me even now about my boy—"He does mansplain, doesn't he?"

She shakes her head quite discernibly even on the grainy Zoom reception. "He's opinionated," she says. "I saw him go from Libertarian in middle school to Socialist a year or two later, and he got there because he loved being challenged. But he really listens to people and their struggles. And he likes to debate. He does that with my boyfriend too."

Whew. The jury may still be out on the mansplaining, but it helps to hear a smart woman clear him of the accusation.

Sienna's boyfriend, Ebrima, overhears us and asks if he can say something. He beams into the camera and then says to Sienna, "When we'd just started dating, you and I had a fight once and Gibran took me downstairs and said, 'Look, here are some things that will help you understand Sienna better.' It really helped me. He's known you since seventh grade!"

Sienna is hearing this for the first time. Her eyes fill with tears.

Sienna says, "A few months ago, when Gibran was visiting Seattle, we were all set to go to a friend's birthday pajama party. I got insecure, again, about my body. Gibran and Ebrima really wanted to go. I got so anxious, I started crying. My boyfriend was frustrated but Gibran was so sweet. He said he would stay by my side through the whole party. I still didn't want to go. So Gibran didn't go either. And he didn't let me feel guilty about it."

I ask if Sienna and Gibran have ever spoken directly about feminism. No, not directly, she says. It was a "given" between them, she says. She speaks of the comfort of the nonspeaking relationship a feminist girl or woman can have with a feminist male friend. "Because I could see he was a feminist, I didn't have to talk about something that would feel awkward to me anyway," she says.

"Why awkward?"

"It's such an intersectional issue. I am a white woman. Gibran and Ebrima[5] are both men of color. I didn't want to impose some white feminist talk on them, but I'll tell you for sure that a lot of the white guys I know, the preppy frat boys who claim to be feminists these days because it's cool, still do terrible things. Gibran and

---

5. Ebrima's parents are immigrants from The Gambia; he was born in New York.

Ebrima don't go about declaring themselves feminists, but they walk the walk."

Gibran's friend Alec Hannaford, a straight, white, cisgender male, recalls talking to Gibran about feminism in their freshman year of high school. "He was in a bit of an 'edgy' contrarian phase. Someone brought up women getting less compensation in the workplace, and Gibran said that was only because of their lower participation in the workplace, not because they receive lower pay for the same work. It seemed like he really wanted to make a point of disputing a main-stream feminist narrative? But he basically did a 180-degree turn on this position over the next couple of years. I think a big turning point for him was reading *The Origin of the Family, Private Property, and the State* by [Friedrich] Engels. His position shifted to one where he saw women as being more disadvantaged. Since capitalist society sort of relies on the nuclear family, and the nuclear family sort of relies on the unpaid labor of women, such as child-rearing."

And then, Alec says this in response to nothing at all: "All in all, I'm sure Gibran will be a good father and husband if he ever decides to have kids."

Gibran's friend since sixth grade, Cal, a white, bisexual male, has a little more of a lighthearted take: "You know the kind of women Gibran likes to date, right? He likes to be slapped around intellectu-ally by his girlfriend."

You will know you have raised a feminist son when his friends say they see the signs.

Gods

On more than one occasion, my mother has referred to Gibran as "a god." She also believes, to this day, that my first husband is a god. She never said this about my second, for which I am thankful. She has also never said that I am a goddess.

In her defense, we Indians are quick to title humans as gods. To be specific, we Hindus, being polytheistic, aren't stingy in assigning divinity even to men we have banished in divorce. And surely some status would come my way from being the mother of a god?

And yet, I was godless enough to be bothered by such a thing. She did it again, on that trip that Gibran and I took to India in the summer before he left for college. I was invited along for a vacation with the god and his grandmother to Rajasthan. Quite honestly, I was deeply moved.

My mother hadn't had a vacation in years. At the airport before our flight to Jaipur, her knee started to hurt badly. My heart cracked open. She had spent all this money on flights and luxury hotels for her grandson, and here she was in extreme pain before her trip had even begun.

She wouldn't dream of canceling. We pumped her full of ibuprofen. It had barely kicked in before she started to fuss over us.

"Gibran beta, do you want dosa? See, at that counter there is dosa. Do you want brownies?"

"I'll get dosas, Naani. Mama and I will go get them. What can we get you?"

"Nothing, nothing."

"You sure? What about coffee?"

"I wanted coffee, but that line is too long. I don't want your Mama and you to stand in that long line. I will get coffee on the flight."

"Yeah, that coffee on the flight will suck. Let's get you coffee now."

"No, no, beta. I want you to rest before the flight."

"Rest before the flight?" Gibran said, wide-eyed. "Because we'll be running on treadmills during the flight?"

My mother laughed uncontrollably, the kind of laughter that crinkled up her face and made her shoulders quake, and it went on and on soundlessly except for the occasional gasp. I had missed this laughter in my life many oceans and resentments away.

"It wasn't *that* funny, Mom," I said, smiling. "Tell me what kind of coffee you want, please. We don't have so much time."

She straightened up a little and shook her head.

"I am feeling much better now. Let me go and get the dosa for Gibran. I want to make sure they give him all the different types of chutneys."

"Jeez, Naani," Gibran said. "Now I know where Mama gets it from."

"Gets what?" I asked.

"This thing of taking care of everyone else. You know, instead of just chilling and getting what *you* want."

My mother and I looked at each other. She smiled at me. Her vacation had begun.

▀▀▀▀▀▀▀▀▀▀▀▀▀▀▀▀▀▀▀▀▀▀▀▀▀

The beauty of Rajasthan came up and crashed into us. Rajasthan, the desert state of India, in the central region of the country's heart. Gibran had never set eyes on quite such a landscape—sand dunes and flat open spaces with no skyscrapers, just short buildings and architecture of an ancient time. Jaipur is also known as the Pink City because of its centuries-old sandstone buildings, all lined up, in hues of salmon pink.

As the teenage boy slept in at our hotel, my mother and I decided to go in search of peacocks. We stepped out into the lush gardens of the hotel and were delighted that we were the only ones there. Everything became hushed. My mother's knee was doing much better.

"Here, Mom" I said. "Stand under this tree."

It was a tree laden thick with frangipani flowers. My mother stood under it, smiling, and I shook the branches so the flowers would rain down all around her. She threw her arms open wide to catch the flowers in the palms of her hands, like that child who knew intimately the timing of trees.

We visited forts and temples all day, and then rushed back to the hotel for their legendary high tea buffet. I had missed high tea buffets in the United States. I brought a plate laden with cucumber sandwiches and a variety of tea cakes back to our table. I started to think that nothing could possibly go wrong. This was the best family vacation in years. I could barely remember a time when my mother and I had laughed in the way we had these past two days.

As I started to sit down, I heard my mother tell Gibran that she hoped his father and I would get back together now that Alec and I were divorced.

I almost dropped my plate in shock. Gibran grinned at me nervously and tried to change the subject as I flopped into the seat next to him.

"No, I mean it, Gibran," my mother said. "They should never have been divorced. He is a god, your father. She should never have left him."

I bit down on a cucumber sandwich because I could think of nothing to say. The butter was rancid. The bread was dry in my mouth. I took a sip of my tea.

"Actually, I would much rather that Mama and Alec got back together," Gibran said. "Mama and my dad have very different lives in two different countries."

I wanted to say something to him about not getting involved in such conversations, not being rude by talking about me in third person while I was right there next to him, not holding the conviction that he got to weigh in like this on my life. But I took another sip of my tea.

"I could never stand that Alec," my mother said. "Your father is a god. You remind me of him."

I got up from my seat and lurched away. Gibran grabbed at my arm and said something about easing up on the drama. I glared at him and shook my arm from his grasp.

This was all it took. A few days in this country and a son could mock his mother.

As people at the nearby tables started to look over, I said, "I should not have come here." And I turned and left.

Gibran and my mother finished their high tea and came upstairs to the room. My mother started to talk to him about how I should never have left and how it was time for me to return to India.

"Too many women are raped here," I heard myself say. "I have never felt safe here."

"Nonsense," my mother said.

I heard myself again, "Mom, I have lost count of the number of times I was molested . . ."

She frowned at me. Gibran stiffened.

"I have told you about my experiences here, Mom," I said. I wanted her to be on my side. I wanted her to remember my stories the way I remembered hers of being beaten by my father. I wanted her to stand by me the way I'd stood by her as a teen, leaving home with her every time she tried to break away from him. And I wanted her to tell me that she knew, that she felt so bad that all this happened to me, that she knew it would all be OK someday, that I will be OK.

"You have told me no such thing," my mother said. "You go about telling other people. You tell this person and that person. You tell lies. You write about these things to get attention. You have never told me anything."

Gibran sat down on his bed and shook his head. He'd heard those stories from me, but this wasn't the best topic for a vacation. I wanted to do the right thing as his mother. *What was the right thing? Should*

I shield him? Or should I show him that it was all right to cry out and ask for the understanding of the people you love?

I knew I had a choice here not to suffer, not to take the bait, not to cry, not to hurl myself out of the hotel window, not to scream, not to slap my mother, not to respond, not to goad her but to understand why she was saying what she was saying. As my mind sat in the swamp of these choices, all it could place on my lips was, "I did tell you. How could you forget? You are my mother."

My mother said nothing. Gibran spoke then. He spoke in the gentlest voice I have heard from my child's throat. "Naani, please listen. Please think about this—if Mama did not tell you about those experiences, think about why she may not have told you. Think about her as a girl growing up here. It would be hard for her to tell you."

My mother looked at him and shook her head. "Why hard? She's lying."

Gibran tried again. "Naani, India is not a good place for women. It's really hard on women here, right Naani? I can see it around me even while visiting. Really hard. Think about why a child may not be able to tell her mother. It's great for me here, as a guy. I'm treated like a god. I'm treated better than Mama. India is hard on girls. Mama was a little girl, and if I were her, I think I would have been very scared. And maybe she found it hard to tell you even after she grew up and became as strong as she is because she knew she wouldn't be believed? Maybe you can believe her *this time*?"

My mother fell silent. She hugged Gibran.

In bringing Gibran to reconnect with my family, a part of me had been afraid of losing him. But I had said a prayer. My prayer was that Gibran, here, in our homeland, amid the fleeting traces of love in our family, would step into his own model of love. He would speak of love in a language none of us had ever used before.

You will know you have raised a feminist son when he uses the voice he has been given—some might even say the voice of a god—to be the best kind of ally. He will kick the pedestal out from under himself and say, "No, thanks."

Growth

The week before Gibran left for college, I told him I wanted to take him out every night to a fancy Seattle restaurant.

"*Any* restaurant?" he asked.

"Any," I said, holding his gaze steady, as if my bank account had my back. But we'd had a rough few years. My time with him was running out. We deserved this.

One of the restaurants he chose was Toulouse Petit, which was reputed to offer the city's best Cajun-Creole cuisine. I made a reservation, we found parking with a little difficulty, and we walked into the restaurant the way we have shown up in restaurants in Seattle since 2003, a single immigrant mother and her only child.

A male host showed us to our table and a beautiful woman server around my son's age came to tell us about the specials. My boy said he was trying to make up his mind between the New York steak au poivre or the Muscovy duck confit.

"What would you recommend?" he asked the young woman.

"Definitely the duck confit," she said.

"I'll get *that* then," my boy said to her with a smile.

When she had gathered up our menus and walked away, I grinned at my son. "Were you *flirting* with her?"

"What?" he said. "*No.*"

"Oh, don't worry, it would be fine if you were. You're eighteen years old. Headed into college and all."

"I know it's OK for me to flirt, Mama," he said, shaking his head. "But it would not be OK for me to flirt with *her.* She's at work. The power dynamic between us and her right now is uneven. She's required to be polite to us, to match her tone to mine. How disgusting would it be if I took advantage of that dynamic?"

He talked to me about how waitstaff at restaurants—especially women—get hit on by men all the time and have to deal with it to earn tips or to not get fired. I held his gaze steady and nodded as if my own social conditioning had my back.

It didn't.

I am a feminist, but I had to raise myself to be one. My son is a feminist because someone raised him that way. He had a head start. I, meanwhile, still sometimes don't hear the starting pistol.

You will know you have raised a feminist son when he respects women in the workplace. You will know you have a raised a feminist son when his feminism branches and flowers beyond yours.

Goal

Dr. Kishonna Gray, the scholar of gaming theory, sees her Black sons' feminism when they nudge her to think differently. She tells me about an instance when she was playing the multiplayer game *Apex Legends* and her boys asked her to play *Overwatch* with them instead. "I was saying *Overwatch* doesn't have a readily identifiable Black woman in the game. *Apex Legends* does. And my kids said, 'But Mom, look at all the other beautiful women of color in the game, we can play with one of them, right?' And I said, 'You know what, you're absolutely right.' Because whereas we might not have all the wins, we are still able to play with the beautiful Indigenous woman in the game. We can't win them all, but we can recognize the wins of other communities."

My white friends Yancy and Emily see their son cheering for feminist victories in his little seven-year-old ways. "We've been watching *The Kicks* with him," says Yancy. "There's soccer and kids who love soccer, so he's hooked. It's teenage girls, so not really his world, but he's *mostly* on board with it. There's an episode where the girls' team has to practice on a gopher-infested field while the boys get the fancy field. The girls' coach—a man, alas, but still—challenges the boys' coach to play for the field. Watching my son cheer so wholeheartedly for the girls' team, and with such a clear grasp of the sexism at the root of the problem was . . . I mean, it was awesome. GOOAAALLLLL!!!! You know what I mean?"

Some of these things may seem like boys just being compassionate, empathetic, kind people. Why label it feminism, you may ask. We label it feminism because their compassion, empathy, and kindness is turned, in its attention, to the female condition, the condition of half of humanity. It is alert to misogyny, which turns the knife just a little more into the cultural wound. Our boys notice the turn of the knife, they name it, they see how they are complicit, they call it out, they amplify, they learn when to be quiet and sit down, they learn when to get out of the way, and they heave together to topple structures that give them an unfair advantage.

Feminism is about love. If we teach our children this new way to love, we will see that love grow and take new forms that will make our hearts burst open at unexpected moments. And, when this happens, we will slow down to feel the world turning, changing. When our boys do or say something that shows us that we have grown feminists, we will celebrate the heck out of the successes. We will shout out our boys' feminism from the rooftops.

We will shout "Goal!"

RESOURCES

How do we make this task of raising feminist boys a cozy one? We bring in books with which to curl up by the fire with a hot chocolate. We listen to audiobooks on family road trips. We binge-watch a miniseries as we eat samosas. What follows are some resources—a global, sometimes-serious, sometimes-humorous annotated bibliography, filmography (mainstream, indie, foreign, obscure), and television recommendations—to help with the task of raising a feminist boy. Included here are cultural products for children across all ages and also for you to cultivate and nurture the feminist within. Most of these were compiled with the help of my own feminist son, and some were recommendations from friends, particularly my friends Victor Evans (who teaches media literacy) and Yancy Hughes Dominick (who teaches philosophy and is raising a feminist son). Treasures upon treasures exist across cultures and languages and imaginations that you or others could add to the list. This is just a tiny starter.

RESOURCES FOR CHILDREN

Books

This list is geared toward young boys; most of these are books to read to your boy or along with him. How I wish I could gather little Gibran back up in my arms and read him just one of the many exciting feminist children's books available nowadays . . .

My First Book of Feminism (for Boys) by Julie Merberg

BABY–3 YEARS

It's never too early to start your boy on the practice of living a feminist life, and this book brings in the fun. Filled with humorous scenarios narrated through rhyme, this book takes everyday oppressions against women—human rights, consent, equality—and turns them into teachable moments that are sweet, simple, and age-appropriate even for toddlers. Use this book to encourage boys to help around the house. It tells them, "If you learn to work hard, you can do something cool—fight fires, bake cakes, fly a spaceship, teach school." Parents will have a blast reading this snuggled up with their sons.

Today I Feel . . . : An Alphabet of Feelings by Madalena Moniz

3–5 YEARS

Such a great way to explore a variety of feelings with your boy in a world that still tells boys to hide their feelings. Psychologists say that naming your feelings is the first step to coping with them. This book takes you through twenty-six feelings, not all of them positive. Give your boy the language to express his emotions with words like "invisible," "nervous," "quiet," and "relaxed."

A Is for Activist by **Innosanto Nagara**

3–7 YEARS

A fun book made to help the youngest among us learn their ABCs, *A Is for Activist* will help cement notions of equality, justice, and courage in your child's head. Combining the fun rhymes associated with this type of book with a genuinely radical outlook, it will send the right message to any kid.

Franny's Father Is a Feminist by **Rhonda Leet**

3–7 YEARS

In this beautifully illustrated book, you'll find an answer to your child's inevitable question: "What's a feminist?" Leet takes a straightforward tack—it's simple, really: Franny's dad raises her to believe she has all the rights he has. This book is a fun, unpretentious depiction of what it means to be a male feminist, and is a great choice for children across genders.

Sleeping Handsome and the Princess Engineer by **Kay Woodward**

3–7 YEARS

In this retelling of a classic fairy tale, a prince is in a deep nap, so a princess with wild engineering skills must find a way to perform an impossible rescue and wake him up. Hilarious and a great entry point for turning the "rescue" narrative on its head.

Snow White and the 77 Dwarfs by **Davide Calì and Raphaëlle Barbanègre**

3–7 YEARS

Another humorous retelling, this time of the Snow White fairy tale. Snow White is running from the wicked witch, all right, but once she picks up after seventy-seven dwarfs with their lazy, messy ways, she realizes she'd be better off with the witch. This is a good one to read with your son so you can talk about how it's not up to girls and women to clean up after them.

From the Stars in the Sky to the Fish in the Sea **by Kai Cheng Thom**

3–8 YEARS

An excellent book about a gender-neutral child named Miu Lan who is trying to decide who they want to be. Their imagination soars—be a fish, be a shooting star, be a flower, be a boy, be a girl. No matter who they choose to be, they will be loved.

Not All Princesses Dress in Pink **by Jane Yolen and Heidi E. Y. Stemple**

3–8 YEARS

Written by a mother-daughter team, this book features delightful and empowered girl characters, none of them dressed in pink but all of them wearing tiaras to celebrate how they sparkle. Lovely illustrations accompany the narrative of sassy girls living their best life playing baseball in stinky socks, climbing trees, getting muddied. Your boy can take delight in girls having a blast.

The Emperor and the Kite **by Jane Yolen and Ed Young**

4–8 YEARS

A good book to turn gender expectations on their head. Princess Djeow Seow is the fourth daughter of the emperor. She is tiny and goes unnoticed, while her brothers are considered to be "four rising suns" in their father's eyes. Her older sisters are hailed as "midnight moons." Djeow Seow spends her time playing with a kite she built. She becomes the unlikely but powerful hero of the story when her father is captured and she can use her kite and her tiny frame to pull off a fabulous rescue.

Grace for President **by Kelly DiPucchio and LeUyen Pham**

4–8 YEARS

Grace for President provides several role models for your children who are their peers while emphasizing that surface-level popularity can be a misleading force.

Julián Is a Mermaid by Jessica Love

4–8 YEARS

A winning, whimsical book, *Julián Is a Mermaid* is full of representation, with lots of different skin tones, body types, and hair. The story of a boy inspired by feminine expressions of his culture teaches your child that our cultural norms are determined every day and that masculinity can be defined by our own hands. For children, self-expression is of paramount importance, and Love emphasizes this rightly.

Kate and the Beanstalk by Mary Pope Osborne and Giselle Potter

4–8 YEARS

This is one of those delightful retellings of a fairy tale that turns gendered storytelling on its head. Kate, not Jack, goes up the beanstalk. And, of course, she has more obstacles than he did. Kate must do practical and magical things to take on the giant and restore love and power to a family. Oh, and there's a giantess who could do with Kate's help to fell the giant.

Mae Among the Stars by Roda Ahmed and Stasia Burrington

4–8 YEARS

A beautiful picture book about Mae Jemison, the NASA astronaut who was the first Black woman to travel to space. It tells the sweet story of little Mae's curiosity, intelligence, and dreams, powered by her parents' encouragement. Boys will find inspiration in this story of a girl with her head among the stars.

Meet Yasmin! by Saadia Faruqi

5–8 YEARS

This is the first in a series of books about a second-grader named Yasmin who has a big imagination. She's a problem solver and has a spirit that takes her exploring. We also meet her multigenerational

Pakistani American family. Other titles in the series include *Yasmin in Charge*, *Yasmin the Explorer*, and *Yasmin the Superhero*.

Rosie Revere, Engineer by Andrea Beaty

5 AND UP

Part of Beaty's broader Questioneers series, *Rosie Revere* is an instant classic, with accomplished, charming, and original illustrations to match a fun, fast-paced story full of interesting characters. *Rosie Revere* contains excellent representation and will leave little doubt in your child's mind that they can and should pursue anything they're passionate about.

The Girl with a Brave Heart: A Tale from Tehran by Rita Jahanforuz and Vali Mintzi

6–9 YEARS

Shiraz is a kindhearted girl living in a family that becomes unhappy after her father dies. In the opening scenes, Shiraz's ball of wool falls into a neighbor's courtyard, and she must summon up her courage to retrieve it. The old woman who answers the door is impatient and wild looking. She tells Shiraz she may have her ball of wool back, if Shiraz helps her around the house. The woman asks Shiraz to do strange things, like smash all the dishes in her filthy kitchen with a hammer. As Shiraz decides what to do, she uses her heart to listen to the woman's requests, with magical results.

Cinderella Liberator by Rebecca Solnit

7–10 YEARS

The writer who gave us landmark feminist essay collections like *Men Explain Things to Me* is a delightful reteller of fairy tales. Cinderella isn't dreaming of a prince but of self-fulfillment. The stepsisters aren't evil, the animals aren't just in service of the humans, and the prince isn't a rescuer. There's no marriage, but there's so much "happily ever after."

The Girl Who Helped Thunder and Other Native American Folktales by James Bruchac and Joseph Bruchac

8–12 YEARS

The title story is just one in this rich collection of twenty-four Native American legends and tales from across the United States. These are beautiful stories from the Cherokee, Cheyenne, Hopi, Lenape, Maidu, Seminole, Seneca, and other tribes. These stories of humans and animals will gift our children accounts of valor and bravery and agency and sacrifice.

Princess Sonora and the Long Sleep by Gail Carson Levine

8–12 YEARS

I had to put this in, yes, because the princess is my namesake, and yes, because her curse is that she is ten times smarter than anyone else. But there are so many lovely feminist moments here, as she clicks not with the rich and handsome prince meant to rescue her but with a shepherd who has so many questions for Sonora (and she, of course, has all the answers).

Stories for Boys Who Dare to Be Different: True Tales of Amazing Boys Who Changed the World without Killing Dragons by Ben Brooks

8–12 YEARS

For middle-grade boys, here are stories of seventy-five men, some famous and others little-known, who broke rules and resisted the limited perceptions of masculinity. This book celebrates boys and men who were introverts, boys who were innovators, boys who were sensitive, boys who were sweet. Boys who learned to lead and follow without violence and with empathy. We're talking Salvador Dalí, Jesse Owens, Ai Weiwei, Barack Obama, Beethoven, and many, many more.

The Boy in the Dress by David **Walliams**

11–15 YEARS

A tender and funny story about a boy whose divorced dad struggles to connect with him and his brother. This boy loves fashion but is afraid to tell people about it. A fashion-savvy girl at school takes him under her wing, and they enjoy getting him dressed up until one day when he goes to school in a dress. This book is about gender and sexuality and also about fathers and sons.

Dating and Sex: A Guide for the 21st Century Teen Boy by Andrew P. Smiler, PhD

15–21 YEARS

This one is a guide, not a storybook. It's something to hand to your teenage boy to help him navigate a deeper understanding of his sexuality and contextualize it within his values and desires. Dr. Smiler explores with empathy and without judgment topics like masturbation, hookups, identity, and more. The most important part of this book is that it will get your feminist son to think about a sexual partner's emotions and truly understand the importance of consent.

Films

As I said in the prologue, movies are where I quietly grew a feminist son. There's something magical about the hush, the anticipation, the shared commitment to the uninterrupted visual story, the beckoning to the imagination. The conversations dissecting the films after are the best part. Here's a small sampling of films to watch with your boy. Add your own, and grow your own feminist filmography.

Babe (1995)

G

The first-ever film I watched with Gibran, *Babe* features a pig who is out of place and does not know his role among other farm animals. But he knows about kindness and gentleness and love. This film will make you cry and cheer with its themes of misfits, belonging, and chosen family.

Charlotte's Web (2006)

G

Read the book by E. B. White and then watch this movie. It's another one featuring a pig, but the protagonist is a girl who builds a feminist alliance among farmyard animals through her courage. Her wit and bravery outshines and upends some of the actions of the males around her. This children's classic shows that girls and women can do anything they set their minds to, and they bring others along.

Finding Nemo (2003)

G

This is the story of a father fish who must go out of his comfort zone to find his son fish. Along the way, he must learn to give up his controlling behaviors. He is aided by a woman fish named Dory, who teaches him to be brave like her.

Mulan (1998; 2020)

G

Watch the animated version from 1998 (G) or the live-action one from 2020 by acclaimed filmmaker Niki Caro (PG-13) about the Chinese princess whose courage turns her into a brave warrior so she can fight for her family and her country.

Toy Story (1995; 1999; 2010; 2019)

G

The four *Toy Story* films were a solid bet during the Gibran-and-Mama years. The first one came out the year Gibran was born and the third was where I wept my heart out as Andy, whose toys the film is about, left for college. That's when I realized that Andy's mom has been a single mother throughout. Sigh. While the first film is about some posturing between the sheriff toy Woody and the newbie Buzz Lightyear, their male rivalry is played to comic effect, and, by *Toy Story 4*, we have solid feminist themes—Bo Peep is transformed from hyperfeminine shepherdess to crook-wielding rescuer of men and their fragile machismo. A toy named Gabby Gabby also offers us a complex female villain. This is another enduring film about chosen family.

Alice Doesn't Live Here Anymore (1974)

PG

A far cry from the films Martin Scorsese is better known for, *Alice Doesn't Live Here Anymore* is a moving story about a mother deciding to recover from tragedy by pursuing her dreams. The eponymous Alice begins the film recently widowed, and decides to return to her hometown to become a singer, taking her bright young son along with her. However, their finances quickly end up causing them problems, and while little goes according to plan, much as in life, they learn to make do. *Alice* gives us a thoughtful and honest picture of a working-class mother's relationship with her son, and makes a case that the connections we make on the margins are often the strongest.

Frozen (2013)

PG

After a whole lot of rescuable and lovestruck princesses, here's a breath of fresh feminist air from Disney. In *Frozen*, sisters Elsa and Anna show what princesses might really want. They defy gender roles and spurn expectations. They rescue each other and rescue themselves. They have little time for falling in love. They raise up their sisterhood. The film's superhit song "Let It Go" is a battle cry for abandoning the "good girl" burden in favor of agency and in defense of women's anger.

The Iron Giant (1999)

PG

Although this film fails on the Bechdel test (it has only one small role for a female character who gets to speak), it does explore some themes of toxic versus gentle masculinity. The story takes place in rural Maine against the backdrop of 1950s Red Scare and Cold War politics. A giant space robot lands on earth and becomes friends with a boy with an overactive imagination. It satirizes the toxically masculine antagonist, Kent Masley, and provides other subtle political commentary about civilization while encouraging self-expression in boyhood. It also features a single mother raising a kind boy.

James and the Giant Peach (1996)

PG

This musical fantasy film is based on Roald Dahl's 1961 story about a boy whose parents are dead and who must escape his cruel aunts. He is given magical beans that produce a house-sized peach. James's friends are a spider, a centipede, an earthworm, a glowworm, a grasshopper, a ladybug, and a silkworm, and they help lead the boy to adventure and freedom. This story is about reimagining life with courage and also about seeking out one's chosen family.

The Princess Bride (1987)

PG

A surreptitiously feminist film. Although the protagonist is a damsel who needs saving, she has increasing agency, and her love interest is a man who respects her and gets out of her way. He fights for her will and her self-determination, which is different from rescuing her for his own gain.

Spirited Away (2001)

PG

A stunning, totally captivating animated feature by noted Japanese director Hayao Miyazaki. When her father makes a wrong turn driving home, ten-year-old Chihiro and her parents stumble upon a seemingly abandoned amusement park. Her mother and father are turned into giant pigs. Chihiro meets the mysterious Haku (Miyu Irino), who explains that the park is a resort for supernatural beings who need a break from their time spent in the earthly realm. Using her wit, kindness, and courage, Chihiro takes on an adventure as she seeks to free her parents.

Bend It Like Beckham (2002)

PG-13

High school senior Jesminder Bhamra has a poster of football star David Beckham in her West London bedroom, not because she has a crush on him but because she wants to *be* him. She wants to play professional football. But her Punjabi-Indian family wants her to shut up and get married. A sweet comedy by British Indian Gurinder Chadha, this film is a girl-power cult classic and features Keira Knightley before she became a star.

Black Panther (2018)

PG-13

Finally, a superhero film with fully realized women characters even within a male-centered narrative. My favorite among these is Shuri, the scientist who heals broken men, drives a high-powered car remotely from her lab in Wakanda through a chase-scene in South Korea, and delivers some of the best lines in the film. Warrior general Okoye and activist Nakia are other strong lead characters. Wakanda itself represents a haven of non-gender-based hierarchies.

He Named Me Malala (2015)

PG-13

This is the story of a girl who was shot on her school bus by a Taliban shooter who was opposed to her going to school. When she recovered, she went right back to school and became an activist for girls' education in her homeland Pakistan and then won the Nobel Peace Prize. She is also a girl who worries about her physics exam, has crushes on sports stars, and teases her brothers. The film centers Malala Yousafzai's relationship with her father, who champions his daughter every day.

Love, Simon (2018)

PG-13

The first mainstream gay teen film ever released in the theater, this film features seventeen-year-old Simon Spier (Nick Robinson), who has yet to tell his family or friends that he's gay, while at the same time falling for an anonymous classmate online.

Princess Mononoke (1997)

PG-13

Another Miyazaki film with a strong female protagonist, *Princess Mononoke* presents a world in which humans and gods struggle over the resources of a vast forest. In it, gender roles differ significantly from our own, but it is through the protagonist of the film, San, that the viewer is given a glimpse into a wilder, less constrained form of womanhood—one that is unabashedly aggressive.

Whale Rider (2002)

PG-13

Whale Rider is about a spirited eleven-year-old born in tragic circumstances on the coastal village of Whangara, New Zealand. Pai must overcome the patriarchal restrictions posed by her village and family and push to live into her identity. At the center of the film is the theme of ancestors and whales. This coming-of-age story about a neglected child's strength also features the subplot of a male heir who rejects his community's expectations of him and leaves town to pursue a career as an artist.

Alex Strangelove (2018)

TV-MA

Alex Truelove, a high school senior, plans to lose his virginity to his girlfriend, but that changes when he meets a handsome and charming gay kid from the other side of town who unwittingly sends him on a roller-coaster journey of sexual identity.

Beautiful Thing (1996)

R

Two young boys—Jamie and Ste—living in the London projects think they could be gay and finally explore their feelings when Ste is allowed to stay over at Jamie's place after an incident with his abusive father.

Blackbird (2014)

R

Another coming-out teen film, but the focus this time is on a gay Black male, Randy, who is coming to terms with his identity while dealing with his overbearing and erratic mother, played by Academy Award–winning actress Mo'Nique.

Eighth Grade (2018)

R

A sweet and smart story about thirteen-year-old Kayla as she makes it through the avalanche of emotions and insecurities that typify the end of middle school in American suburbia. Kayla vlogs her thoughts on a life that's more positive and upbeat than her reality. The film is a sensitive portrayal of friendships and loneliness and also depicts an uncomfortable scene of Kayla's first #MeToo experience. I watched this film with Gibran and he said that scene just broke his heart.

Mustang (2015)

R

Deniz Gamze Ergüven's semiautobiographical feature debut depicts a group of five Turkish sisters, orphaned and living with their grandparents. The gap in ages between the girls and their guardians is a source of much tension in this coming-of-age film, as the protagonists chafe against the mores of a conservative section of Turkish society.

Pariah (2011)

R

Pariah follows Alike (Adepero Oduye), a Black teenage lesbian in Brooklyn who is dealing with her homophobic mother (Kim Wayans). A sweet and poignant story about family, friendships, and loneliness. It premiered at the 2011 Sundance Film Festival and was awarded the Excellence in Cinematography Award.

20th Century Women (2016)

R

This movie may as well have been titled *How to Raise a Feminist Son*. Written and directed by Mike Mills based on his own upbringing in 1970s California, *20th Century Women* displays, to indelible effect, the impact that different types of women can have on a boy. Centered around three women, each of whom relates to the protagonist, Jamie, on a very different level, the amalgamation and interplay of their personalities end up shaping a major part of Jamie's worldview. The film approaches the question of how our boys relate to the many different sorts of women in their lives with the utmost delicateness and care.

This Is Everything: Gigi Gorgeous (2019)

NR

Director Barbara Kopple creates an intimate documentary of "Gigi Gorgeous" Lazzarato, a well-known and popular internet celebrity, by using old photos, film, family interviews, and Gigi's early web appearances where she documented her gender-transitioning process.

Television

Remember the "co-viewing" suggested by media scholars? I did a lot of co-viewing with Gibran on lazy evenings and weekends over the years. I envy your co-viewing of all these shows with the boy in your life. I wish I could eavesdrop on your conversations.

Dora the Explorer (2000–2019)

TV-Y

This little Latina girl saved our children's imagination when she burst onto American television screens in 2000 (incidentally, the year Gibran and I arrived in America). Dora and her monkey, Boots, her talking backpack, and a host of other animated friends go traveling, exploring, and solving puzzles.

Molly of Denali (2019–)

TV-Y

PBS gives us this Indigenous heroine who solves problems using research and information. We follow the daily adventures of ten-year-old Alaska native Molly Mabray, her family, her dog, Suki, and her friends Tooey and Trini. Molly is played by fourteen-year-old Sovereign Bill of Auburn, Washington, who is a member of the Muckleshoot Indian tribe in Washington and the T'ak Dein Taan clan of the Tlingit tribe from the Alaska community of Hoonah. Yancy watches this show with his seven-year-old boy and reports that it's great fun!

Loud House (2016–)

TV-Y7

This animated show follows the adventures of eleven-year-old Lincoln, who has ten sisters and lives in a very loud and chaotic house. His best friend, Clyde, has two dads and they are all often involved in the escapades.

The Powerpuff Girls (1998–2005)

TV-Y7

I loved, loved, loved that Gibran was crazy about *The Powerpuff Girls* as a little boy. I would sing along with the very catchy title song ("Here they come just in time . . . the Powerpuff Girls!").

Three sisters—Blossom, Bubbles, and Buttercup—are created in a lab by Professor Utonium, and they come through for their native Townsville every time the evil Mojo Jojo wreaks havoc.

Andi Mack (2017–2019)

TV-G

The coming-of-age series follows the life of the thirteen-year-old title character, played by Peyton Elizabeth Lee. In the second season, Andi's best friend, Cyrus, begins to realize that he too has feelings for Andi's crush, Jonah.

The Kicks (2015)

TV-G

This Amazon original show is a recommendation from Yancy and his son. It's based on a book series by Olympic gold medalist and US Women's National Team soccer player Alex Morgan. Devin is the star player on her soccer team until her family moves to California during the school year. After learning that her new team, The Kicks, is on a monthslong losing streak and in need of an inspiring leader, Devin must rise to the challenge and become a competitive force who can lead the team to victory. Yancy says the focus on a women's team is a great gender-equalizer for his soccer-loving boy. The show tells stories about unequal treatment of boys' and girls' teams—an excellent conversation starter.

Kim Possible (2002–2007)

TV-G

During its run, this show gave kids a great example of an empowered, sassy, fun-loving crime-fighter in Kim Possible. The adolescent Kim uses her smarts and her good friendships to navigate the world of high school cheerleading and high-stakes criminals in this comedy-adventure series. Her sidekick is her buddy Ron Stoppable.

Degrassi: The Next Generation (2001–2015)

TV-PG

The long-running, multiple-award-winning Canadian drama series follows the goings-on of a diverse cast of characters as they endure the angst of blossoming sexuality, growing up, drugs, and dealing with their parents. Numerous LGBTQ and nonconforming characters have been featured throughout the seasons.

Glee (2009–2015)

TV-PG

The McKinley High School's glee club—New Directions—is a place where ambitious and talented students can find strength, acceptance, and their voice. Through dance and fun and interpersonal tensions, the show navigates the treacherous terrain of adolescent love, gender, and sexuality.

My So-Called Life (1994–1995)

TV-PG

This show is all teen angst. It follows Angela, a high schooler in constant turmoil over her exposure to boys, friends, drugs, sex . . . The cast includes Ricki (Wilson Cruz), her best friend, who is coming to terms with his sexuality. *My So-Called Life* addresses a full range of topics, including everything from homelessness and homophobia to budding relationships.

Steven Universe (2013–2019)

TV-PG

The first show on Cartoon Network created by Rebecca Sugar, *Steven Universe* is as close as we'll get to an unabashedly intersectional feminist children's show. Filled with thrilling fights and catchy music, *Steven Universe* is about a boy raised by three genderless (but women-presenting) guardians: the heroic, world-protecting Crystal Gems. The Gems are Steven's primary role models, and the series engages with LGBTQ issues to a truly impressive extent. This series is an excellent way to introduce your son to a number of sensitive issues, especially how to recognize and prevent toxic masculinity.

Supergirl (2015–)

TV-PG

As the title suggests, the show follows the adventures of Supergirl, Kara Zor-El, who escaped planet Krypton to Earth where she grows up with the Danvers family, including her foster sister, Alex. Alex, a major character, has navigated a few relationships with women throughout the show.

Aggretsuko (2018–)

TV-14

A lighthearted but hilarious Netflix show from Sanrio, the creators of Hello Kitty, *Aggretsuko* is a bingeable animated series about a typically diminutive red panda, Aggretsuko, who works at an accounting firm. But Aggretsuko likes to blow off the many stresses of being a Japanese working woman (microaggressions at work, constant social pressure to marry) by singing death metal music at a karaoke bar every night. *Aggretsuko* is a fun satire of office life that uses humor to deliver poignant moments and real insight.

The Baker and the Beauty (2020)

TV-14

This ABC show centers on a Latinx-family who owns a Miami bakery and shows how their life is turned upside when the son, Amos, begins dating an A-lister. The cast includes Amos's sister, Natalie

(Belissa Escobedo), who is coming to terms with her sexuality, including navigating her first crush and coming out to her parents.

Black Lightning (2018–)

TV-14

Based on one of DC Comics' first Black superheroes, *Black Lightning* focuses on Jefferson Pierce, principal of a charter school, as he is forced to return to his former vigilante persona of Black Lightning. Jefferson is a complex but heroic figure, unafraid to demonstrate his vulnerability and emotions to his family, his students, and even the criminals he hopes to reform. Written by a majority-Black writing staff, *Black Lightning* provides plenty of action while carefully considering many aspects of Black masculinity.

Borgen (2010–2013)

TV-14

Borgen is about the fictional first female prime minister of Denmark. Beyond giving the viewer a glimpse of life as the most powerful woman in a country, and the complications that come with that, *Borgen* has a refreshingly grounded focus on reproductive rights, particularly as they apply to working women.

Buffy the Vampire Slayer (1997–2003)

TV-14

The series followed the adventures of Buffy, a slayer whose mission is to seek out and destroy vampires, demons, and other forces of darkness. Buffy has a "Scooby gang" that aids her in her battles with evil, including Willow, who later in the series comes to terms with her sexuality and navigates a relationship with Tara.

The Fosters (2013–2018)

TV-14

The show centers on Stef, a dedicated police officer, who is in a relationship with Lena. The couple creates a close-knit nontraditional family, including Stef's biological son, Brandon; adopted twins, Mariana and Jesus; and foster children, Callie and Jude.

A Million Little Things (2020)

TV-14

This soapy drama follows the lives of friends whose world are shattered with someone in their circle unexpectantly dies by suicide. The cast includes Danny Dixon (Chance Hurstfield), a twelve-year-old boy who is navigating his sexuality, including his first kiss with a boy in his class.

Puella Magi Madoka Magica (2011)

TV-14

For those who enjoy anime, or perhaps whose sons do, *Puella Magi Madoka Magica* is a fascinating subversion of the various feminine archetypes that appear in mainstream Japanese media. What at first appears to be a straightforward "magical girl" premise (think *Sailor Moon*) metamorphoses into something far more sinister as the girls at the center of the plot find that their powers, and the enemies they face, are not what they seem. *Madoka* is a stunning metaphor for the inequities in women's depiction in anime in particular, and in Japanese media at large.

Pose (2018–)

TV-MA

Victor Evans urges us watch this show with our adolescent kids. It's a drama television series about New York City's Black and Latino LGBTQ and gender-nonconforming ballroom culture scene in the 1980s and, in the second season, early 1990s. Glamorous and riveting.

UnREAL (2015–2018)

TV-MA

This drama series, cocreated by a former reality television producer, takes us behind the curtain of the entertainment that dominates many young people's lives. The main character, Rachel Goldberg, is a producer on a dating show who struggles with the frequent requests made of her to compromise her scruples. The series is an entertaining look at how the media molds young people, and young women in particular, into whatever best suits the purposes of the viewing public at that moment.

When They See Us (2019)

TV-MA

When They See Us, created and directed by Ava DuVernay, tells the gut-wrenching story of the Central Park Five, a group of teenagers wrongfully accused of raping a white woman in a highly racially politicized environment in 1989. The miniseries speaks for itself, and, with the story itself, stands as a testament to the strength of Black and brown families in the face of structural injustice, and shows us how boys and men of color are profiled in their attitudes to women.

RESOURCES FOR ADULTS

Here's a list of books, films, and other tools for adults to find inspiration, information, and instruction in the raising of boys. As I said in an early chapter, the world is conspiring to raise kind boys. These resources are just one part of that wonderful conspiracy.

Books

Between the World and Me by Ta-Nehisi Coates

Written as a letter from a father to his son, this book lays bare the racism and the fears and hopes of an African American father for his country and for his son. The book is about America, and it is about white America's gaze on Black masculinity, in particular the Black male body that is murdered, incarcerated, policed, and seen as suspect. Coates also provides hope to his son: "This is your country, this is your world, this is your body, and you must find some way to live within the all of it." A must-read for its tenderness as well as its call to action in a violent nation.

Boys & Sex: Young Men on Hookups, Love, Porn, Consent, and Navigating the New Masculinity by Peggy Orenstein

Orenstein interviewed young men and got them to open up about the confusion and pain our boys have been feeling around sex and sexuality. Again, here, we find boys and men who are aching to connect while our society—including media and porn—push them to be emotionally detached, insulting, even violating in matters as tender as love and sexuality. We can do better, Orenstein says, and we start by talking to our boys about intimacy and vulnerability.

Good Talk: A Memoir in Conversations by Mira Jacob

Novelist Mira Jacob's graphic memoir will move you deeply with its honest, funny, very relatable moments. Jacob is South Asian and her husband is Jewish. The "good talks" in the book are those moments in which her son raises awkward yet profound questions about biracial identity, love, and culture. Jacob uses these to reflect on her growing years. Stylish, humorous, and increasingly relevant, this book also models how one may navigate our kids' world of urgent and beautiful questions.

How to Raise a Boy: The Power of Connection to Build Good Men by Michael C. Reichert

Full of clinical insights and resources, this book is drawn from the author's years of work as a psychologist. Reichert calls for a change in the culture so our boys may flourish. Listen to them, encourage them to have close friends, fill their lives with good role models and coaches, and let them talk about their feelings—these are just some of the many tips Reichert offers for nurturing a healthy boyhood.

Mediocre: The Dangerous Legacy of White Male America by Ijeoma Oluo

The author of *New York Times* best seller *So You Want to Talk About Race* turns her incisive examination to white male identity in America. Where does violent masculinity intersect with misogyny and racism? Oluo asks. What happens when success is defined by status over women and people of color, instead of by actual accomplishments? Delving into an analysis of American history, Oluo shows us that white male supremacy crushes women and people of color, yes, but also damages white men themselves. What lessons can we learn for raising our boys from Oluo's instruction on how to imagine a new male identity free from racism and sexism?

***Operating Instructions: A Journal of My Son's First Year* by Anne Lamott**

I laughed and cried my way through this book. Anne Lamott writes about all those delightful and nerve-wracking moments of the first few days and months of having a baby. A sweet, funny mother-son memoir, this book is about so many other emotions that flood a mother's life as she turns to the task of mothering. Lamott also bares her sharp wit on masculinity and what may lie ahead for her baby boy.

***The Power of Discord: Why the Ups and Downs of Relationships Are the Secret to Building Intimacy, Resilience, and Trust* by Ed Tronick and Claudia M. Gold**

Psychologist Dr. Ed Tronick is the man behind the "Still-Face Experiment" (watchable on YouTube) in which a mother first plays with her delighted baby expressively and then switches to a still face. The baby does all it can to get the mother to respond. The experiment tells us so much about how humans crave connection, and Dr. Tronick and pediatrician Dr. Claudia Gold show us how we may use this for teaching our boys to maintain their emotional core and continue to connect deeply and unabashedly so we all may go on to lead more fulfilling lives with our partners, our families, our friends, and our colleagues.

***Raising Cain: Protecting the Emotional Life of Boys* by Dan Kindlon and Michael Thompson**

Two child psychologists share their combined thirty-five years of experience working with boys to draw attention to a nation of boys who are hurting—sad, afraid, angry, lonely, silent, addicted, suicidal. They discuss how societal forces and destructive emotional messaging in our everyday interactions with our boys threaten their humanity. We teach them to believe that "cool" equals macho strength and stoicism. The authors encourage parents to raise boys with values such as warmth and empathy and free them of the current impossible and painful standards of manhood.

Sister Outsider: Essays and Speeches by Audre Lorde

In particular, Lorde's essay titled "Man Child: A Black Lesbian Feminist's Response" is a powerful, brilliant thesis on how to raise a son in a feminist paradigm within a sexist and racist society. Her son Jonathan is turning fourteen when she writes this essay. Although she says she has no golden message for the raising of sons by lesbian mothers, Lorde provides one of the most profound examinations into masculinity and sexuality from the point of view of a mother that you will read anywhere. The sons of lesbians, she says, "have the advantage of our blueprints for survival." Raising Black children in a racist and sexist society calls for teaching survival and love and how not to be overwhelmed by fear. She wants to raise a Black man who will not take the cruel tools of white men trained on him and turn it on women. This essay becomes more and more relevant with every passing year.

We Should All Be Feminists by Chimamanda Ngozi Adichie

In this large-hearted essay compiled into a tiny book, Adichie recalls running for class monitor in her school but the teacher giving the position to a boy. "What was even more interesting was that this boy was a sweet, gentle soul who had no interest in patrolling the class with a stick. While *I* was full of ambition to do so." Adichie narrates this and other memories while issuing a call for twenty-first-century feminism to be more inclusive and therefore beneficial to all. She lays out the intersections of gender and culture as she recalls her coming to feminism in Nigeria and then reckoning with its denial across the world. Men, especially, must speak up, she says.

When Boys Become Boys: Development, Relationships, and Masculinity by Judy Y. Chu

Dr. Chu and Dr. Carol Gilligan did a study that followed boys from pre-kindergarten through first grade. They found these boys to be tender, emotionally perceptive, craving emotional connection, and articulate about all of this. They also found that society started to teach these boys to shed these "feminine" qualities to prove they are boys. Our boys receive messages to be stoic, self-sufficient, competitive, even aggressive, to be accepted as "real boys." What they lose is far more precious and indeed something they later say they crave—the emotional connection that is part of their humanity. Let's return those good things to our boys, these researchers say.

Films

The Mask You Live In (2015)

In ninety minutes, this documentary film by Jennifer Siebel Newsom cuts to the heart of the beast we have created: toxic masculinity. Little boys and young men open up about how they are schooled in stoicism and in hating women. Psychologists and researchers raise alarm about the health of our boys. Cultural critics and academics reveal how media socialize our children into becoming a shell of their whole human selves. What we learn in this film is how we must move with urgency if we are to rescue our boys and return them to their unmasked joys.

Tough Guise 2: Violence, Manhood, and American Culture (2013)

Over the years in my media literacy classes when I have screened *Tough Guise* (2000) and *Tough Guise 2* (2013), young men in my classroom are either moved or become defensive. Pioneering anti-violence educator, cultural theorist, and author Jackson Katz has documented time and again how America embeds a violent ethic in its boys as if violence is synonymous with manhood. Katz examines masculinity across racial and class lines and goes deep into issues of mass shootings, homophobia, and American militarism, all of which are fattened on messages through media, video games, advertising, sports culture, and our own deep-rooted and twisted notions of how boys become men.

Other Resources

Decisions That Matter: An Interactive Experience

This is a short, interactive video game created by students at Carnegie Mellon University on ways to prevent sexual assault. In roughly ten minutes, the player makes decisions throughout a typical college day with friends. The player's decisions ultimately lead to a character being assaulted or not. At the end, the actors, students of the College of Fine Arts, bring the characters to life and explain their emotional responses to the outcome. Have your college-bound boy play this and then discuss with you.
www.andrew.cmu.edu/course/53-610

"The Urgency of Intersectionality"

I have used the term "intersectionality" several times in this book because it is, to me, a foundation to being a feminist. We should all be grateful to Dr. Kimberlé Crenshaw for giving a name to a sensibility without which feminism would be incomplete or even warped. In this TED Talk, Dr. Crenshaw explains how race and gender bias systematically exclude women of color, especially Black women, from socioeconomic and other privileges.
www.ted.com/talks/kimberle_crenshaw_the_urgency_of_intersectionality

ACKNOWLEDGMENTS

A thousand thanks to the people who made this book possible. Thanks to the fabulous team at Sasquatch Books/Penguin Random House, especially my editor Hannah Elnan, for her wisdom and wit and cake treats. Thanks also to my wonderful agent Soumeya Bendimerad Roberts.

I am grateful to those who read early drafts of this book—Theo Nestor, Rick Simonson, Ranjit Arab, and Novera King. My beta readers were invaluable—thank you, Ramon Isao, Amber Flame, Ruchika Tulshyan, and Jenny Abrami.

Thanks also to my student researchers over the years—Anina Walas, Phoebe Kim, Schuyler Dull, and Alec Downing. I thank the faculty, staff, and students of Seattle University, in particular my colleagues in the Department of Communication and Media. Thank you, Verna McKinnon-Hipps. Thanks also to my writing companions—Novera, Kim, Ellie, Abby, David, Anna, Francoise, and Waverly (whom I miss so much).

For giving me a residency and an office to quietly write in, I thank Hugo House. Residencies like PLAYA, L'Ancienne Auberge, and the home of Grace Nordhoff and Jonathan Beard helped me turn all my attention to craft. My deepest gratitude to Hedgebrook writing retreat for always feeding the hungriest parts of my soul.

Thanks also to Theo Nestor, the kind of friend, mentor, and sister you need, especially when writing a book such as this one. For the parts of this book that are memoir, I thank all those who enriched my life. I am grateful to my sister, for standing up for me, for walking out with me.

My most tender thanks, of course, is to my son—for all the laughter.

HOW TO RAISE A FEMINIST SON: A READER'S GUIDE

▬▬▬▬▬▬▬▬▬▬▬

A CONVERSATION WITH
IJEOMA OLUO AND SONORA JHA

———————————————
▀▀▀▀▀▀▀▀▀▀▀▀▀▀▀▀▀▀▀▀▀▀▀▀▀

This discussion originally occurred live at Town Hall Seattle on April 7, 2021. It has been edited and condensed for brevity.

IJEOMA OLUO is a writer, speaker, and self-proclaimed internet yeller. She is the author of the #1 *New York Times* best seller *So You Want to Talk About Race* and *Mediocre: The Dangerous Legacy of White Male America*. Her work on race has been featured in the *New York Times* and the *Washington Post* among many periodicals, printed and otherwise. Oluo was named to the 2021 TIME100 Next list and has been twice named to the Root 100.

Ijeoma Oluo: I would love to see if we remember our early conversations similarly because I don't know if you know that it was the Hedgebrook [Writers' Retreat] trip when I began *Mediocre* that we also talked about this book.

Sonora Jha: Yes, and I'm so happy that we're doing this together because I saw in your first chapter of *Mediocre* you talk about how the conversations at the farmhouse table at Hedgebrook were about men and mediocrity and the way we were not able to get ahead, and I was working on some chapters of this book, so you were probing that question and I was probing this question of a mother and boyhood and boys of color, and I remember we were talking way into the night. Those were great conversations—I remember being so inspired by what you'd already done because you had just finished *So You Want to Talk About Race* and it had been launched and you were enjoying the glory of that, or at least I hope you were enjoying the glory of that, and then we were in this space of creating.

IO: For people who aren't familiar, Hedgebrook is a writing retreat for women to take a break from all of the things that pull us away from being able to create, and it's a wonderful, immersive experience, and we were both there together along with some other absolutely amazing women, and I remember we were all talking about our projects and all the problems we were having as writers dealing with these dudes and it was there that I had the inspiration for *Mediocre* but then you emailed me years later and said, "Hey, remember this conversation we had? The book is almost done!" and it was so exciting to see.

SJ: And you were so gracious to agree to give me a blurb. There was so much going on in your life at the time and your blurb for my book was just perfect, so thank you for that too.

IO: Well, I want to say the blurb wasn't a charity thing. The book was something I turned to after we had our house fire, and I was trying to just sit and have some solace and read, and this was a book that really made me think about the ways in which I had raised my sons. I have two sons, one is nineteen and one is thirteen. I was nineteen when I was pregnant with my older son and twenty when he was born, so looking at where I am now as a woman and as a feminist you go back and think: *What did I instinctually do, and what would I redo?* And so I loved this life history with your son. I would like to know what inspired you to think, *This is the way I'm going to write about this* because there are so many ways to write about feminism but this is so deeply personal; it's this really beautiful history of your life together. What made you decide that this was the way you were going to write it?

SJ: It's so interesting that you asked me but I feel like I had to write it this way because I was writing a memoir off and on, and then all these things would keep happening in the world, like the

#MeToo movement, and my son and I were having these conversations about rape culture and dating culture. At the time, my boy was getting ready to go to college, and we were just beginning to talk about things like campus rapes in society. Then there were the Black Lives Matter protests and so many other things—police brutality and seeing what toxic masculinity looked like—and now the phrase has become this loaded one but really it is what it is. So I would start writing these political essays that were also getting laced with my personal stories about my son and those would get such overwhelming responses from people. I realized: *this* is what my memoir has to be about. I was writing a mother-son memoir and it just started to gel together, and then the journalist in me said I needed to talk to other people so I did the interviews, and then the academic in me said, *Of course there's a lot of research out there* and the feminist scholar in me said, *Pull from all of this and weave it together and see what comes of that.* So I feel like it satisfies all those parts of me. The personal parts are like a mother saying to a younger sister: let's do this, let's raise better men.

IO: That's beautiful. It's interesting, so often when people talk about feminists they say that we don't like men or we hate men and I feel like there's such optimism and such love in the honest way you look at what is probably the most important man in your life—which is your son—and the way you approach your duty in raising him. I was wondering if you could talk a little bit about what it means to love a man as a feminist? What does it mean to live in that and act in that while also of course loving yourself?

SJ: Wow, that's a great question. You know, when I found out that I was having a boy—and back then in 1995 we were totally assigning a gender even before we gave birth—I was sad, and I write about that in the book. I cried because I wanted to have a girl, because I had really bad role models of men in my family, and violence, so I was actually scared of what it would be like to raise a boy. Is he going to grow up and shout at me? Is he going to be out of control? But then there was this baby and how could that happen? And then I thought, *If I love him, first of all I want him to grow up to be tender and gentle and sweet* and then I want him to be able to have those qualities that I saw men wanting but not being able to own, like being able to cry, being able to express love and be kind to people and not see that as a blotch on their masculinity. So it was an act of love. And it was really something I was responding to in my son as well because he *wanted* to be sweet. So I think that was my love that wanted to raise him as a feminist and wanted to give him what feminism affords to boys. And also to love myself. So you know I write in the book how I wasn't one of those moms that was cooking for my son all the time, like he hates my cooking. We were eating frozen pizza; I was a single mom! You know, I couldn't help with homework and sometimes I was working late and he was managing on his own. I was following my own career, enjoying life, dating, and all of those things. I think that showed him that women can live full lives and be self-actualizing rather than self-sacrificing. Now that he's a man, I see that he values that in women.

IO: I definitely saw that and I've always felt with my sons that it matters for them to see me pursue my dreams, to see me own my space and to be protective of myself and to seek out joy and to be a whole person. There was one part of the book that really struck me that I hadn't realized I had really kept from my kids, where you talked about having honest conversations about sexual abuse and sexual assault with your son. That was something that I as a survivor hadn't done and it hit me because part of me was like, *Oh, even now I could go back, with this relationship I have with my kids, and actually be honest about that* but then I started thinking about how this speaks to many of the ways in which we really do protect boys from the pain that patriarchy costs us, even while we try to raise them with these positive values. Actually, I think oftentimes we shortchange them and think that they can't handle it but of course *we're* handling it, right, we're handling the direct impacts of it and so I was kind of curious about what it was like to begin to have these conversations. Was it scary? Was it just something you naturally knew you should do? Have you heard from other people about whether or not they did that as well?

SJ: I didn't know how to do it. I was in moments of anguish when I would tell him, you know, "I'm crying because of this," and I would say, "Hey, some things happened in my childhood." It was at an age-appropriate time, when he was fourteen and fifteen and knew about sex and sexuality, and he was quiet and stunned. He said, "Oh gosh, that's terrible. Were you scared?"—he was that age where they can ask questions that are full of tenderness rather than "I don't want to talk about this." I write about how later I felt like I should have done it differently because he did say later that at that age he was a little bit alarmed about our safety in the world and so I felt bad about that. So I mean I feel like people can do it with the help of a therapist, but it's also, now that he's a little bit older and he realizes, *OK, we're safe, right*—I mean to the extent that anyone is safe, especially people of color and women—he feels like he benefited from it. One of his friends, a young woman, says he really listens and he believes.

You can have this conversation because you're saying, *We're carrying this, this happens to us,* why are we protecting them? By protecting boys, we're not protecting the girls that it could still happen to. It's like the Chanel Miller case. In her book *Know My Name*, she talks about the Stanford rapist Brock Turner and she talks about being raped and about how these two guys from Sweden saw the assault taking place and came and chased down Brock Turner. It struck me: these guys were from Sweden; they weren't US guys, because there they talk about consent, they've trained boys to think about what consent is so when they saw this happening they knew something was wrong. This woman was unconscious. So we have to have those conversations and it makes them just better human beings.

IO: Absolutely. And this book does a great job of illustrating how we need to activate young men and boys into seeing the responsibility that they have in society as social creatures and the influence they have on their peers. Not only the control they have over their own actions but the responsibility they have as active participants in male society to really step in there. I really appreciate the trust that you seem to show in your son to be able to do that. That's one thing I really love about the book is you're honest and you sit with times where you're disappointed. I've seen this too as a parent, recognizing that you can still have faith in them but be honest and say, "Hey, that was disappointing."

SJ: My son disappoints me all the time! The job is never done. But thank god we have the language. We can turn it around and say, "Hey, this is what you're doing" and they get it and they can understand that it's not pleasant for me to be mansplained to, and there's also humor around it.

IO: Oh yeah, I remember my newly licensed sixteen-year-old trying to explain to me how to drive. And I was just like, "Are you kidding me? Because you've literally been in the car your entire life as I've been getting you safely from point A to point B."

SJ: Exactly!

IO: It's amazing how society comes in and really wants to pull boys away from themselves and as a parent you're in this tug of war. But I think we have to have faith that they can get it. They are capable of pushing back just like we are. Because the truth is—and I say this about race as well—Black children aren't given a primer for how to navigate a racist world, right, and how to push back against all of the harmful things that they're told about themselves and their role in society, and women aren't either. We are finding ways and we're naming things and writing things and working toward it and as a society I think we have to have as much faith in men. And that faith comes with that responsibility of saying, "I am disappointed because I know you can do better."

SJ: Yes!

IO: I think that's important, talking about how to raise a feminist son, but I think it's also talking about it not as if men are the end-all and be-all of accomplishment or safety. It's really about loving women and people harmed by patriarchy and we do this through the ways we raise our sons. I think that that's an important distinction because often when we're trying to "sell" feminism to men it lives and dies in the benefits for men and then the humanity of people who are most harmed by patriarchy—most women and femmes and nonbinary people—are kind of secondary, and where it doesn't seem to benefit men directly then they don't address the issues. I find the same with race often when we try to "sell" anti-racism to white people, then it lives and dies within their own growth and benefit. But this is clearly grounded in love for women and really it is about our humanity and recognizing our worth and making sure that we are raising sons who recognize our worth, and not just thinking about the great benefit to them in freeing them from patriarchy. And I would say, if you're a parent of a boy, you see how incredibly toxic and hurtful patriarchy is from a very early age, but at the end of the day, it's also about always being firm in the value of women in our society.

SJ: And that's why it also had to be about me living a feminist life and him finding the friends that would support that: girlfriends, women friends, and friends across gender with whom he can listen to their experiences instead of centering himself, and knowing how to get out of the way. Of course then people say, "Why would you disadvantage your son?" So, I was raised in a Brahman family and as a middle-class Brahman family living in Bombay or Bangalore, with his father being in advertising, we could have had a lot of benefits for my son. He would have been very different if he were raised in India. But then of course the challenges of raising a brown-skinned boy in America . . . I think when people say, "Why would you take away those advantages?" and then you realize it comes down to: How do you want to live your life? How do you see oppressing people or being rude to women or claiming more space than should be yours as an advantage? I know that my son feels like a better human being because we have these conversations and the sweetest thing that our kids can say to us is that "I wouldn't exchange my life for anyone else's."

IO: That's wonderful to hear and I think that's important when we look at liberation. When we're talking about feminism and when we're talking about anti-racism, it's important to be aware of the desire to trade in true liberation for your proximity to the power structures that exist, and so whether it's caste in India or talking about race here, it's important to remember that always there's going to be this lure to tie yourself and especially to tie your sons or your partner to these systems of power thinking that it will get you something more than you could get if you let it go in search of true liberation. Reading your life story and knowing so many other amazing women of color who have decided this—and I would say oftentimes for many of us it's decided for us because we don't actually have that much proximity to power—but we have to let it go and say, *Actually, no, there has to be a greater liberation out there.* I think that a lot of times people will bill it as selfish but it's an amazing adventure to actually be able to take your children on. I hope that people can see this when they read the book and recognize that those relationships wait for them and that that feeling waits for you.

You know, I don't write a lot about my kids—yet, at least—but we get these moments where you can see reflected the things you've taught and I'll always remember someone messaging me and saying, "Hey, did you know that your son is arguing with a relative on Facebook about abortion rights right now?" And he had all these facts and stats and links. I think because this is my job, both my kids do the whole "I don't want to talk about any of these things because you're so annoying about it all the time" thing, and so it was funny to watch him just actively in there talking to one of his aunts and saying, you know, "You need to understand choice matters." What they're doing is that they're walking the walk, they're doing the work without claiming it.

SJ: So my son says, "I don't like the performative aspect, like nowadays a lot of guys will just say they're feminists and they're not really." I'm sure you'll agree that with boys of color, feminism to them is just an extension of the rights that are needed for everyone else. Like you're saying that women deserve a full experience of humanity—if they are full human beings entitled to opinions and everything else, right, then humanity itself must be extended to everyone else. I mean, that's intersectionality at work and that's why your sons are on there doing that work because they recognize that this is all part of that whole fabric that is changing. I'm glad that they're doing it and Facebook is a great place to go have those conversations.

IO: Yeah, I either catch him on Facebook or catch him in the chat function of his video games—which is hilarious—you know, they have their headphones on so they don't realize they're shouting the whole time and I'll hear him say, "One more homophobic remark and you are banned permanently from this group!"

SJ: [*laughs*]

IO: Everywhere it can go, you know. I hope that we recognize that everywhere matters and everywhere that we allow this kind of oppressive behavior to continue to flourish is going to come back and harm us in all spaces.

SJ: Yes, greatness is not about power and taking up space and being in these positions, it's about all kinds of other things—so greatness may still be yours but if you can learn to be tender, to apologize, to be a follower and get out of the way, those are the things that I wish for our masculinity in the future.

IO: That's a wonderful image and I hope that people will take that to heart. I think that's a great way to end our conversation and I want to thank you so much for having me.

SJ: Thank you!

QUESTIONS AND TOPICS FOR DISCUSSION

1. Who is the boy (or boys) you had in mind while reading this book? Why do you want to raise him as a feminist?

2. Which parts of the book did you find most helpful or relate to the most? Did you enjoy the personal stories from the author's life, the research and interviews with others, or the to-do lists at the end of each chapter? Was there a chapter that especially resonated?

3. What do you find hardest about raising a feminist boy? What do you find most joyful or freeing?

4. On page 44, the author writes, "Literature builds empathy and empathy builds solidarity, especially as a toddler boy imagines the wide, wide world and, one day, helps reimagine it." Look at your boy's bookshelf—are there opportunities to build his empathy there?

5. Is your instinct to edit (or limit) the media your boy engages with, or to let him watch or read whatever he wants and circle back to discuss afterward? Has your approach changed as your child has grown? Did the book encourage you to rethink any of your own rules and rubrics about media usage?

6. Who are your "goddesses"? Where do you take inspiration from when raising a feminist boy?

7. The author writes, "What we needed to talk about is proactively going after the problem and training men to read women the way women have been trained to read men" (page 136). What do you want the next generation of men to understand about what it means to live in a woman's body? What do you wish men had known? What will you teach your boy?

8. What expectations do you hold regarding your boy's body? Where might you let go of those in service of *all* of our freedom to be in our bodies?

9. In Chapter Ten, the author writes, "So what are the ways in which a feminist boy might slip up in his growing years? He may use his fists on the playground. He may say to a buddy, 'That's so gay!' He may push a girl off a swing. He may tease his sister for her games and toys and sports and ways of being in the world that society whispers in his ear are 'less than.' He may bully his peers. He may call a classmate a slut. He may join his friends in rating their female peers based on their faces and bodies. He may try to coerce girls into sex as a conquest. He may try to shut a girl down when she's smarter than him. He may try to lash out at a girl when she laughs at him. He may try to talk a girl down when she shares her dreams" (page 173).

   What is your worst fear about what your boy could say or do? How do you think you would react? What would you want to do afterward?

10. What are your thoughts on the author's choice to raise her son "here among the oppressed" (page 190)?

11. For those reading as a group, how will you keep each other accountable on the long journey of raising feminist boys?

12. Who else in your life needs to read this book? Who else can you enlist in the job of raising a feminist boy?

ABOUT THE AUTHOR

Ellie Kozlowski

SONORA JHA, PhD, is an essayist, novelist, researcher, and professor of journalism at Seattle University. She is the author of the novel *Foreign*, and her op-eds and essays have appeared in the *New York Times*, the *Seattle Times*, the Establishment, DAME, and in several anthologies. She grew up in Mumbai and has been chief of the metropolitan bureau for the *Times of India* and contributing editor for *East* magazine in Singapore. She teaches fiction and essay writing for Hugo House, Hedgebrook Writers' Retreat, and Seattle Public Library. She is an alumna and board member of Hedgebrook Writers' Retreat, and has served on the jury for awards for Artist Trust, Hedgebrook, and Hugo House.